THIS IS THE BULLFIGHT

THIS

by John Leibold

IS THE BULLFIGHT

SOUTH BRUNSWICK AND NEW YORK:
A. S. BARNES AND COMPANY

LONDON:
THOMAS YOSELOFF LTD

© 1971 by A. S. Barnes and Co., Inc.
Library of Congress Catalogue Card Number: 72-88282

A. S. Barnes and Co., Inc.
Cranbury, New Jersey 08512

Thomas Yoseloff Ltd
108 New Bond Street
London W1Y OQX, England

Photographs by Luis Arenas

SBN 498 07449 8
Printed in the United States of America

To Anne

CONTENTS

AUTHOR'S NOTE

There is no set of official written rules which really describes and limits all the action which takes place in the bullring. In the Spanish government regulation governing the bullfight, published in 1962, 10 of the 13 chapters are concerned with the organization, administration and material prerequisites for the fight while only three chapters deal with the action of the fight itself. Over the years however, precedent and tradition have defined and limited the action which occurs in the bullring more effectively than any official rule book could possibly have done.

In the following pages when I have used the term "the rules of bullfighting," I am referring to the currently accepted standards of the informed enthusiast based upon this precedent and tradition. Any reference to "the regulation" is to the official Spanish government publication *Reglamento de Espectaculos Taurinos* mentioned above, a complete translation of which is included as an appendix to the text.

ACKNOWLEDGMENTS

Sources of information for a book such as this are many and varied. It is impossible to remember or acknowledge all of them. A few special books and people however deserve special mention.

Books: *Death in the Afternoon* by Ernest Hemingway, Scribners, New York. Still the best book on the subject in English.
Encyclopedie de la Corrida by A. La Front, Prisma, Paris. An organized, illustrated, analytical study of every aspect of the bullfight.
Los Toros, Vols. I, II, III, and IV by Jose Maria de Cossio, Espasa-Calpe, S.A., Madrid. The final authority.

People: Special thanks are due Elena Vialo for her fine translation of the official bullfight regulation, her incisive editorial comment and her meticulous manuscript correction.

THIS IS THE BULLFIGHT

1.

WHAT IS THE BULLFIGHT?

It was nearly four in the morning and the bar was almost empty. We took a table in the back and sat down with a bottle of wine to finish off the evening.

On the wall there were framed photographs of a young bullfighter I had never seen before. When I asked about him the owner showed me the scar on his neck and told me they were pictures taken before the goring, before he had lost his courage and had gotten sick and become a bartender.

"I was very good," he said, "and then after the goring I couldn't do it anymore."

He spoke of it all calmly as something which was over and done with, like a war or a sickness. Then he took out his wallet and showed me a picture of his nephew who was only 11 years old and too young to fight regularly, but who took after his uncle in his yearning to be a bullfighter.

"He's very brave," the owner said proudly, "we tested him with a small bull last year and he did very well. See in the picture how he's standing his ground without flinching."

He looked at me keenly.

"Would you like to see what he can do?" he said, and then quickly before I could reply he turned and opened a door behind the bar.

"Juanito wake up," he shouted. "Get in here. Some people want to see you. Get up. Get out of bed."

A woman's voice muttered querously, but he shouted again and in a moment a sleepy-eyed boy stumbled into the room yawning and rubbing his eyes.

His uncle reached down under the bar and pulled out an old muleta and a long wooden stick and thrust them at him.

"Here," he said, "they want to see what you can do."

The boy took the muleta and the stick and adjusted them in his right hand. Then as he swung the cloth, he looked past us and his eyes gleamed.

"Haho. Toro," he said, throwing back his head and advancing the muleta in the accepted manner.

As we watched, the bull appeared in front of the cloth and when he swung the muleta you could almost hear the sudden rush of hooves and the grunt as the bull turned and charged back again. Three times he took him on the right and then he switched the cloth behind his back and sent him away under his left arm. As he turned on his heel and came strutting back toward us with the bull perfectly set, we started to applaud. The owner leaned forward and we were back in the bar.

"You see," he said, "what do you think of that?"

"Terrific," I said.

The owner looked at the boy affectionately.

"Maybe one day he will be a bullfighter," he said, "meanwhile he has to work and run errands and help his uncle clean up around here."

The boy fingered the stick and the cloth.

"Shall I do something more," he said.

"No," said his uncle, "go back to bed. You have to get up in an hour and fetch the water before they turn it off at the pump again."

He took back the muleta and the stick and put them under the bar. The boy yawned sleepily and shook hands with us and wandered off to bed. We sat and drank our wine without saying anything while the owner stood quietly alone behind the bar staring out into space, not thinking of us or anything else there around him.

The bullfight is a spectacle or pageant
> **a battle**
> **a sport**
> **a ballet**
> **a ritual sacrifice**
> **a tragedy**
> **a sadistic orgy**
> **a craft**
> **an art**

Bullfighting has been variously described as all of these things at various times by various people. Without going too far into detail, it is worth examining each of these descriptions in turn, in order to clarify to some extent at least, what bullfighting really is or is not all about.

The bullfight is a spectacle.

The spectacle or pageant aspect of the bullfight is immediately apparent to even the most casual observer. The trumpet calls, the music, the costumes, the color, the movement, the play of light and shadow, all these contribute to keep the eye engrossed as the various phases of the bullfight succeed each other with predetermined regularity. For the newcomer, especially, the richness and variety of the spectacle are almost overwhelming and tend to obscure the fundamental austerity of the basic action. It is generally not until the second or third fight that any degree of perspective is obtained and the details of the fight begin to take on any real importance. No matter how familiar the details may become, however, the spectacle aspect of the bullfight never really fades and even the most cynical oldtimer never completely loses sight of the colorful pageantry that makes the bullfight the unique spectacle that it is.

The bullfight is a battle.

The gladitorial or battle aspect of the bullfight is really inescapable, more because of the resemblance of the arena to the Roman coliseum perhaps than because of any real resemblance between the bullfight and the ancient Roman games. As even a cursory examination of the action will indicate, the bullfighter does not really fight the bull in any ordinary sense of the word, and with the exception of the action of the picadores and the single vital thrust delivered with the sword in the last act of the fight, no real attack or physical contact is ever made by the men with the bull which might serve to qualify the action as a real battle or gladitorial contest.

The bullfight is a sport.

Bullfighting is sometimes thought of as a sport, in the sense that big-game hunting and fishing are called sports, for bullfighting really originated as a sort of big game hunt under controlled conditions. In the beginning, wild bulls were captured and loosed in the arena to be killed by noblemen from horseback to demonstrate their prowess before the other nobles and the court. This led naturally to the breeding of animals especially for this event and to the development of an entire ritual to accompany it. Eventually this ritual was refined by precedent and tradition into a set of rules of conduct for both man and beast and the bullfight became something more than just an exhibition of a man's ability to kill a wild animal. But bullfighting is not, and never has been, a fair contest between evenly matched opponents in any sense of the word. On the one hand the bull is overwhelmingly stronger, better armed and more powerful than the man, while on the other the man is infinitely more intelligent, skillful and resourceful than the bull. The man decides and chooses the terms on which he will meet the bull, which weapons he will use, the degree of danger he will risk, the time and place of the meeting, and even the extent to which the bull must be weakened before he will meet him in any direct, frontal attack. None of these things are decided or chosen on the basis of providing a fair contest, but rather to insure the smooth development of the action to a predetermined end.

In bullfighting there is no such thing as a winner or a loser, but only a good, or interesting, or poor, or dull bullfight. Sporting terms can be applied to the bullfight, but these terms are a foreign importation and mean nothing to the native enthusiast. In these terms the bull always loses, since he is always killed, but in these same terms the man often loses, whenever he is outclassed by the bull and must resort to expedients in order to bring about the death of the bull, since he is expected to be able to do this gracefully and without effort. Such terms are meaningless however, since if the bull is exceptionally good, and the man exceptionally capable, they both may win, in the sense that they have both fullfilled their appointed roles to perfection, and neither could have showed to such advantage without the other.

The bullfight is a ballet.

The bullfight is sometimes described as a ballet . . . "a tragic ballet in which the man and the bull dance together through a choreography of exquisite plastic beauty. The assistants both mounted and on foot are the chorus, and the opening scenes of violent movement and color in which they take part finally give way to a tragic *pas de deux* between the matador and the bull which ends only when the bull is dead."

Delightful as this description may be, neither the man nor the bull really "dance" a ballet in any ordinary sense of the word, although at times they do move through a series of rhythmic figures of enormous plastic beauty and emotional intensity. Despite this fact, however, the comparison is still basically a misleading one, and the spectator who does not realize this is due for an unpleasant surprise when he sees his first bullfight and finds, not the pretty aesthetics of the ballet stage, but the stark beauty of the bullring. The lover of ballet should be forewarned of the ugly realities of blood and raw violence which from the opening moments distinguish this "ballet" from all others elsewhere in the world.

The bullfight is a ritual sacrifice.

The bullfight bears considerable resemblance to certain ancient religious ceremonies in which the ritual sacrifice of a venerated animal was made to appease the gods. Viewed in this way the bull is of course the sacrifice, the bullfighters are the high priests, and the spectators the worshipers and faithful followers of this pagan blood cult.

While such resemblances or parallels cannot be denied, and although among real enthusiasts there is sometimes an almost mystical appreciation of the bull, no real religious significance of any kind is ever attributed to the bullfight by either the bullfighters or the spectators. People do not consciously go to the bullfight to participate in a blood cult, and they do not believe that any gods are appeased by the death of the bull, nor that any power will devolve upon them as a result of it. Whether they do these things unconsciously or not is a matter of conjecture, and hardly suffices for classifying the bullfight in this way.

The bullfight is a tragedy.

Sometimes the bullfight is described as a tragedy, a dramatic composition in three or seven acts culminating in the classic death or destruction of the bull. A certain comparison between the traditional sequence of the bullfight and the basic construction of classical drama is, of course, undeniable. However, besides giving the bullfight a literary flavor or form which it does not really possess, such a description is also inherently mistaken. It fails to consider that the matter of fundamental importance in the bullfight is not the fact that the bull dies or is destroyed, but rather that the man triumphs and lives. An understanding of this fundamental point is absolutely essential to any real grasp of the nature of the bullfight.

The emphasis placed upon the death of the bull and the concept of the bull as a tragic figure is relatively new in the history of bullfighting, and appears to be a foreign importation or interpretation which is entirely unintelligible to the native enthusiast.

The bullfight is a sadistic orgy.

With regard to the popular conception of bullfight spectators as twisted individuals who derive a sadistic sexual satisfaction from the action at the bullfight, it should be noted that the ordinary spectator does not go to the bullfight to enjoy the blood or pain or suffering of either the bull or the man, and derives no specific pleasure of any kind from these things. Rather, he accepts these aspects of the bullfight as an inevitable part of the spectacle and is displeased when they intrude too forcefully on the smooth flow of the action, as for example, when a man is gored or the bull is accidentally crippled, or disabled or punished beyond the absolute minimum necessary for the proper control of the fight. There are, of course, in every crowd a few sick individuals whose appreciation of the fight is as twisted as they are, but their reaction is hardly of other than clinical interest and cannot be seriously considered as typical.

The bullfight is a craft.

The craft of bullfighting refers to the mastery of the mechanical aspects of the bullfight, and can be learned by anyone with good native intelligence, normal reflexes and adequate body coordination. Included in this category are not only the correct use and practiced handling of all the instruments of the trade i.e. the cape, the muleta and the sword, but the mastery of the fundamental concept called *lidia* as well.

Lidia in its largest sense means combat of any kind, but in bullring terminology it refers to ringcraft or strategy, i.e., the correct application of sound principles in the conduct of the bullfight.

Good lidia brings out the best qualities of even the poorest bull, while bad lidia can ruin the bravest and noblest animal and make him appear both cowardly and vicious. Under good lidia the bull moves through the appointed phases of the fight smoothly and easily, without unnecessary punishment or injury and arrives at the phase of the muleta in the best possible condition for a brilliant and artistic faena. Under bad lidia he goes to pieces quickly, becomes crafty, unmanageable and so dangerous or exhausted that the bullfighter must kill him immediately.

If the bullfighter is a master of good lidia, the bullfight moves like clock-work. Everyone performs his appointed duties neatly and efficiently. There is no messy flopping of capes, no confusion of movement, no working at cross-purposes, no waste motion of any kind. The bull and the bullfight are under control.

The quality of good lidia in a bullfight distinguishes the first from the second-rate and separates the better from the best. It presupposes a sound knowledge of the habits and peculiarities of fighting bulls and a certain amount of experience in working with them. More than this however, it supposes a profound realization of the fact that each bull has a different personality and as a consequence must be fought in a different way. This latter fact is of the first importance and is the basis of all good lidia. It is one of the fundamental elements of good bullfighting and one of the necessary qualities of the great bullfighter. As such it is very rare.

The bullfight is an art.

It is almost a cliché to state that bullfighting is an art in the sense that interpretive dancing is an art, or to state that the aesthetic emotion derived from it is similar to that derived from classic ballet. On the other hand, some critics have compared its aesthetic appeal to that of sculpture, and deny it as a major art only because of its impermanence.

While the rhythmic beauty of certain phases of the bullfight cannot be denied, and while the plastic beauty of line and mass at certain moments seems stopped and molded in time as solidly as any group in stone, neither of these definitions or comparisons is really entirely satisfactory either to the bullfighter or to the spectators. For bullfighting is neither dancing nor sculpture. Bullfighting is an art all its own. It is an art in the sense that it is the graceful illustration of a philosophy of life. And it is an art, too, in the sense that (when well done) what is done is aesthetically pleasing and satisfying to the informed observer.

Fundamentally the bullfighter is illustrating or demonstrating his conviction that, if a man goes forward to face danger and the unknown with sufficient courage and confidence, he can do beautiful things and triumph no matter what the odds, but that if he is faint-hearted or unsure of himself, nothing can be accomplished. Actually he is stating his faith in the innate ability of man to triumph over his animal existence. He does this by triumphing, not over the lowest and basest elements of that existence, but rather over one of the finest and noblest examples of it. Through his actions in the ring with cape, muleta and sword the bullfighter illustrates the truth of his statement in an aesthetically pleasing and satisfying way by creating graceful and inspired solutions to the problems inherent in dominating and killing the bull. The beauty and emotion that can be created and communicated by these actions cannot adequately be described and must be seen to be appreciated or believed. It is this beauty and this emotion, however, which are the essence of bullfighting and raise it from the category of a cruel or clever craft to the rank of a vibrant and living art.

The bullfight is a spectacle.

The bullfight is a battle.

The bullfight is a sport.

The bullfight is a ballet.

The bullfight is a ritual sacrifice.

The bullfight is a tragedy.

The bullfight is an art.

2.

THE BULLS

We were sitting over in the sun in the first row waiting for the bullfighter to step out when suddenly somebody put his hand on my shoulder and crowded me to one side. I looked up to see who it was and there he was stepping past me over the cable. As I watched he crouched low and leaned out and leaped forward across the passageway into the ring.

He was wearing an old pair of jeans and a dirty shirt and was clutching the usual homemade muleta in one hand and he looked like any one of thousands you might see anyplace. He might have pulled it off all right, there wasn't anyone near enough to stop him, but his foot caught on the fence as he cleared the passageway and instead of landing on his feet he pitched forward headfirst into the ring.

The bull was only a few yards away and, as the kid fell, the movement caught the bull's eye and he swung around and charged all in one fluid motion, so quickly that no one had a chance to move or swing a cape or anything.

From where we were sitting we could only see the kid for a moment as he reached back and groped for the fence, trying to get to his feet. Then the bull was on him and we couldn't see anything except the pulsating, driving, hindquarters of the bull as he thrust and shoved and gored at the writhing body caught in the angle against the fence. Each time the bull surged forward we could see the heavy body muscles tense and strain under the hide and hear the thud of the horns as they dug into the fence.

The men in the ring leaped forward and those in the passageway were flopping capes, but all the bull was interested in was the body on the ground and they had a hard time getting him away. Finally one of the men ran forward and grabbed the bull's tail and pulled hard enough to hurt him and someone else picked him up with the movement of a cape and took him away to the center of the ring.

The attendants leaped over the fence and started to pick up the kid to carry him to the infirmary, but suddenly they stopped and stepped back and he stood up without their help and started brushing off his clothes.

He was all right. It was unbelievable but he hadn't been hurt. One of his eyes was beginning to puff up a little and there was a scrape across his forehead and his clothes were in tatters, but he hadn't been gored and nothing seemed to be broken anywhere. He was all right. It was a miracle.

We watched silently as he stood there, and then as we began to breathe again he suddenly started to cry. He was a big, loutish-looking kid and, as he came through the opening in the fence to meet the police, you could see the tears running down his cheeks and the hurt look on his face.

Nobody looked at him. He had missed his big chance. He was nobody.

Out in the middle of the ring the bullfighter stepped forward and swung his cape. As the bull charged, the crowd roared.

The bulls are the basic element of the bullfight. They are the raw material, the steel and stone from which the bullfight is built. Without decent raw material there can be no sound structure, no bullfight. In order to really understand what the bullfight is all about, some understanding of the qualities that go to make up the ideal fighting bull is absolutely necessary.

Fighting bulls are thoroughbreds in the same sense that race horses are thoroughbreds; that is, they all have registered pedigrees and all are descended originally from the same, pure-blood ancestors.

Like racehorses, fighting bulls have been selectively bred to eliminate all undesirable qualities and to conserve or improve the original basic physical and temperamental characteristics of the race in all their purity. Above all, fighting bulls are not domestic animals in any sense of the word, and bear as little relation either temperamentally or physically to the ox or farm-bull as a race horse does to a draught or plough-horse.

There is no need to train or teach fighting bulls how to fight, and until they enter the bullring, except for a brief testing and branding interlude, fighting bulls lead a perfectly quiet and unmolested life at pasture on the open range until they are fought in the ring. They are naturally aggressive, however, when challenged, and are bred to preserve this quality which they exercise by fighting among themselves on the open range. Bulls are colorblind to the extent that they cannot distinguish one color from another and they charge the cloth because it moves, not because it is red. Bulls do not charge blindly, nor do they charge with their eyes shut. On the contrary the entire principle of the bullfight is based on the fact that the bull will follow the slightest movement of the cloth as it changes direction in the hands of the bullfighter.

With regard to physical appearance, the fighting bull may be identified by certain basic characteristics. He has a small head, a fine tail, smooth skin, wide-set eyes, deep chest and well-developed hind-quarters. His horns are sharply pointed, curving forward and up, neither too short nor too long, neither too open nor closed, neither too high nor too low. The throwing muscle at the back of the neck (called the *morrillo)* is remarkably developed. He has slim legs and small feet, and is nervous, sensitive and remarkably fast. In general, he is strongly but finely built with a heavily muscled body that carries no excess weight or fat.

The full-grown bull (four through six years old) generally weighs a little under half a ton (500 kilos), and stands about five feet at the shoulder. Above a certain minimum weight of approximately 900 pounds (450 kilos), age is always of greater importance than size. Larger bulls are often seen, but unless the additional weight is well-developed muscle, greater size is of little or no importance. Sheer bulk is undesirable and is generally a hindrance. The fighting bull, by his well-developed muscular structure, should give an impression of latent strength and power even in repose. Bulls which are merely heavy through excess fat will not give this impression, no matter how big they are.

In theory, all bulls fought and killed in the ring (in a corrida de toros) are at least four and no more than six years old. Younger bulls are generally not sufficiently developed or strong enough to support the punishment of the fight, while older bulls are too crafty and too wise to permit brilliance with the cloth. Despite this fact and the provision of the regulation which prohibits it, both younger and older bulls are often fought every season. The younger bulls are generally fought by the stars who are able to choose the animals they will fight, while the older bulls are fought by the novices and the second category bullfighters who have no other choice. The age of the bull is prescribed by the regulation and is checked after the fight by veterinarians who examine the bull's teeth and horns.

The basic qualities of the fighting bull are bravery, nobility and strength.
The qualities of bravery, nobility and strength are not evenly distributed in all bulls and never to exactly the same extent in any two bulls. Bulls from the same ranch or herd, however, tend to display the same qualities to a similar degree. Thus some herds are noted for their exceptional bravery, but will possess the other qualities to a lesser degree. Individual bulls, or strings of bulls, may be exceptions to this rule and occasionally one particular bull from a particular ranch will possess all three qualities to a remarkable degree, while other bulls from that ranch will be only average. If a bull lacks all three qualities, which sometimes occurs especially in

bulls which have been crossed with tame cattle, he cannot be fought and does not really qualify as a fighting bull at all.

With respect to fighting bulls, bravery may be defined as a positive response to punishment. That is to say that when attacked or punished, as for instance by the picadors during the bullfight, the fighting bull responds by forcing under the goad to the point where he would drop of exhaustion before relinquishing the attack.

A really brave bull will ignore all pain and punishment and appears to be unaware of wounds or weakness. He is undaunted by any odds and will attack anything that moves no matter what its size or how much it may hurt him. Brave bulls have fought lions, tigers and even elephants and have been known to attack automobiles, trucks and locomotives. The bravery of a really brave bull is awe-inspiring and almost unbelievable. It is a tribute to the success of selective breeding that most of the bulls fought in the ring, while falling short of the ideal, are extraordinarily brave, and that the ideally brave bull described above is seen at least once and often several times every season in most of the larger bull rings of Spain.

Those bulls which fall short of the ideal to the extent that they absolutely refuse to fight are called *manso* or tame. This is a relative term, however, and, except for an occasional throwback, there is no comparison between the bravery of fighting bulls and ordinary beef cattle, no matter how vicious or wild the cattle may be or how tame the fighting bull.

Nobility with regard to fighting bulls refers to the straightforwardness of the bull's conduct. It is characterized by a frank, open rush toward whatever threatens, meeting danger or attack or its threat head-on, without craftiness or cunning, without a sidestep or a moment's hesitation.

In its purest form, nobility also refers to a bull's refusal to attack a fallen man or fallen horse until he has regained his feet, or to attack at all unless challenged. It is a kind of regal dignity which disdains all unfair advantage or craftiness. There have been cases of fighting bulls so noble that they could permit themselves to be stroked and petted and even permit children to mount on their back while later in the plaza they fought savagely with the picadores and charged every challenging movement of the cape and muleta until they died.

The strength of the bull is fundamental to any bullfight. Unless the bull has the strength to absorb the punishment he must take, and expend the energy he must expend, in charging and recharging again and again, the element of danger so necessary to the bullfight is completely lacking and it cannot be taken seriously.

The pathetic spectacle of a fighting bull stumbling and falling helplessly about the ring, unable to attack or defend himself because he lacks sufficient strength, robs the bullfight of all dignity and interest and is in absolute contrast to the bull which charges hard and fast with power enough to throw the mounted picador over his head or against the fence almost without effort again and again. This is the bull which charges time and again untiringly and dies hard, fighting to the last; his mouth clamped shut, wounded and weakened, but dangerous and strong enough to kill a man even in his death agony.

These qualities of bravery, nobility and strength are unique in the fighting bull and the bullfight is based upon the assumption that all the bulls to be fought will have all these qualities to a greater or lesser degree.

The ideal concept of the bullfight limits the role of the bull to one of straightforward, ferocious brute force. Bulls which unite these qualities dominate the plaza with their force, vigor and personality and transform the bullfight from a pretty or pathetic show into something which has been variously described as art, tragedy, or mortal combat, something—that particular something—which makes and has made the bullfight the unique spectacle it is. To the extent that the bull is sly, cunning, crafty, or weak and defensive, to that extent the bull is not fulfilling his assigned role and the bullfight is not a success.

In addition to the basic qualities of bravery, nobility and strength, bulls are sometimes also classified by type with respect to other physical characteristics or the manner in which they conduct themselves in the ring during the fight. Some of the most common terms used to designate them in this fashion are: *boyante*, *codicioso*, *con sentido*, *que cortan terrero*, *abanto*, *incierto*, *blando*, *huido* and *burriciego*.

A boyante bull (also called *franco, sencillo,* or *claro*) is a thoroughly brave bull which responds immediately to every movement in the ring and every command or challenge offered by the cloth. It is one which charges frankly without hesitation in a straight line time after time. This is the ideal bull that all bullfighters dream about.

A codicioso or *revoltoso* bull is an extremely, almost excessively, brave bull, but one which turns quickly after each pass and constantly renews the attack without waiting to be challenged. It is one which seems to be glued or stuck to the man and gives him no time to recover. Such bulls are extremely dangerous in case of an accident in which the man is caught or falls, since the bull will be immediately upon him.

A bull con sentido is one which either already knows, or learns immediately, the difference between the cloth and the man who is handling it. Such bulls seem to know all about the bullfight and the deception inherent in the manipulation of the cloth and seek out the man behind the cloth. Bulls with sentido are usually either older (five or six years old) , or have had previous contact with men on foot, or sometimes have been fought before. In addition to the sentido or knowledge that they have they may also be either brave or tame.

Bulls que cortan terreno (or *que se ciñen*) are those which cut in toward the man in the midst of a pass. They do not completely ignore the cloth or hook at the man, trying to catch him, as a bull con sentido might do, but simply cut the trajectory of the cloth and lean in toward the man as they pass him. If the man moves or is running, as in placing the banderillas, they will cut sharply in trying to intercept him.

An abanto bull does not appear to be particularly interested in fighting when he first enters the ring and attacks without decision or any real follow-through. Such bulls generally settle down after the first few passes with the cape and may become very smooth and even boyante as the fight progresses.

An incierto or uncertain bull is easily distracted from the cloth sometimes even by things outside the ring, and seems unable to decide whether to charge or not. This is often a sign that the bull is lacking in bravery and always makes the bull difficult to fight since the man can never be sure that the bull is really interested in the cloth.

A blando or soft bull does not force under the pic or give the picador a chance to punish him, but rather desists at the first punishment. Such bulls often reach the muleta without having been worn down sufficiently and are difficult to fight because of this.

A huido bull flees from the bullfighter and tries to escape by jumping the fence or evading the men in the ring. Huido bulls will only charge when they feel they are cornered and cannot escape. They are dangerous because their actions are unpredictable.

Burriciego bulls are bulls with impaired sight, whether by being near or far sighted or through some accident or disease. They can be extremely dangerous if they do not see well enough to follow the cloth.

A stud or seed bull on the range. Carefully selected for his strength, bravery, and general physical appearance, he leads a life of ease and tranquility with his harem of cows on the open range. He is older and wiser and consequently more dangerous than the bulls which are fought in the ring and the men on horseback maintain a respectful distance as they separate him from the herd for the photographer.

Brave cows with their calves. The calves are born in late Fall and remain with their mothers throughout the first year. The cows are lighter-boned and without the massive neck and forequarters that characterize the fighting bull. Since the essential quality of bravery in fighting bulls is transmitted primarily through the female rather than the male, an elaborate system of testing has been evolved to determine which cows are the most aggressive.

Testing bull calves on the open range. The men overtake the calf from behind
and, by a skillfull touch of the pole at the base of the tail, tip him over at full
gallop. The extent of the calf's bravery is judged by his behavior as he scrambles
to his feet. If he charges repeatedly at the horsemen present he is judged fit for
the bullfight. If he tries to avoid a fight he is destined for the slaughterhouse.
Extremely brave calves are marked as potential stud or seed bulls and are retested
at a later date. Bull calves are never worked with cape or muleta unless they are
destined as seed bulls.

Fullgrown bulls being driven in for shipping to the bullring. The three black bulls are surrounded by tame steers. The steers have been trained to obey the herders' commands, and this, plus the strong herd instinct of the fighting bulls, permits these aggressive animals to be moved with a minimum of difficulty and danger.

Separating a bull in the corrals. The public is sometimes permitted to view this operation, particularly during the big fairs. An elaborate system of chutes and rope-operated doors is necessary to separate the bulls once they are in the corrals. The pole is used to attract or prod a reluctant animal in the proper direction.

Bulls on exhibition to the public in Seville. During the big spring fairs in Seville and Madrid the public can see and compare bulls from the various ranches as they rest in the corrals. The bulls in the photograph are all from the same ranch and have been chosen for the same general characteristics of conformation and color. Bulls from different ranches or different breeds are never mixed as they would fight and kill each other.

A small young bull in the ring at Seville. Although the horns are fairly large and well set, the body is still undeveloped and the face is immature. The bull is less than four years old and is being fought in a novillada or minor bullfight. A bull of this size and age is unacceptable for a regular bullfight or full corrida.

A large young bull with small "banana" horns and too much weight for his frame. Despite his impressive bulk he is not really a fit animal for the bullring. The excess weight will tell during the fight and leave him shortwinded and weak after his fight with the picadores, while the size of his horns takes away all real merit from anything the man may do with the cloth.

A large, full-grown bull on the range. Note the power and strength of the heavily muscled body. Although the horns are not especially large, they are adequate and together with his age and size are sufficient to make him a serious and difficult adversary for even the most skillful matador. Such bulls are generally shunned by the big stars who prefer younger, smaller and more manageable animals.

3.

THE BULLFIGHTERS

It could have happened in any small town anywhere. The bulls were big and ugly and over six years old, with heavy horns and plenty of strength and speed. There were six of them and the three kids who were supposed to fight them were all as green as grass. When the first bull came out, one of the men gave him a quick run and got out of the way.

The first kid didn't have any idea how an old bull should be fought or what it was all about. He came out with a lot of steam and enthusiasm and tried to do something pretty and the bull caught him in the groin on the second pass and threw him ten feet through the air against the wall. Somebody took the bull away, and the ring attendants rushed the kid out of the ring to the infirmary, while the second kid got ready to come out to kill the bull.

The second kid had sense enough not to try to do anything pretty, but the bull was too much for him anyway. When he made a mistake, the bull caught him in the thigh and ripped his leg open to the bone. As he went down, the bull ripped at him again, and then there were capes everywhere, and then his men had him under the arms and were running with him to the infirmary too.

The bull ran free out to the center of ring and turned and stopped with his head up, waiting. The stands were in a turmoil.

The third kid stood behind the fence looking at the bull without any expression on his face. Suddenly he threw down his cape.

"I won't do it," he said. "I'm not going out there. It's suicide. I'm not going to try."

He refused to fight. Everyone talked to him, but in the end they had to call it off and refund all the tickets. They arrested the kid and took him to jail, as much

41

to protect him from the crowd as anything else. The next day his family paid the fine and they let him go.

A few days later a reporter from one of the bullfight papers interviewed him in his home. When he asked the kid why he hadn't even tried to kill the bull the kid just looked at him.

"There were five more just like him waiting for me in the pens," he said. "The bull knew more about bullfighting than I did. My two friends were laying on the table in the infirmary with only one general practitioner to care for them. If I got gored there wouldn't even have been anyone to give me first aid. Better to go to jail than to die."

It was a sensible explanation but, in the editorial, they criticized what they called his lack of enthusiasm and in the end he never got another chance to fight anywhere after that, ever again.

If the bulls are the steel and stone from which the bullfight is built, the bullfighters are the architects responsible for that construction. Without the bulls there is no bullfight, but without this particular bullfighter there will be some other construction, some other bullfight. It is the bullfighters who form the raw material into an artistic whole, who construct and build and form the material presented to them in accordance with the basic rules and regulations of their art—an art refined and developed through the years and at present enjoying a renaissance, an art whose underlying concept however has not changed through three centuries.

Originally, all bulls were fought from horseback and the men who fought them were all aristocrats. However, when bullfighters began fighting on foot, the common man began to dominate all bullfighting and has continued to do so until today. While the great majority of bullfighters come from modest circumstances, occasionally the son of a wealthy family will be found among them. These men are generally from families with a bullfighting tradition and have fathers, brothers, uncles, or others who were bullfighters or associated with bullfighting in some way, and with whom bullfighting is a way of life. Thus the Bienvenida, Vásquez, Dominguín and Ordóñez families, to mention only a few of the currently famous ones. These, however, are the exceptions. The others, the majority, come from the poorer classes, for bullfighting, like boxing, provides a chance for the poor but talented to reach for fame and fortune. There is a saying in Spanish that the best training for a bullfighter is a long apprenticeship in hunger. It is perhaps significant that, among the top 20 most popular bullfighters in Spain today, only one or two are from families with more than an average income and the vast majority are from extremely poor and modest circumstances.

Ordinarily bullfighters begin their apprenticeship by practicing or playing as children. Where this is not the case, the various passes and other actions involving cape, muleta and sword must be learned through long hours of formal practice until they can be done smoothly and perfectly almost without thinking.

Bullfighters from wealthy families generally start young and learn from professionals. They also have the advantage of an introduction into the bullfight world and are assured of being well managed from the start. Bullfighters from poorer families learn what they can when they can. Sometimes in an attempt to attract the attention of a promoter or a manager they will jump into the ring during a regular bullfight and attempt a pass or two with an improvised cape or a bit of cloth on a stick. Those who attempt this sort of thing are called *espontáneos* or spontaneous ones, although this action is, of course, planned ahead of time and is anything but spontaneous. Espontaneos generally choose the moment before the bullfighter steps into the ring for the opening capework, to make their leap into the ring, since at this time the bull is still fresh and strong and still charges from a distance at anything that moves. While the espontaneo is often greeted by the public with applause or sympathy, his intervention is always detrimental to the smooth progression of the regular fight and often spoils the bull for the man who has to kill him. In order to limit the number of these interruptions, the regulation provides that all espontáneos be fined approximately ten dollars or spend several days in jail, or both. In addition espontáneos are barred from fighting in any bullring anywhere in Spain for a period of two years. Since the object of leaping into the ring is to attract the notice of a promoter who will back their career, this penalty has real teeth in it. In spite of this fact, no series of bullfights is without its espontáneo and sometimes there will be more than one of these interruptions in a single afternoon.

Most of the bullfighters from poorer families begin their apprenticeship as unpaid performers in village fights called *capeas*. These fights take place without picadores, with difficult and dangerous animals which are not killed and have often been fought before. With luck they survive this trial and go on to organized performances without picadores but with smaller animals in regular rings in small towns throughout the country. If they are consistently successful in these fights they may graduate to regular performances in larger towns with larger animals and the aid of picadores. At this point they are called *matadores de novillos* or *novilleros*. When they feel they have gained sufficient experience to compete as real professionals they may become fullfldged bullfighters or *matadores de toros*. The long road from first amateur fight to full professional status generally takes five or six years or more. Breaking in is difficult and painful. Like young club fighters bullfighters from poor families must hustle for a chance to fight and to show what they can do. They must be ready to fight anywhere and under any conditions at any time, often beyond their ability, against old and dangerous animals which no established matador would ever consider facing. Against such animals they must try to start and then try again, often with disastrous results and a big wound for their trouble. They are often exploited by promoters and are generally badly managed, particularly in the early stages of their career. In the face of these handicaps it is not surprising that only the most determined—and lucky—survive to become real professionals.

The physical requirements of a bullfighter more closely resemble those of a fencer than any other type of athlete. A certain amount of physical strength is of course necessary but more important are stamina, speed, excellent reflexes and strong wrists.

Size is of importance in a bullfighter to the extent that a very short man will have difficulty in reaching high enough to place the sword properly and will be obliged to expose himself more in order to kill correctly. An extremely tall man, on the other hand, will find it difficult not to appear awkward or ridiculous in certain circumstances or positions, especially if the bull is not particularly big or dangerous. Most bullfighters are slim and lean from the constant exercise involved in practicing with the heavy cape and muleta. Although a few of heavier build give the impression of being stout there are no really fat bullfighters. The age of the bullfighter is of importance only with regard to whether or not it restricts the man's physical activity.

Many bullfighters have begun their careers as child prodigies, fighting little bulls in exhibitions as professionals often as early as 10 or 12. Ordinarily, however, they make their first professional appearance in their early teens. The regulation provides that they may not become full matadores before they are 18 and must have written permission from their parents or guardians until they are 21. With only a few rare exceptions, bullfighters find the life physically exhausting and retire before they are 35.

The prime qualities of a bullfighter are courage, integrity and artistry.

The qualities of courage, integrity and artistry are not found to the same extent in all bullfighters. While all bullfighters of the first rank must possess all three qualities in order to arrive at and maintain their positions, only a few great figures throughout the history of bullfighting have ever possessed all three qualities to an exceptional degree. Such men are the touchstones against which all others are compared. Normally, however, a bullfighter will possess only one, or at the most two, of these qualities to a really outstanding degree and his reputation will be based upon this combination. Thus, there are bullfighters of exceptional courage and artistry, who lack the necessary integrity to make them great. There are others of great courage and integrity who simply do not have the skill or artistry to raise them to the pinnacle. Still others have the integrity and the artistry but lack the necessary courage to perform at a peak consistently.

The courage of the bullfighter is distinguished from the bravery of the bull since the man is always aware of the danger he faces and must overcome the natural fear he experiences in the face of that danger while the bull has no such problem. The domination of this fear is always a conscious effort for some men and sometimes even assumes the proportion of a violent inner struggle which renders them physically ill. For others the domination of this fear is the spice of life and one of the major reasons for being a bullfighter.

Without the necessary courage it is, of course, impossible for the bullfighter to perform. However, some bullfighters are so talented that they are pardoned their relative lack of courage because of the things they can do when they are able to conquer their fear. On the other hand, certain bullfighters have built their reputations on an almost limitless courage which is comparable only to the mystical bravery of the bulls.

Whatever the man's reaction to his fear, it is obvious that any man who regularly goes into the bullring must have courage of a kind far above and beyond that of the average person. To have chosen such a dangerous and punishing profession at all supposes a courage of a sort not common. This courage is, of course, taken for granted, much as the courage of a boxer or a trapeze artist is taken for granted, and unless it is either present or lacking to an exceptional degree the courage of a bullfighter is never mentioned.

In order to fully appreciate the courage of the bullfighter some grasp of the real danger he faces is essential. In the first place wounds are a part of the business. These wounds are inflicted by the bull's horns which not only puncture and slash the man's body but rip, tear and dislocate it as well. The horn wounds received by the bullfighter are of a particularly nasty and disagreeable kind since they generally occur in the upper thigh or lower abdomen and often involve serious damage to the intestines and other organs as well as danger to the femoral arteries. Prior to the advent of penicillin, any serious wound of this kind was generally fatal due to peritonitis and gangrene. With the use of antibiotics, however, fatalities are now kept to a minimum but crippling and punishing wounds are as common as ever.

Most young bullfighters are wounded a half-dozen or more times before they ever really achieve status as matadores or full professionals.

Although death is no longer a serious consideration statistically for the bullfighter, bullfighting involves a particular type of terror and fascination which exists elsewhere only in hand-to-hand combat and to a lesser degree in certain types of big game hunting. For the danger inherent in bullfighting is not the impersonal curve or oil slick of motor racing, nor the loose stone or weak rope of mountain climbing. It is not the accident that a misstep or poor timing provokes. It is the terror of facing vibrant, living, animal force just a few feet away which is doing everything possible and using every skill available to kill you in the nastiest possible fashion. This situation is doubly compounded since the bullfighter must not only kill and dispose of this living animal neatly and quickly with only a straight sword as a weapon, but he must first perform certain intricate and graceful movements designed to increase the danger to its absolute maximum in order to demonstrate absolute domination of the situation and absolute lack of fear to a critical audience. In the final analysis, it is really this facet of his profession which distinguishes the bullfighter from other brave men in other dangerous ways of life. Often these wounds are not serious and only serve as a prelude for what is to come. For sooner or later nearly all bullfighters receive a really serious goring, one which threatens to cripple them or kill them. And it is with this wound that the bullfighter reaches a critical point in his career. With a serious goring the bullfighter's physical reserves are temporarily exhausted and he has a long period of inactivity in the hospital during which his imagination has time to function and he has time to think and weigh all the alternatives of his chosen profession. It is the same thing that happens to a front-line soldier when he is seriously wounded and sent to the rear areas to a field hospital. While he is being cured of his wounds he is cared for and coddled, the protective psychology that he has gradually developed in action is completely relaxed and the hazards that he once accepted as normal and inevitable assume disproportionate importance in his eyes. This is a common phenomenon and men of exceptional courage have passed through it. Some have never recovered their former courage, while others have only been able to do so through some special effort of will. Even for the exceptional man whose courage never seems to falter no matter what occurs, it is a trial and an effort and takes its toll in nervous energy. In a long career it is not unusual for a top-flight matador to have received ten or 15 serious or critical horn wounds and 20 to 30 lesser ones. The bullfighter must be able to face these wounds and recover from them with his courage and nerves intact.

The integrity of the bullfighter is in contrast to the nobility of the bull. Where the bull is noble, that is, with a straightforward open attack, without vice or viciousness, the man must match this nobility with an integrity that refuses all easy solutions and cheap effects, that does not take unfair advantage of the bull's weaknesses, and that does not pretend difficulty where none exists. Above all the man must not try to sell the public on the fact that he is doing something difficult when he is not.

With a particularly noble bull it is relatively easy for even a young and fairly inexperienced bullfighter to show to some advantage without actually exposing himself to any serious danger, while an experienced bullfighter can do so with hardly any risk whatsoever. Even with an ordinary bull, one which exhibits no unusual nobility, an experienced bullfighter can "cheat" to a considerable extent once the bull has started to follow the cloth. This cheating can take many forms but usually consists of the man stepping or swaying back from the bull's line of charge only to lean forward once the horns of the bull have passed thus giving the impression of great danger where none exists. When, as sometimes happens, an experienced bullfighter not only utilizes such tricks, but attempts to pass them off as passes of real merit, his honesty and integrity as a bullfighter must be seriously questioned.

The man must have the integrity and confidence to throw aside all such tricks and meet the bull on his own ground. The straight forward, open attack of the noble bull demands that the man crowd in on the trajectory of the charge in order to reduce his margin of safety once more to the absolute minimum and increase the danger again to the maximum. It demands that the man attempt the simplest and most difficult passes in their purest form without any sidesteps or other reflex motion to protect himself. It demands that the man commit himself absolutely and completely to the charge of the bull, exposing himself in utter confidence despite his knowledge that the bull may do something unusual that may cost him a goring.

Where the man is not able to do this the bullfight takes on something of the character of an assassination, and the sympathy of the spectators goes out to the bull to such an extent that the real emotion of the bullfight is obscured by a feeling of pity for the underdog. When the man disdains all such trickery and meets the bull squarely, giving not an inch and accepting no easy solution, the bullfight regains its dignity and the bullfighter again becomes the central figure and focus of all attention.

The intelligence and artistry of the bullfighter is in contrast to the strength and power of the bull.

Through his intelligence the man is able to outmaneuver the bull, and by giving way to his superior strength and power rather than opposing it, is able to force the bull to exhaust himself, much as a fisherman exhausts a trout by playing him on a line hardly strong enough to support his weight. In bullfighting this is further complicated by the fact that the bull is not even attached to the line or cloth with which he is being played. As a consequence the skill involved is not only different but greater.

Beyond the basic skill or craft involved in dominating and killing the bull, however, the bullfighter also exploits the plastic beauty of line, motion

and mass in a constantly changing rhythmic pattern in order to communicate an idea and emotion which is aesthetically pleasing and satisfying to the beholder.

It is only by means of his intelligence that the man is able to fully exploit his knowledge of the habits and characteristics of fighting bulls and, despite their superior strength, speed and armament, is able to control, dominate and kill them in the open ring with no other weapon than a sword and a piece of cloth on a stick. He is able to do these things gracefully in the face of danger only through the skill and dexterity he has acquired through many hours of practice and through the self-discipline which enables him to overcome his natural tendency to step away or flee from the charging bull.

It is through his ability to create an aesthetically satisfying effect while improvising within the rigid framework of the bullfight, however, that the contrast between the intelligence and artistry of the bullfighter and the power and strength of the bull is most strongly apparent. It is this contrast which is the most striking characteristic of the bullfighter and is the basis for the fundamental conflict and emotion. Where the bull is too clever or the man too sluggish or stupid, this contrast is lost and the bullfight is a failure.

The peculiar combination of qualities that make up a bullfighter are unique in the world of spectacle and in the world of sport. Many sports require integrity and courage. Many spectacles require integrity and art, but no example of sport or spectacle requires all three qualities to the degree that bullfighting does.

The ideal concept of the bullfight demands that the bullfighter, disdaining all trickery, face the straightforward, brute force of the bull's attack with cool courage, confidence and absolute integrity, relying entirely on his knowledge and skill in manipulating the cloth in order to temper and control the bull's charge. This ideal concept demands that the man deliberately flirt with danger, not only ignoring the possible consequences of an accident, but contemptuously increasing the risk to the maximum in order to improvise a rhythmic pattern of movements and postures which build naturally in emotional intensity to an aesthetic climax. Whenever the man is prudent, fearful, uncertain, dishonest, incompetent or uninspired, the man is not fulfilling his assigned role and the bullfight is not a success.

In addition to the basic qualities of courage, integrity and artistry, bullfighters are sometimes also classified with respect to their style of fighting as belonging to either the Ronda or the Seville school of bullfighting.

Neither of these classifications has anything to do with whether or not the man happens to be from Ronda or Seville, nor do they mean that he has actually attended a school for bullfighters in either of these places or anywhere else. They serve simply to describe two fundamental and contrasting approaches to bullfighting.

The Ronda School is characterized by deep emotional impact and the simple intensity and emphasis of each movement. This is the style of the introvert for whom bullfighting is essentially some deep, personal, almost religious, relationship between man and animal. It is sober, intense, austere, and is characterized by an extremely limited repertoire and range of passes. It places little emphasis on technique for its own sake.

The Seville school on the other hand is characterized by graceful nonchalance and carefree, flowery, expansive actions and gestures. This is the style of the extrovert for whom bullfighting is some lighthearted, devil-may-care game or contest. It is a brilliant, colorful, happy style of fighting and is characterized by a dazzling technical competence in wide variety of passes which stress the mans skill with both cape and muleta.

Boys playing in an empty lot. A stick, a cloth and an old set of horns, but already there is a certain style, a certain art in the set of the young body as the "bull" sweeps by under perfect control.

Serious practice at a country home. The equipment is more expensive and the apparatus more elaborate, but the concentration is the same for the well-to-do young apprentice shown training here under the critical eye of his tutors.

Testing cows in a private ring on a ranch. The cows are worked with cape and muleta prior to being picked by the man on horseback. The cow's reaction to the cloth as well as her behavior under the pic are of importance in deciding her future as a breeding animal. Guests of all ages sometimes participate in the action but ordinarily the play of the cows is reserved for professionals who are invited for this purpose and take advantage of the occasion to practice with these lighter, less dangerous animals.

The maletillas. After the guests and professionals have finished working with the animal the rancher sometimes permits one of the young apprentice bullfighters, who has come miles for this chance, to make a few passes before the cow is taken from the ring. This is the only real practice that some of these young men ever get. It is a unique opportunity since it gives them a chance to demonstrate their ability before those who are in a position to do something for them. Only a few of the young men watching from behind the wall will be given a chance, and they watch critically as the lucky one who has been chosen sets himself for his first pass.

The espontaneo. The young man has crept down from the cheap seats with a homemade muleta and leaped into the ring to make a few passes in the hope of attracting the attention of a manager or some other influential person. The bull has not yet been picked and is not ready for such close work. The young man's timing with the cloth is poor and he has just realized that the bull is not going to follow it past his body as he should.

The inevitable. The bull has ignored the cloth and swung his head in the direction of the moving figure of the man. Luckily, the horn has only penetrated the cloth of the shirt and if the matador and his assistants reach the scene in time, the young man may escape with nothing more than a few bruises. The public tends to sympathize with the espontaneo, but this interruption in the normal sequence of the action usually ruins the bull for the regular fight which is to follow and seldom provides the young man who has risked his life with more than a stiff fine and a short stay in jail.

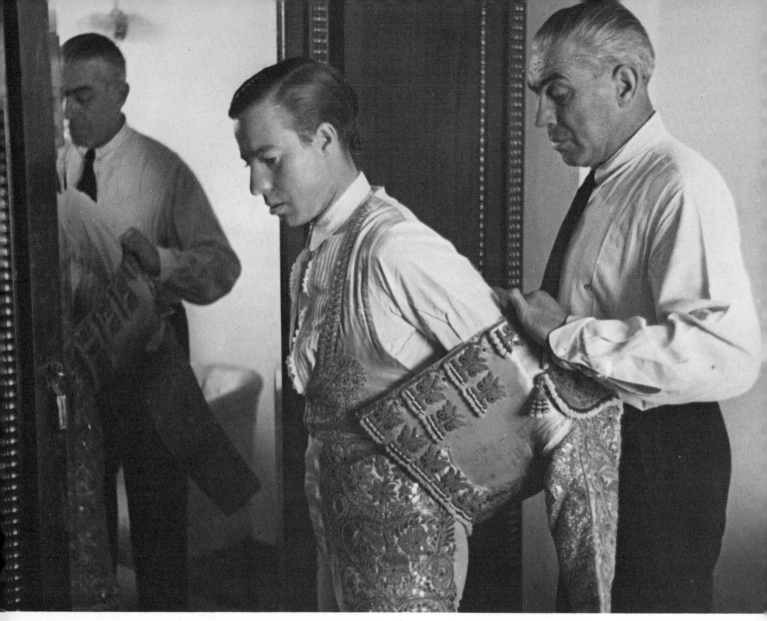

A young professional dressing for the fight. The young man is thoughtful and serious as his swordhandler helps him into the embroidered silk jacket of his suit of lights. The older man is serious and thoughtful too.

The young and the old.

The old and the young.

In the midst of the action the man has slipped and fallen. The bull whirls and is on him. The man has kept his head and thrown the cape in one direction while he rolls away in the other. The bull is following the large movement of the cloth and with luck the man will be able to get to his feet, unaided, to continue the fight.

A near miss. The bull barely misses the man with his horns, while the force of his charge brushes the man's body aside.

The accident. The man has misjudged the distance or made some other fundamental mistake and the bull has caught him with a tremendous chop of the right horn. The bull is big and well armed and if the man escapes without a serious wound he can count himself lucky.

The bull has thrown the man and is about to gore him a second time. The man knows the bull is close beside him and is trying to cover his head with his hands and lie still in the hope that the bull will ignore him and go away.

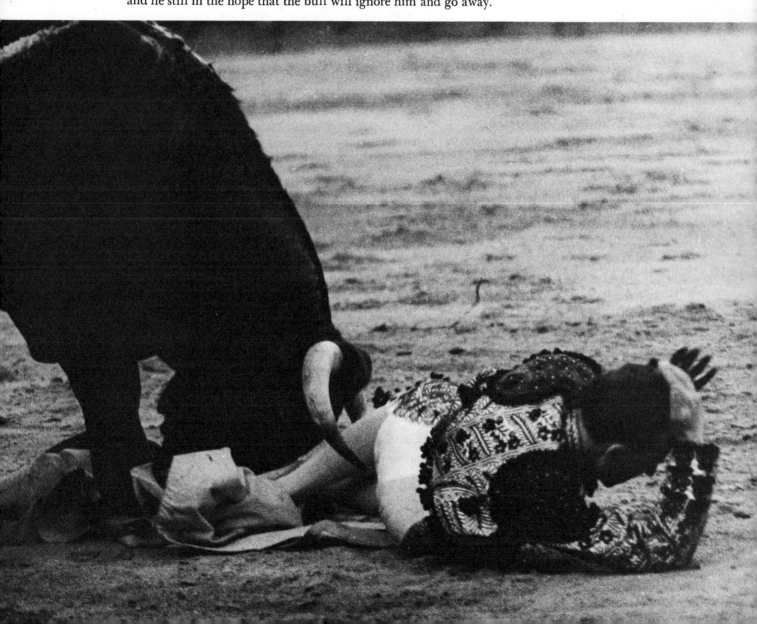

The *Quite*. With the man at the mercy of the bull everyone rushes forward to take the bull away. The man behind the bull has pulled on the bull's tail to hurt him and distract him from the man on the ground, while the others have raced close with their capes to center his attention elsewhere. The bull is fixed on the man at the far left and in another moment the others will be free to pickup the fallen man and race with him to the infirmary.

Racing to the infirmary. Almost before his wound has had a chance to begin to bleed, the men have lifted the man and are racing with him to the infirmary. The bull is still loose in the ring and the man in the center is watching to be sure he is at a safe distance while the workmen in the foreground is reaching toward the fence to help swing open the gate so they can get out of the ring.

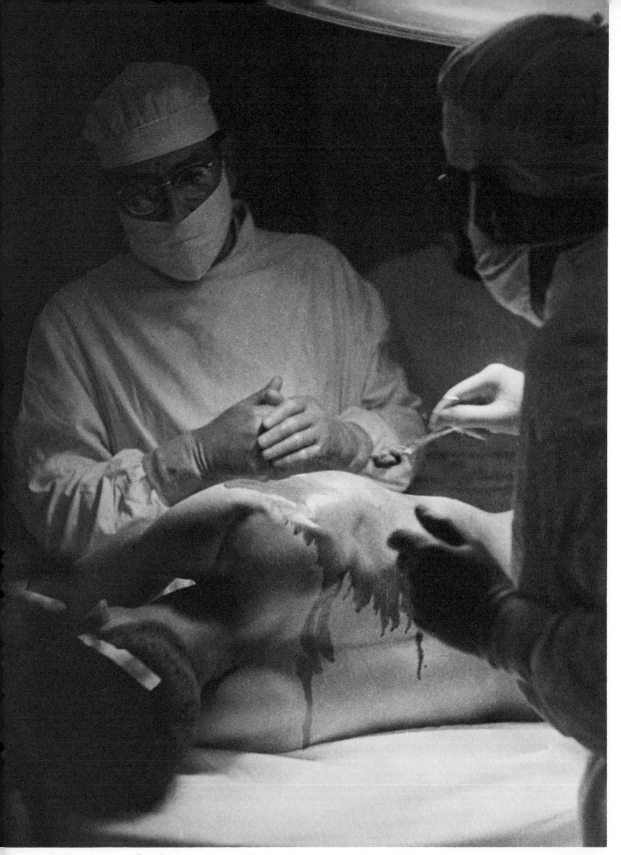

On the operating table. The hospital staff have filed in from their special ringside seats near the door to the infirmary and have washed and dressed for the operation by the time the man has been stripped and placed on the table. Here the chief surgeon makes his appraisal of the situation and in a moment the operation will begin. This picture was taken in Seville. In the smaller towns and villages there often is no infirmary and no specialized hospital staff and sometimes not even a good general practitioner.

Convalescence. In a hospital bed, with a three-day growth of beard, the man becomes a husband and father again.

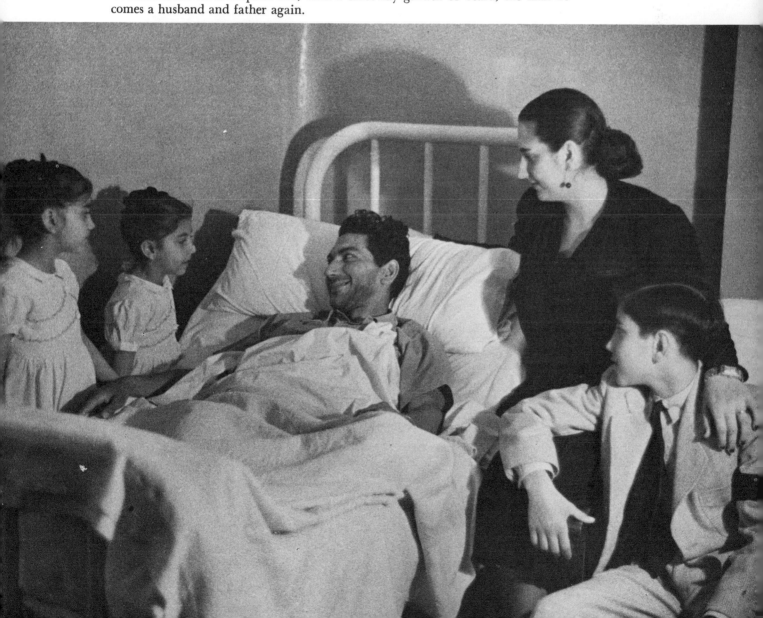

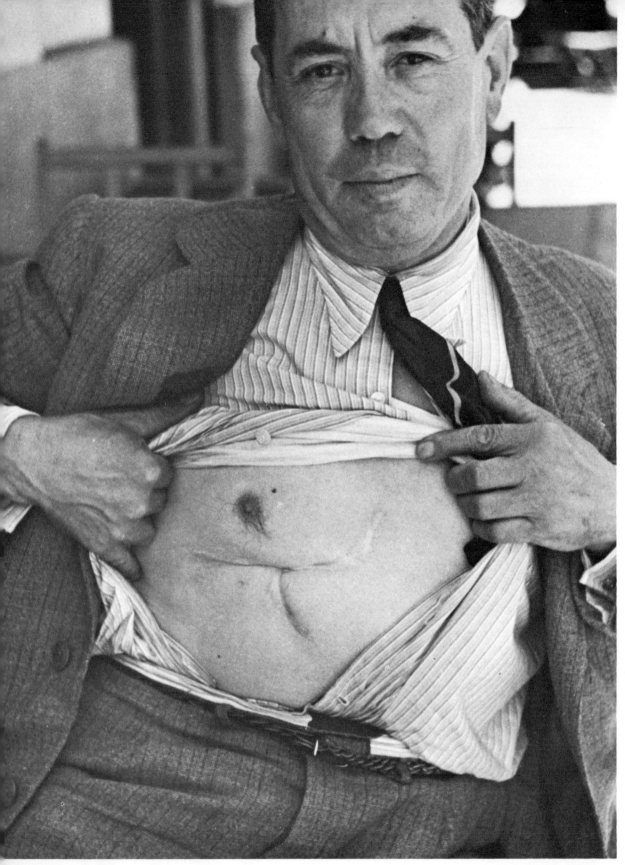

The crippling wound. And years later if you should ask what happened that he never made it, the man would show you the wound that took one of his lungs and nearly took his life.

4.

THE SPECTATORS

The kid came down along the fence carrying the sword and muleta in one hand and his hat in the other. Just as he reached us he stopped and looked up at the stands. Then he threw back his head and raised his arms.

We turned around to look, and there, behind us, up in the stands, an old man stood up and took off his hat. They stood looking at each other a moment. Then the kid spoke.

"For you father," he said, "the greatest bullfighter and the greatest teacher who ever lived, I dedicate the death of this bull, the first of my professional career."

As he finished speaking he turned on his heel and threw his hat back over his shoulder toward the stands. Somebody caught it and passed it up to the old man who took it and sat down, blinking proudly, as he watched the kid walk out toward the bull in the center of the ring.

It should have been a triumph. We were all for him and certainly the kid gave it everything he had but it was a difficult bull and he had a hard time just staying on his feet much less trying to do anything pretty. It still would have been all right, even then, but when it came time to kill the kid lost his nerve and by the time it was all over the crowd was whistling and jeering and we were all trying not to look at the old man sitting stony faced in the stands. The kid was crying from rage and frustration and when finally the bull was dead and he came over to retrieve his hat a hush came over the crowd.

The kid couldn't quite bring himself to look up at the stands but the old man stood up tall and proud, and called to him fiercely.

"Look at me!" he said, "Hold up your head. Have you no pride? If you want to be a bullfighter learn first to be a man."

Then as the kid looked up, he threw back his hat to him and they stood looking at each other a long moment more. The kid turned as pale as death as he looked up into the stands and then suddenly he spun on his heel and walked away with his chin up, without saying a word, while the old man sat down again without speaking or looking at anyone.

Not all the people who go to the bullfight are enthusiasts or really understand and appreciate it for what it is.

Only a small percentage of the people in Spain go to bullfights, and only an even smaller percentage have the opportunity to go often. Contrary to popular belief, bullfighting is not the most popular entertainment in Spain, and the vast majority of the people not only seldom or never go to the fights but really know little or nothing about them beyond some of the basic nomenclature and the names of a few stars. Among those that do go to the fights only those in the major cities such as Madrid, Barcelona and Sevilla have the opportunity to see more than a dozen fights of one kind or another each year. As a consequence, only those enthusiasts in the larger urban centers really have any wide, first-hand knowledge of the status of current bullfighting.

Some people go to the bullfight to be seen.

Some people go to the bullfight to be seen, the same way that they go to the theater or the opera or other public entertainments to be seen. They go for the prestige and what might be called the social aspects of the occasion. These spectators fill the expensive seats at the big fights and are generally more concerned with the impression they are making than with the action in the ring. They add their voices to the general acclamation or abuse of the crowd, automatically following the lead of the majority. Such people have only a superficial grasp of the mechanics of the fight and no real feeling for it. They go to see others and be seen themselves and are interested in the fight itself in only the most superficial way. Generally the people who go to the bullfight to be seen represent only a small percentage of the total public at any fight; however, at the occasional big charity fights and benefit festivals their proportion is often much greater.

Many people go to the bullfight to be entertained.

The great majority of the people go to the bullfight to be entertained. They go to see action in the ring and preferably a triumph for the matador. They know something of the mechanics of the bullfight but they are often unable to distinguish between first-rate and second-rate, and tend to applaud anything that gives them an emotional thrill, no matter how cheap or vulgar. They are not always an easy public, however, since they often demand that the man attempt impossible things with difficult bulls and become enraged when he refuses to do so. On the other hand they expect all professional bullfighters to conduct themselves as professionals and are not interested in seeing them resolve private, psychological, physical or moral problems in the ring. As a consequence they are often harsh and cruel in their treatment of individual fighters who show weakness, fear or indecision in the same way that they would be with a trapeze artist, for example, who showed these same qualities in the midst of his act.

Nevertheless these people are as generous with their rewards as they are unpitying in their demands, and generally tend to give two ears when one would be enough; but they are also as capricious and illogical as a young girl and have no memory beyond the present moment, so that the man who triumphs with his first bull may be booed from the ring by them after his second. Despite all this, they arrive at a fairly accurate estimate of each man's worth and ability which over the years establishes his reputation for all time. As a consequence, it is this public which has the last voice and it is this public with which the bullfighter must come to terms if he is to be a success.

Other spectators are tourists.

The third large group of spectators are tourists seeing a bullfight for the first, second, or perhaps third time. They frequently know little or nothing about the mechanics of the fight but are extremely interested in understanding what it is all about and in absorbing impressions and watching their own reactions to the various aspects of the fight. They are most often too preoccupied with these things and too timid or unsure of themselves in a strange atmosphere to do more than add their voice to the rest of the crowd if the bullfighter triumphs or guard a discreet silence if he fails. They stand out from the crowd because of their dress or aspect, but otherwise hardly voice an opinion or make an impression.

An exception to this occurs in the resort towns where, during the height of the season, tourists often far outnumber all other categories of spectators. Under such circumstances the uninformed reaction of the crowd is without serious reference and the bullfight degenerates into a cheap circus act where meaningless bravado is often wildly applauded and significant artistry is sometimes booed from the ring.

Only a very small minority really understands and appreciates the bullfight.

There are two other important groups of spectators which, taken together, are smaller than any of the other groups alone. These are the real enthusiasts, the men who go to every fight, who follow the fights in the papers and magazines, who discuss bullfighting and bullfighters among themselves, and who are completely familiar with all the mechanics of the fight as well as the background and ability of most of the fighters.

Within this group there is a small, hard-core minority which really understands and appreciates the bullfight in its purest form and for whom the bullfight is really a profound emotional and aesthetic experience. The rest, the majority of this minority fall into the category of these who know a great deal about the mechanics of the fight but are really more interested in refining and confirming their knowledge of the fight than in savoring the beauty of it.

It should be understood that these two groups taken together hardly ever represent more than a very small percentage, perhaps never more than five percent of the total number of spectators. This small percentage, however, sets the tone of the bullfight and keeps the request for ears and other trophies under control. When this percentage drops too low the standards of the bullfight deteriorate rapidly.

Some people go to the bullfight to be seen.

Many people go to the bullfight to be entertained.

Other spectators are tourists.

Only a small minority really understand and appreciate the bullfight.

Professional interest is special and different.

5.

BULLRINGS AND SEATING

The kid didn't have much talent and he wasn't very brave and finally the crowd got tired of watching and began to whistle and jeer.

He knew he had to do something, so he swung the cloth into his left hand and throwing back his head challenged the bull the way he had seen the big stars do. The bull came at him like an express train but he had misjudged the distances and the bull caught him by the leg and spun him high in the air. He hung for a moment twisting on the horn and then as the bull tossed his head again he crashed to the sand and lay still. Everyone dashed forward to take the bull away and two of his men raced out and caught him under the arms and started to run with him to the infirmary.

Before they reached the fence the kid came to. As soon as he realized what they were doing he started fighting to get free. He was like a wild man and they couldn't hold him. His trousers were torn and there was a lot of blood running down his leg but he had such a crazy look on his face that they finally let him go.

He threw them off and just stood there a moment. Then he lurched around and started back toward the bull. He hardly took a step before his leg buckled under him and he started to go down. It looked like he was finished then but he managed to catch himself in time and staggered forward again like a drunken man, a step at a time.

The bull was alone in the center of the ring watching him come and when his leg gave way a second time the bull lowered his head and got ready to charge. The kid tried to get up but his leg wouldn't hold him. Finally when he saw that it was no good he started crawling on his hands and knees, inching himself along, trying to reach the sword and muleta lying there in the sand. Just as he reached them the bull charged.

75

The kid flattened himself to the ground and the bull went by with a rush right over him. Then the kid was on his knees and using the sword as a cane, was struggling to his feet again. He stood on one leg and shook out the cloth in his left hand and then, leaning heavily on the sword, he limped staggeringly toward the bull who had turned and was waiting for him.

Everyone was on his feet yelling at him to stop but he didn't hear them and when the bull charged again he made an aborted kind of movement with the cloth and stuck out the sword and then the bull smashed into him and it was all over.

The sword hit bone just above the right shoulder and, as the bull smashed into him, the kid crashed back into the sand and lay still. Somebody took the bull away and this time as they ran with the kid from the ring he lay still as death in their arms.

As they carried him out below us into the infirmary the old timer sitting in front of me shook his head disdainfully.

"Ridiculous," he said. "A clown. What kind of a bullfighter is that? What was he trying to prove? He didn't even know what he was doing. Fools like that shouldn't be permitted in the ring."

The bullring (or *plaza*) is an amphitheater of tiered seats enclosing a smooth, flat, circular patch of hard-packed, yellow sand. Bullrings in Spain vary in size from large, three-tiered structures, such as those in Madrid and Barcelona which hold 23 or 26 thousand people, to small village rings capable of holding only four or five thousand or even less.

Most bullrings are permanent structures of brick and stone, but in recent years there have been a number of portable or temporary rings made of wood and steel which can be put up and taken down in a few hours and which are rented to towns for specific occasions.

Although there is no standard size specified by the regulation, normally the action area of the bullring is some 50 yards in diameter. Sometimes it is so small that the men are actually crowded in their work, while in rings like Madrid and Barcelona, at times, they seem lost in an immense expanse of deserted sand. In general, beyond a certain vital minimum, the size of this area varies in direct proportion to the seating capacity of the arena.

In permanent bullrings the action area of the ring is separated from the tiered seats by an inner wooden fence, five and a half feet high, and an outer higher fence or wall at least seven feet high. This outer fence, which is the foundation of the tiered seats, is surmounted by a pair of steel cables for extra security. The protected corridor between these two fences varies from five and a half to six feet in width and provides a place to stand and move about for all those connected with the fight who are not involved in the action of the moment.

Prior to the introduction of prefabricated bullrings and even today in certain outlying districts, the smaller towns or pueblos transform the main square of the town into a bullring once or twice a year by the simple expedient of blocking off all streets exiting from it with high-sided farm carts. These carts, beside forming an effective barrier, also provide seats for the spectators who cannot find a place at some window or balcony overlooking the square.

All permanent bullrings, and most temporary ones, include a small chapel, an infirmary and a set of corrals as auxiliary structures or as part of the ring itself.

It is sometimes, but not always, possible to visit the various parts of the bullring in the morning prior to the fight. This usually entails tipping the doorman or bullring superintendent, or in better organized rings, paying a standard fee for a visitor's ticket. If possible, this is a worthwhile orientation and a curious back-stage insight into the bullfight. It is also a good opportunity to buy souvenirs such as banderillas, horns, etc., generally not available elsewhere. In some rings it is even possible to view the bulls in the corrals and to watch the *apartado* or separation of the bulls as they are shunted into the *chiqueros* or stalls under the stands. This latter operation takes place at exactly noon on the day of the fight.

All bullrings, whatever their size, are arbitrarily divided into a number of pie-shaped segments or sections called *tendidos*, which are numbered for ticket-reference purposes.

Since the word tendido also refers to general admission seats, there is sometimes a certain amount of confusion with regard to this designation and it is worth knowing that it can mean either one particular numbered part of the arena or the kind of seat that is desired.

Generally speaking, seats in the bullring are divided into three classifications: those in the shade (*sombra*), those in the sun and shade (*sol y sombra*) and those in the sun (*sol*).

Shade (sombra) means that the seats are in the shade from the beginning throughout the fight. Sun and shade (sol y sombra) means that the seats are in the sun at the beginning of the fight but will be reached by the shade after the second or third bull. Sun (sol) means that the seats are in the sun throughout the fight.

Seats in the shade are always the most expensive, seats in the sun and shade are less expensive and seats in the sun are least expensive.

The difference in cost for these classifications has been established because the bullfighting season stretches through the terrible heat of the Spanish summer. While it is undeniable that on a sunny day in midsummer the seats in the shade are vastly more comfortable, in early spring or late fall, or on the occasional cool or cloudy day in midsummer this is not always true and on such occasions the cheaper seats in the sun are worth considering as a practical economy.

Within these three classifications, seats are also graded with regard to price from lowest and closest to the action, to highest and most distant. Thus the first row or ringside (*barrera*) within any of the classifications is the most expensive of that classification followed by the second row (*contrabarrera*) the third row (*delantera*) and the general admission (*tendido*), with rows numbered from one to 10 or 20 or 30, which are cheaper still. Some of the very largest rings such as Madrid, Sevilla and Barcelona have a covered section even higher than the tendido which is called the *grada* and sometimes, as in Madrid and Barcelona, another section higher still called the *andanada*, the seats of which are even cheaper than the grada.

For anyone attending his first bullfight, or for the newcomer in general, the higher and cheaper seats are by far the best for several reasons. To begin with, the spectacle aspect of the fight is more impressive, since the added distance gives a more comprehensive view of all the action and the pageantry can be more fully appreciated. In addition, certain sometimes unpleasant details, such as the action of the picadores or a messy job of killing, will lose some of their stark reality and disagreeable effect from a position slightly removed. Finally, the psychological aspect of the bullfighter, interesting but distracting, and really only a sidelight on the bullfight, assumes too much importance from close up. This is especially true for the newcomer who tends to watch the reaction of the man and to become too involved with him to the detriment of an overall appreciation of the action.

A further interesting aspect of the higher seats is the fact that all of the action in the ring seems to take place in something like slow motion. This same optical effect occurs in watching motion pictures of bullfights and when viewing the action through field-glasses or binoculars. Whatever the reasons for this curious effect, it provides the spectator with an opportunity to view the action in the ring with greater clarity and perspective and to appreciate the fine points in all their aesthetic intensity.

There are certain drawbacks, of course, to sitting high up in the plaza. The seats are more difficult to reach, especially if you arrive late. They are not as comfortable as those at ringside since not only do you have someone's knees in *your* back, but your knees are in someone's back in front of you. Also the seats in the cheaper sections are not as widely spaced and the higher you go the more crowded together you will be.

As a final word with regard to seating, it may be worthwhile to mention that aside from the comfort involved, and strictly from the point of view of seeing the bullfight, certain sections of the stands are more desirable than others. While these vary with the individual characteristics of each bullring, it is worth remembering that little fighting is ever done in front of the gate of the bullpen (*toril*) , through which the bull enters the arena, and as a rule, more fighting occurs in the shade than in the sun.

The bullfighter avoids the area near the toril because the bull goes on the defensive in that area and as a consequence becomes almost impossible to fight brilliantly or at all. The bullfighter's preference for the shade corresponds to the proximity of help in case of need in the form of the handlers and capemen behind the fence (*barrera*) in that area. Another consideration is of course that it is cooler and more comfortable in the shade and unless the bull requires otherwise the man prefers to be comfortable.

6.

BUYING TICKETS

As the sword went in high up between the shoulders, the bull turned, took a step, then stopped and coughed.

The kid waved everyone away and stood, with his hand up, looking at the bull. The bull looked at the kid and took a step toward him. The kid stepped back. The bull coughed again and started after the kid a step at a time. The kid backed slowly away.

Finally the bull stopped.

The sword had reached some vital spot deep inside him and suddenly you could see him forget about the kid and start fighting to stay on his feet. He locked his legs stiff and spread them wide apart to brace himself and stood there swaying from side to side. The kid stood with his hand up insistently, watching him struggle. The bull swayed back and forth with his legs locked, holding on. Finally he swayed too far, his weight overbalanced, and he stumbled forward in a stiff legged lunge. For a moment it looked as though he might go over, then he recovered and braced himself and started swaying as before. The men started forward to turn him with their capes but the kid waved them back impatiently. The bull stood still, fighting to stay on his feet, fighting to stay alive.

The kid stood watching the bull a moment more, then he stepped forward and swung the muleta lightly in front of him. The bull accepted this final challenge, staggered forward in a last stiff legged charge, stumbled, recovered, stumbled again, fought to keep his feet under him and finally in one last desperate lunge crashed over dead in the sand.

The kid looked down at the dead bull.

Suddenly he leaned forward and touched him gently, almost tenderly. It had been a bad fight and on the kid's face there was a look of sadness, a touch of sorrow,

80

something of regret. A moment more he stood there, then he straightened, turned, and walked back across the ring with his head down while we all sat silently watching him go.

If possible reserve your tickets ahead of time.

If you know that you will be going to certain specific fights, for example, during the fair in Sevilla in April or to Pamplona in July, write to the bullring ticket office (*Empresa, Plaza de Toros*) or to the mayor's office (*Ayuntamiento*) of the town or city and ask them if they can reserve the tickets you want. Be sure to write several months in advance and remember to specify the kind and number of tickets you want. Also ask whether or not you can pay for them by mail with a check or international money order and if not, how long they can hold them for you. Not all bullrings make it a policy to reserve tickets, so this procedure may not always work, but if it does it will certainly eliminate a great deal of last-minute scrambling, especially if the fight in question is a particularly popular one. If possible, write in Spanish, but if not, English will do in all but the very smallest towns.

If this is not possible, tickets first go on sale in the resale (20 percent) places four or five days ahead of the bullfight.

These are little stalls or ticket-windows scattered throughout the business center of the larger towns and cities. In smaller towns or villages they are located in the main square or plaza. Here tickets to all shows and sporting events are resold at an official standard mark-up of 20 percent. There is often a large choice of seats at these agencies and because of the 20 percent commission, tickets of some kind generally remain available from this source until a few hours before the fight is scheduled to begin.

Tickets go on sale at the official ticket-office only during certain hours, a day or two prior to the fight, and at the last minute at the bullring itself if there are any left. The times and places for official sale are marked on the billboards announcing the fight.

The cheapest way to get seats, of course, is to go to the bullring itself an hour or two prior to the fight or else trace down the central ticket office of the bullring which may be located anywhere in the center of town and is only open during certain hours of the day. Here you can stand in line, wait your turn, and buy your ticket at its face value like all the natives and hard-core enthusiasts without it costing a cent more than the purchase price marked on the program. This supposes an almost unlimited amount of free time and if the fight is a popular one you run the risk of arriving at the window only to find that they are sold out.

If you are not able to get tickets any other way, there is always the recourse of buying any ticket you can find from one of the regular scalpers that haunt the area around the bullring immediately prior to the fight.

Scalpers' prices are, of course, gauged to the demand. As a consequence, unless the fight is so popular that it is a sell-out (posting the sign, *NO HAY BILLETES*), there are always a few scalpers caught with tickets they cannot sell at the very last minute. Thus, if you must buy from scalpers, the longer you wait the better your bargaining position becomes. Unless you are skilled at such bargaining, however, you may still end up paying too much for poor seats high up in the sun when you think you are buying seats low down in the shade.

Finally, the simplest way to get tickets to the bullfight is to have someone buy them for you.

If you are staying at one of the better hotels, the man at the desk will be glad to send one of the bellhops out for them or he may have a few tickets to dispose of as a personal service or for a friend. Unless you specify (and insist), the tickets will be of the better and more expensive kind and in any case a tip and a commission will be expected.

A more economical and more prosaic way is to go to the bullfight on a guided tour through a tourist agency. In this case, the tickets will ordinarily be of the general admission type and the guide generally provides some kind of running commentary on the action in the ring.

7

GETTING SEATED

He couldn't kill the bull. He went in with the sword ten times but he couldn't find the spot. Finally he had to give it up. The bull was on the defensive and each time he started in the bull almost got him.

His men closed in flopping their capes, first on one side, then on the other, trying to help him, trying to get the bull's head down so he would have a chance. It wasn't any use.

He came over to the fence to get a fresh sword and you could see that he had really lost all control. His hands were shaking and his voice wouldn't behave and his eyes were wild with fear. His manager and his sword handler took him aside and tried to talk some sense to him but he was too far gone to listen and in the end he just brushed them aside and grabbed a new sword and rushed back out into the ring.

He tried desperately five more times after that, but each time the bull was ready for him. By this time the crowd was whistling and jeering and throwing cushions into the ring and the kid's face was white with rage and fear and frustration.

He tried over and over again after that, until the bull's back was a bloody mess of chopped meat, until he was so tired he couldn't raise his arm high enough to make the proper movement anymore and finally he just stood there, beaten.

The crowd was furious. People were throwing bottles and cushions and anything they could get their hands on into the ring and were screaming insults and obscenities in a deafening roar. The police had stepped out and were watching the crowd and the kid was standing there in the ring, facing them, taking it all, with a terrible desperate look on his face, knowing he was finished as a bullfighter and a man in that town, forever.

Wear light, comfortable clothes which will not show dust or dirt too easily, and if you are in the mountains or it is a cool day carry some kind of sweater or light coat or shawl to put on as the sun goes down.

A bullfight is a formal affair and most Spaniards dress up for it. Unless you are sitting high up in the sun in the cheapest seats, dress as you might for a theater matinee or some other fairly formal afternoon entertainment. Extremes in clothing are seldom seen except on foreigners. Wild sport shirts, T-shirts, jeans, stretch-pants, shorts and other such informal sports attire attract a great deal of attention and are really not suitable. In the cheaper seats, of course, there is less formality about dress, but even high up in the sun, conservative standards of dress are maintained and extreme undress is whistled and jeered. Two absolute "Dont's" are very low-cut sun dresses for the women and bare torso exhibitionism by the men.

Leave your still camera behind but bring a movie camera if you have one.

It is practically impossible to take good action-photos at the bullfight from a seat in the stands. Even with a telephoto lens the results are usually less than satisfying. It is doubly difficult if you are not thoroughly familiar with what is happening and cannot anticipate the precise moment which is the height of the action. Most souvenir stores have a wide assortment of color slides covering every phase of the fight and many photography shops sell black and white prints by professionals which are far superior to anything you can hope to achieve.

A movie camera, on the other hand, since it captures all the action, will provide a real souvenir, especially if you have the opportunity of filming a good fight. Take plenty of film with you and expect to use it, since there is at least an hour of solid action in every bullfight. Much of this action will not be worth filming, of course, but nothing is more frustrating than to be sitting with an empty camera when the fight of the afternoon takes place right below you. You can cover more of the action in greater detail if you have some sort of telephoto attachment for your camera. In any case unless you are seated at ringside you will be troubled by the people in front of you and the angle will not show the action to best advantage. If you intend to take pictures be sure to take the sun into account when buying your tickets.

Bring binoculars, if you can, no matter where you happen to be sitting.

Unless you are extremely lucky, a good part of the action will probably take place on the far side of the ring. If you happen to be fairly high up in the stands this can be a matter of several hundred feet or more. Even if you are at ringside the action may be 50 or 60 yards away. It is a great advantage at such times to be able to step up close and take a look at the action.

Besides the obvious advantages of being able to see more clearly, binoculars are extremely useful in verifying certain details not immediately apparent from a distance, i.e., the exact placement of the sword at the time of the kill, the way the man is holding the muleta, the degree of punishment the bull has received from the picador, etc. It is interesting, too, to have an occasional glimpse at the man's face to observe the concentration, confidence, joy, fear, and terror that is reflected there or to peek into the backstage world of the sword-handlers and assistants over behind the fence. Binoculars should be used sparingly for a close-up and not continuously throughout the fight since they distort depth perception and tend to give a false idea of the speed and majesty of the bullfighter's movements and the distance he is working from the bull.

Arrange to get to the bullring early enough.

Make allowances for traffic jams and finding a place to park if you are driving. Try to arrive on foot in front of the bullring with your ticket in your pocket at least 15 minutes prior to the fight. If this is your very first fight try to get there even earlier. Arriving early will give you time not only to get to your seat comfortably but to savor the hustle and bustle and the excitement of the hurrying crowd, without being too hurried yourself. In any case remember that no matter what happens, the bullfight will start exactly on time and the regulation specifically prescribes that if you arrive late you will not be permitted to go to your seat until the bull which is being fought has been killed.

If your seat is in the sun or the sun and shade, wear some kind of a hat or cap or buy a cardboard sunshade from one of the small boys in front of the bullring for a peseta or two.

Without some kind of head-covering you will not be able to tolerate the sun and will find it difficult to see any action that takes place in the shade across the ring. A wide-brimmed, high-crowned straw hat is the best shelter, of course, but attracts a great deal of attention and is not worn except by foreigners in any of the larger cities. An ordinary straw hat or light panama is more often seen and a soft cloth cap which can be tucked in a pocket or a hand bag is probably the most convenient. The cardboard sunshades sold at the ring are satisfactory and cheap but are ugly and uncomfortable and troublesome to keep on if there is any wind. Sunglasses are a matter of preference but tend to obscure the color and contrast of the light and shadow which are an integral part of the spectacle.

Fans for the women are certainly a part of the Spanish scene and are always agreeable in the heat.

While a fan will not really cool anyone at a bullfight, it does give a certain measure of relief through the air movement and used judiciously will help to keep makeup from running.

Take time also to rent cushions from the Red Cross attendants inside the bullring under the stands.

The cushions are well worth the few extra pesetas they cost to rent, since seats in the bullring are almost always concrete or brick, and, if in the sun, are sometimes hot enough to burn through light summer clothes. These cushions should not be taken with you when you leave and are not to be thrown into the arena under any circumstances.

If an usher shows you to your seat, a small tip of a peseta or two is in order. If there is no usher to help you, verify your tickets against the row and seat numbers to be sure you are in the right spot.

Do not be surprised to find someone already sitting in your seats. This is a standard trick of sharpsters who hope that you will not appear and thus have better seats than they paid for. There is seldom any difficulty about claiming your seats. Since you have your tickets and he has none, as soon as you wave them in front of his face the sharpster will get up and move. If there should be any difficulty, check your row and seat number with the people in the row behind, and if there is still some doubt call an usher.

As you get settled in your seat, you will see below you the hard packed, yellow sand of the bullring, smooth, empty and untouched except for two concentric circles painted in white or red.

These circles in the sand are of importance with reference to the action of the picadores, as well as the other phases of the fight, and are named after the parts of the ring they encircle. The inner circle is called the line of the *medios* since it encircles all the central section of the ring called the medios. The larger of the two circles, the one closer to the fence is called the *tercio* line, since it encircles that part of the ring between it and the medios called the tercios. The part of the ring between the tercio line and the wall is called the *tablas*.

Note the movement and life of the crowd in the stands.

If you arrive early enough and if the fight is a particularly important one or if the fight happens to be the daily high point of one of the big fairs you will have an opportunity to watch the excitement build slowly to an almost unbelievable pitch of intensity before the first bull appears.

Locate the presidential box high up on the shady side of the ring. This is generally distinguished by an awning of red velvet or red and yellow bunting or some similar type of drapery which makes it readily recognizable.

Since the president is charged with the over-all conduct of the fight it is worth knowing where to look for guidance or enlightenment with regard to what is happening in the ring. The presidential box generally remains empty until a moment or two before the fight is to begin, when the officials come forward to take their places. A round of applause generally greets their appearance since it means that the fight is about to begin.

Note across the way behind the fence the dark solid door of the toril through which the bull will enter the ring and above it the kettle drum and trumpet men who will signal the different stages of the fight as they are ordered by the president.

In most rings the weight of each bull is posted above the toril door while the bull is being fought. This weight is in kilos and is of interest since all bulls which are fought must meet certain minimum weight standards specified in the regulation. These standards vary depending upon the category of the plaza and whether the bullfight is a novillada or a full corrida.

Note the spot where the bright yellow and red fighting capes are draped over the wooden fence; the bullfighter's assistants and handlers are already busy in the little passageway behind, cleaning swords, folding capes and making other preparations for the bullfight.

This is the spot the bullfighters will work from and return to when not occupied in the ring. If you happen to be seated at ringside right behind this spot you will have somewhat the same impression as you might have from watching a stage show from the wings of the theater. Such a viewpoint, while very interesting with regard to the performers, is essentially distracting from the main action of the bullfight.

Behind the fence over in the sun almost directly across from the presidential box the bullfighters will be forming up for the entrance parade or *paseo*.

The bullfighters will be in one of the big doorways behind the fence under the stands. They will have just come from offering a prayer in the chapel and will be adjusting their dress capes, or with them already adjusted will be posing for photographers or chatting with friends. They will be standing quietly to the side, as much in the shade as possible in order to avoid the heat, while they wait for the fight to begin.

As the time approaches for the fight to begin keep your eyes on the president's box and watch as he drapes a white handkerchief across the railing in front of him and signals the fight to start.

8.

THE PASEO

He was incredibly brave. His whole reputation was based on that. It was what people came to see. It was what made him a drawing card. It was why people talked about him. It was what made him a star.

Inevitably he was caught and gored. But always lightly. Nothing serious. Then one day, as he was placing a spectacular pair of banderillas, he pushed it too far. The horn caught him just above the pubic hair and opened him up nearly to the sternum. It was like a razor slash and, as his belly split open, his guts started to fall out onto the ground.

He caught himself with both hands and started to stumble toward the fence. Then his men had him in their arms and were racing with him to the infirmary. As they came by beneath us you could see his intestines like sausages spurting out beneath his fingers. His face was gray as dust, but he was still conscious and he was holding onto himself for dear life.

He spent four hours on the operating table. They had to wash and repack his entire abdominal cavity. When he came out of the ether they told him how close it had been and showed him the stack of get well telegrams that had come pouring in.

He didn't say anything at first, then he said, "Call all the newspapers. Tell them I'm just as I was before. Tell them I haven't changed. Tell them I'll be back. That it won't make any difference."

We all thought he was finished for the season but three weeks later, with the stitches still in place, he was back in the ring fighting again just as he had before. He wore a heavy elastic bandage to keep the stitches from tearing loose and when the bull caught him he bled internally, but he kept right on fighting, and eventually the wound healed and when the season ended he was number one on anybody's list of the top ten young bullfighters in Spain.

As the clock marks the hour the bullfight is to begin, the president reaches down and drapes a white handkerchief across the railing in front of him.

With regard to the president it is worth knowing that all of the formal order of the bullfight is under his direction. The president himself need not be an expert on bulls or bullfighting and he is generally some high government official or dignitary. However, to insure that his decisions are knowledgeable he is accompanied by an assessor or expert (generally a former bullfighter or enthusiast) who counsels him in his decisions and indicates what should be done. The final decision of what action should be taken, however, rests with the president and he may ignore the advice of the experts if he so desires.

From his box high up overlooking the arena the president signals his order to two trumpet men and a drummer and to the *alguaciles* who communicate these orders to the men in and about the ring.

The president's signals are generally accomplished by showing a handkerchief; a white one to signal the beginning of the *paseo,* the entrance of the bull and the other changes of *tercio* (phases of the fight), a red one to signal the use of black banderillas (for cowardly bulls who will not charge the picadores), a green one to signal the entrance of the tame steers and their removal of the bull alive from the ring if the bullfighter is unable to kill him in the allotted time, and a blue one (rarely used) to grant a tour of the ring to an especially brave bull after he has been killed.

The white handkerchief is also used by the president to signal his consent to the demands of the crowd for one or two ears as recompense to the triumphant matador after the fight. For more detailed instructions he has a telephone which communicates directly with the ringside and the alguaciles stationed there.

At this signal from the president, two men (called *alguaciles*) ride out into the arena. The alguaciles, dressed in costumes of the time of Phillip II, ride slowly out across the arena together and salute the president, then wheel and spur around the periphery of the ring. They meet in front of the big doorway across from the presidential box where the bullfighters have been waiting. As they rein up, gates in the fence are swung open and the matadores step a pace or two into the ring.

The alguaciles receive all of the president's orders and see that they are carried out. They are the official police force of the bullfight. During the fight they may be seen behind the fence, waving the picadores into place, calling to the bullfighters or the ring attendants, and generally maintaining some semblence of order. After the bull is dead, if the fight has been a success, the alguacil comes forward to receive the ear or ears which have been cut and carries them to the bullfighter in the name of the public and the president.

The matadores form up abreast of each other. Behind each matador in single file follow his three *banderilleros* (foot assistants who place the banderillas) and two *picadores* (mounted assistants who pic the bull). Behind these are two extra picadores, the mule teams which drag out the dead bull, and finally a number of ring attendants whose duties include smoothing and brushing the sand of the arena and helping the picadores to remount. The total number of men and horses makes an attractive and colorful spectacle as the parade moves out across the ring to the sound of a *pasodoble* from the band.

The matadores are dressed in brilliantly colored suits (called *trajes de luces*) spangled with silver and gold, while their assistants wear suits spangled only with silver or decorated with black embroidery. Except for the ornate decoration and the quality of the material the costume of the matadores and that of the banderilleros is basically the same. This costume includes long white stockings over which are worn a pair of silk, rose colored stockings, both of which come well up over the knee. After these, there are a pair of patent leather slippers without heels, a white shirt with a frilled front, a pair of stiff, heavily brocaded, silk trousers which fasten just below the knee to hold the stockings in place, a narrow silk tie and a wide silk sash. Each man wears a large, black, silk-covered button fastened to the hair at the back of his head as a symbol of the long hair or pigtail which was once worn by all bullfighters. He also wears a fancy, embroidered vest and a short, heavily brocaded and embroidered silk jacket. His hat is a peculiarly shaped, furry, black affair with two pendulous "ears." Across his left shoulder or arm he carries a highly brocaded and embroidered, silk dress cape which at the time of the paseo he winds tightly about his left arm and body. Many bullfighters bandage their hands and wrists as an aid and support in handling the heavy cape, muleta and sword but no armor or special protection of any kind is worn for any of the vital areas of the body, and except to mould the figure of the man, this costume gives no protection against the horns of the bull. The entire costume weighs nearly 20 pounds and restricts the movement of the man considerably. In recent years, several stars have made efforts to revise this costume, primarily in order to reduce the weight, but little real progress has been made and the costume remains essentially the way it has been for the last hundred years.

The picadores wear the same white frilled shirt, the tie, the sash and the embroidered vest that the matadores and the banderilleros do, but the jacket differs in that the elbows and shoulders are more heavily reinforced and sometimes padded with leather as protection against heavy falls taken from the horse. The right leg of the picador and sometimes the left, is protected from the ankle to the thigh by a sort of flexible, steel, armor plate which is hidden under heavy yellow trousers that come down nearly to the ankle. The lower part of the leg is protected by heavy leather spats or leggings and heavy boots with triple soles reinforced with steel. The picador also wears a heavy, hard-crowned, wide-brimmed hat and the entire costume is designed to offer as much protection as possible to the man, particularly to those parts most exposed to the horns of the bull.

If any of the bullfighters is wearing a wide black band around his left arm it signifies that he is in mourning for some close relative who has recently died. On rare occasions all three bullfighters may wear this band to commemorate the death of some famous bullfighter who perhaps died in that plaza or recently elsewhere.

If any of the bullfighters is carrying his hat in his hand it means that this is his first appearance in this plaza. An exception to this is the bullfighter who has an unhealed head wound of some kind and has been authorized to remain uncovered because of it.

As the band strikes up a pasodoble the bullfighters cross themselves and step out behind the alguaciles in the paseo.

As the band strikes up and the men step out, watch the free-swinging way they walk with their left arm holding the short dress cape in place and their right arm swinging free. Note the different way each bullfighter carries himself. Some strut, some plod, some go in determined strides, some go pensively or almost hesitantly, many of the younger ones, and some of the older ones too, come tentatively, holding themselves carefully together, hardly daring to breathe. As the procession moves across the ring to the sounds of the music, the color, pageantry and spectacle of the bullfight are most striking.

The paseo breaks up against the barrera in front of the presidents box where everyone bows in salute to this authority. Then the picadores ride out of the arena, the mule teams and attendants leave by another door and the matadores and banderilleros after a few practice swings with the fighting capes, take their places behind the barrera clearing the ring.

Watch as the procession breaks up against the fence and the bullfighters pass the short dress capes across the fence to their assistants. Note that these fancy capes are passed up to the stands to be draped across the barrera in front of the spectators, thus adding an additional bit of color to the spectacle.

As the bullfighters take the large fighting capes from their assistants, pay particular attention to the way they spread these capes and begin a series of trial passes to warm up and get the feel of the cape and to note whether or not the wind is sufficient to disturb the full, free-flowing swing of the folds of the cape. Watch the men as they practice slow, easy, graceful passes; beautiful, easy, languid passes which give an idea of what the man is capable of doing if everything works out perfectly and if the bull turns out to be the bull every bullfighter dreams about. Since only very rarely is the bull as cooperative as he might be or the man as relaxed and at ease as he is at this moment, you will seldom or never see such perfect passes duplicated later during the fight, and, if the bulls are difficult or the men particularly incompetent, these are apt to be the only beautiful passes you may see all afternoon, so it is well to savor them while you can.

As the ring clears, the alguaciles ride again around the periphery. One of them returns, receives from the president the key to the toril or bull pen, carries it to the attendant in charge of this gate and spurs his horse from the arena.

In some rings the alguaciles actually receive the key to the toril, while in other rings this is only done symbolically. In some rings too the president actually throws this key or the object symbolizing it to the alguacil who attempts to catch it in his hat, while in other rings the key or object is handed up to the alguacil by someone behind the fence.

The toril attendants looks around the ring to be sure it is empty, then up at the president's box. The president signals and, as the trumpets sound, the attendant turns, fits the key to the lock, and swings open the gate.

The toril gate opens onto a passageway which runs back under the stands to the individual pens or stalls (*los chiqueros*) where the bulls are kept in readiness for the fight. This passageway and the pens themselves are kept in semi-darkness and the animals are given food and water and permitted to rest undisturbed once they have entered there. Since each pen gives directly onto the passageway, the bulls can be let out in the desired order without difficulty. It should be understood that the bulls are not molested in the pens and that they are not kept in darkness to blind them as is so often supposed. They are in a darkened room for the same reason that the bullfighter is at the hotel, to rest and compose themselves for the effort they will be called upon to make within a very few hours. Just prior to being released into the arena, the *divisa*—a small barb with the colors of the ranch or *ganadéria*—is thrust into the hump of muscle on top of the shoulders and this barb and the open door with light at the end of it are sufficient to speed the bull into the ring.

All eyes focus on the toril gate in anticipation of the explosion of the bull into the arena. The bullfight proper is about to begin.

As the ring clears and the president signals for the entrance of the first bull, look around for the senior bullfighter, who will generally be standing quietly behind one of the *burladeros* or entrances into the ring itself. If you are close enough you will be able to see that he is standing tense and alert, his eyes fixed on the toril gate, awaiting the first glimpse of the bull.

The trumpets. Across from the president's box, above the toril gate, the trumpets echo the president's signal to begin. The iron bull's head is a decoration in Seville which distinguishes the toril gate from the other entrances to the ring.

The alguaciles (or ring police) cross the ring to salute the president.

The matadores step into the ring. As they face the ring, the senior matador is always on the left, the next in seniority is on the right, and the youngest is in the middle. Behind them, each man's banderilleros and picadores line up for the paseo.

The paseo. The alguaciles lead the parade across the ring and out toward the president's box.

The paseo. The men stride across the ring to the sound of the music while the crowd applauds.

At the fence. Ordinarily the men simply bow and turn away as they reach the fence below the president's box, but on this occasion they observe a moment of silence for a comrade who was killed in the ring only a few days before.

The picadores salute the president and turn to ride out of the ring.

The bullfighters take a few practice swings with the fighting capes, then step out of the ring as the trumpet signals the entrance of the first bull.

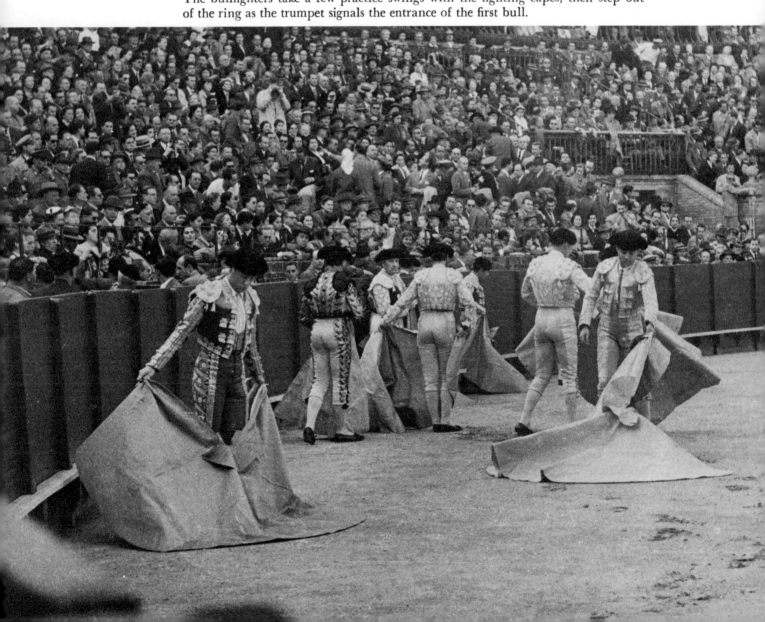

9.

RUNNING THE BULL

Just before the end of the season he was terribly gored. The bull ripped through the muscles in his thigh and tore out the femoral artery so that the blood jumped six feet in the air as they ran with him to the infirmary.

For a while they thought he was going to die. Then they thought they might have to cut off his leg. For two months he was on the critical list. Then slowly he began to recover.

By February they were talking about a limited season if the leg responded to treatment. Then he was up and around and training again. Finally his first fight was scheduled for the end of April in Seville.

As he came limping across the ring in the paseo the crowd gave him a standing ovation. Later in his first bull he tried to live up to his reputation but he couldn't keep his feet still. You could see him trying but no matter what he did his feet would jump back in the midst of every pass. Everyone was quiet, watching, hoping he would be able to make it. Once someone over in the sun started to whistle but the crowd shushed them and when, finally, the bull was dead, the ring was absolutely silent.

Later, when he came out for his second bull you could see he had made up his mind to stand still no matter what happened but as he set himself to take the first charge his legs were twitching, and suddenly I knew he wasn't going to be able to do it. He knew it too and as the bull came by his feet skipped back so that he almost slipped and fell. He tried to pretend that he had slipped, that it had been an accident, but the second time it was the same and after that even though he tried he couldn't pretend any more. It wasn't a pleasant thing to watch and the crowd began to get impatient with him and this time, when someone

101

started to whistle, one by one, others joined in until suddenly the noise was deafening. I thought it was the end of him but finally somehow in desperation he locked his feet in place and mustering all his courage made one pass that looked like something. It wasn't much but it was enough to stop the whistles. And a part of the crowd breathed the first faint breath of a sigh in acknowledgement. You could almost hear his heart beat as he limped forward to take the bull again. And then while the crowd breathed and then cried and then roared, suddenly, he was holding the bull perfectly with the cape, pulling him closer and closer, with no thought of flinching or hesitation. And when finally he broke the series and stepped away the ovation that crashed across the arena was like nothing anyone had ever heard before.

The rest of the fight was like a dream. Suddenly everything was possible. At one point he was so close, so confident, so very sure of himself, that he tapped the tip of one horn with his wounded leg to incite a charge. And when finally the bull was ready, he killed him with one sword, in the grand manner, high up between the shoulders, the way he had always done before he was gored.

It was a moving thing to see and as they carried him around beneath us on their shoulders the old timer next to me stood up with tears in his eyes and clapped until his hands were sore.

That was the beginning of his limited season. He went on to fight more than 70 times that year and finished the season as he always had, as one of the top ten in Spain.

The bullpen door is opened. There is a long moment of anticipation. The bullfighter stands behind one burladero, his assistants behind the others. They watch the door of the bullpen. From across the ring one can see deep into the dark corridor under the stands. Suddenly there is a stir of movement. Then the bull is in the arena.

The bull is one of the major elements in the bullfight; to a large extent everything depends on the type of animal he turns out to be. A bull which attacks frankly and openly, which charges from a distance with his head low and all the speed at his command contributes immeasurably to the possibility of a brilliant fight, while a bull which advances slowly and carefully, his head high, intent on catching the man, practically eliminates all possibility of the bullfighter doing anything graceful or brilliant, no matter how much knowledge and skill he may have or how hard he may try. While a defensive fight between a difficult bull and a skilled matador is of exceptional interest to the real enthusiast, there is little of the brilliant show and languid passes which are one ideal of the bullfight, and to the ordinary spectator the fight will appear dull and boring, or worse.

It is a dramatic moment. The bull surges into the empty ring. He is strong and powerful and alert and carries his head high. He circles quickly, stepping lightly for all his weight, looking for any challenger.

The regulation prescribes that if the bull enters the ring with some defect which prevents him from being fought correctly, i.e., if he is lame, or has a broken horn, or is so tame that he will not charge the cape or the horse at all, he must be removed from the ring and another bull substituted for him. On the other hand, if the bull enters the ring in good condition, but during the fight becomes lame, or breaks a horn, or goes completely on the defensive after the first pic, he may or may not be removed from the ring, but in any case no substitute need be provided.

The action of removing the bull alive from the ring is accomplished with the help of trained steers which guide the bull out to the corrales. This is a colorful and distracting action and, if the bullfight is dull and uninteresting, the crowd sometimes has a tendency to imagine lameness, or some other defect, in the bull in the hope of seeing it. If the bull is removed from the ring alive for any reason, the regulation requires that he be killed immediately.

Note then the way the bull enters the ring, whether he explodes like a bomb or enters slowly and carefully . . . cautiously . . . defensively. Note the size of the bull, and his build and general appearance, the amount of hard muscle tissue he displays or the lack of it. Bulls, like other animals, are hard and physically fit or soft and out of condition. The strength and stamina of the bull obviously have a decided influence on the kind of fight the bullfighter will be able to achieve. A soft, fat bull, no matter how big and heavy, like a soft, fat man, will have little steam, tire quickly and probably toss his head petuantly in his frustration at not being able to do well. Strength, stamina and muscle are, then, the important fundamental physical qualities in the bull. Beware of being impressed by sheer size or bulk.

Note what a beautiful animal the bull is, especially in action. If this is your first bullfight you may be surprised at the speed and liquid grace of an animal of his size and your admiration and perhaps your sympathy may go out to him. This is quite a normal reaction and if the bullfighters are incompetent or outclassed it will seem a sad thing, a disgusting thing, to see such a beautiful animal killed by such a clown. In this respect there is really nothing that can be said. Even the most hardcore enthusiast will admit that there is no excuse for a bad bullfight except that it demonstrates in a negative way what a good bullfight ought to be.

Note the size of the bull's horns and whether they point out and up or curve in toward each other. Those that point out and up are not only more impressive but are actually more dangerous to the bullfighter and will necessarily influence the way he fights this particular bull.

Behind the barrera the bullfighter and his assistants watch the bull for a moment, then one of the assistants steps through an opening in the fence and waves his cape. As the bull charges, the man ducks back through the opening behind the fence and another assistant further along steps out and waves his cape. As the bull charges this new movement, the man steps out of danger and a third assistant repeats the maneuver.

The bullfighter's assistants do not engage in this game of hide-and-seek to infuriate the bull or because they are afraid of him, but rather to sound out his reactions and test his vision.

Each bull has his own personality and characteristic make-up. Some are brave and tricky, some are brave and bold. Some are not so brave and others are outright cowards. Some are cowardly or fearful at first and become braver as the fight continues. Others start well and finish badly. These preliminary rushes give the men some opportunity to decide what this bull is like before committing themselves fully to the fight.

Watch whether the bull is attracted from a distance and how he commits himself to the attack; whether he charges immediately and how he follows through the charge as first one and then another of the bullfighter's assistants step out from behind the fence to wave a cape and then duck back again. Watch to see whether the bull charges completely right up to the fence or whether he backs off or runs wildly about and away.

A bull which backs off pawing the ground in an attempt to nerve himself up to charge is bluffing and generally turns out to be difficult to fight. One which jumps or attempts to jump the fence at any time during the fight generally demonstrates a lack of bravery that will be apparent in his fight with the horses and particularly later, during the muleta faena.

Finally one man slips through an opening in the fence and runs farther out into the ring, waving his cape to attract the attention of the bull. Halfway out he stops and takes a stand to await the bull's charge.

Note the concentration of the bullfighter behind the fence as he watches the action. Sometimes the bullfighter does not bother to wait for his assistants to run the bull or make the first pass, but rather comes straight out himself to pass the bull and test him himself. This generally supposes either exceptional enthusiasm or exceptional knowledge of bulls and is fairly rare. Most bullfighters prefer to wait and follow the formal testing action of their assistants in order to be able to exploit the insight this gives them.

The bull whirls, lowers his head and charges at the movement. As the bull charges, the man swings the cape away from his body. The bull follows the

wide arc of the movement in a powerful but inaccurate charge, first on the right side, then on the left. Finally holding the cape in only one hand the assistant draws the bull in closer to the fence by casting the cape back and forth in two or three long swings, much as a man might cast a trout line, playing the bull in so that the bullfighter can step out and pick him up.

During this action the matador watches from behind the fence noting the speed of the charge, the amount of follow-through, the way in which the bull tosses his head, which horn he favors, whether he hooks to the right or left, and other important details which have significant bearing or how this bull should be fought.

The bullfighter watches particularly for those characteristics which promise to make for a difficult fight, i.e., a bull which throws out his front feet and slows down hooking at the cape as he reaches the peak of his charge, one which is extremely fast and constantly on top of the man, giving him no time to get set, one which charges frankly enough but throws his head to one side or the other unexpectedly as he passes the man threatening to gore him.

He is interested in knowing, too, which horn the bull favors, since a right-horned bull is easier to pass if the man stands to the left of the bull, and vice-versa, and this can have a direct bearing on the extent of his repertory throughout the fight.

The sign of a real maestro is the ability to correct the bull's defects during the course of the fight so that he improves to the point where the man can fight him brilliantly. The sign of an incompetent beginner is the systematic spoiling of a good bull so that he ends up vicious and dangerous through the inept handling he has received.

As a spectator, it is important to note the bull's condition and defects (or lack of them) at this time if one is to really understand the action and weigh the ability of the bullfighter.

As the bull comes in close to the fence, the assistant gives a last swing to the cape and ducks out of the ring. At the same moment the bullfighter steps through the fence and approaches the bull.

Note whether the assistant turns the bull smoothly, without violence and without false starts, and whether he passes the bull on to the bullfighter smoothly without getting tangled in his own cape or caught against the fence by the bull. Finally, note whether the bull has really been brought under some degree of control or whether he is still allowed to run loose as he pleases. It should be remembered that bulls are like temperamental horses—they must be firmly in hand at all times or they become uncontrollable.

The bull explodes into the ring. With his head held high he surveys the arena. His weight of 495 kilograms (over 1,000 pounds) is posted above the toril gate as prescribed by regulation and well exceeds the minimum required for a major bullfight.

The bull tries to leap the fence. Despite his size and an impressive set of horns, the bull demonstrates a lack of bravery by attempting to escape from the ring. If he clears the fence, the men in the passageway will suddenly find themselves exposed to danger and those who have nowhere else to go will have to leap over the fence into the ring and then back out again as the bull runs through the passage and is shunted back into the ring.

Tame steers are brought in to take out a defective bull. If when entering the ring the bull has a broken horn, a crippled leg, or some other defect which renders him unfit for the bullfight, he must be removed and another bull substituted for him. If the defect occurs after the bull has entered the ring, the president need not have the bull removed even though the bull cannot be fought in any way whatsoever.

10.

OPENING CAPEWORK

He had been a pretty big name once, but he had had a bad goring and hadn't fought for several years. He was out of condition and fat and soft and had lost his touch with the cape and the muleta as well as the sword, but he needed the money and thought he could make a comeback.

When he appeared in the ring, the crowd gave him a small round of applause for old times sake and he smiled and tried to look slim and elegant, but he was a big man with a big belly now and in his rented suit he looked like a clown.

He didn't do much with his first bull, but the bull was difficult and the crowd was still with him so it was all right. But his second bull was smooth as silk and, when the crowd saw that he couldn't keep his feet still, they started to whistle and jeer. He knew he was losing them so, when it came time for the muleta, he dedicated the bull to the stands with a big flourish that promised he would give it everything he had.

It looked for a minute like he might pull it off. He began with a pretty good series of right handed passes and I thought he might be able to get something going, but his timing was off and after a while the bull started catching the cloth with his horns and tossing his head and pretty soon the bull's charge was so erratic that he couldn't have stood still anymore even if he had wanted to. He tried to cover it up by switching the muleta to his left hand, but the bull was more difficult on the left and he couldn't pass him on that side either. Finally he tried the right again and then, in desperation, again the left.

By this time the stands were in an uproar, with people jeering and whistling and shouting "ole" mockingly each time he tried to do anything. He saw he had lost them, but he still wanted to prove he had something so suddenly, he put his feet together and started doing manoletinas.

They were the closest manoletinas I had ever seen, so close that the right horn was almost fraying the braid on his trousers each time the bull went by. After the first one he didn't look at the bull any more but kept his eyes fixed on the stands, looking up at the crowd as he cited the bull, spinning against the charge with the muleta spread by the sword held straight out in his right hand.

It was a hair raising thing to watch, but the crowd kept on whistling and jeering and shouting mocking oles and finally he had to stop. They knew he wasn't looking up at the stands because he had the bull under control and wanted to show how great that control was, but only because he was so scared he couldn't keep his feet still if he looked at the horns.

Later, after he had finally killed the bull and was walking back across the ring, some joker over in the sun got a laugh with a bad joke about big bellies and small balls of courage, but they didn't whistle him anymore because they knew he knew he was all washed up and they wouldn't ever have to watch him in the ring again.

As the matador steps into the ring and approaches the bull, he unfurls his cape and holds it out in front of him toward the bull. This is the matador's first direct contact with the bull. It is his first attempt to dominate him and often it is an indication of how the fight with this particular bull will progress.

Watch as the matador steps from behind the fence to pick up the bull in the folds of his cape. Note his attitude and bearing, whether or not he steps out with confidence and decision, or whether he approaches the bull hesitantly, timidly, with the excessive caution of a man unsure of himself.

The cape used by the matador varies with the size of the man but is roughly five feet from the collar to the hem. When spread out flat it forms a nearly complete circle of cloth almost ten feet in diameter. Capes used by the matador are of heavy silk lined with stiff cotton percale. They are reddish purple on the outside and yellow inside. The capes used by the banderilleros are similar except that they are generally made entirely of cotton percale.

The matador generally begins with certain wide, two-handed passes with the cape. The bull follows the movement and returns to follow it again. As the matador finds him responding to the cloth, he straightens his own body and draws the bull closer.

Watch carefully the first few tentative passes and note whether from the very beginning the bullfighter is able to get the bull interested in the cape, whether he is able to exert any control over the bull's charge or whether on the contrary the bull still runs loose in the ring. Note the elegance, the grace (or the lack of it) with which even these first few passes are performed and, as the bull's charge becomes less wild and more concentrated, note how the man tries to settle himself, how he strikes an attitude of defiance, raises the cape and calls the bull.

In general, the merit of all cape passes lies in the manner in which they are performed. The bullfighter must call the bull with decision. He must pick him up smoothly in the folds of the cape, move the cape quietly just ahead of the horns and, while swinging the cape, control the course of the bull past his own body. At the end of the pass he must show the bull the way out, then step forward and pick him up again smoothly for the next pass. While doing all these things he must pull the bull closer and closer to his body, calmly watching the horns brush by his legs until an absolute limit is reached beyond which it is physically impossible for the bull to pass without catching him.

When he finds the bull turning too closely on him at the end of the pass he must move calmly and easily from one position to the next, ahead of the bull, taking the bull with him but never being forced by him. In every case he must carefully judge and never exceed the absolute minimum distance at which he can pass the bull.

Defective capework is characterized by a general disorder in which certain specific traits are easily recognizable. If the matador moves the cape too briskly or too quickly, if he steps back as the animal passes by, or loses control and lets him get away at the end of the pass, or worse, if he passes the animal at a comfortable distance only to lean in or step in after the horn is past in order to give the impression that he has been very close, then no matter how pretty or graceful the pass has been it is of no merit and is worthless as far as the bullfight is concerned.

If the matador is calm, relaxed and confident in his knowledge and skill and is able to pass the bull as close as he wishes and is able to break the rhythm when he chooses, the ascendency of his control over the bull is established and communicated. If he is nervous, hesitant or unsure, or if he is unable to set up a rhythmic series of passes, his control over the bull remains in doubt and he communicates none of the emotion proper to sound bullfighting.

The classic two-handed pass with the cape is called the *veronica*. It is performed by the man holding the cape out in front of his body toward the bull. As the bull charges, the man swings the cape from right to left or left to right ahead of the bull, an inch or two in front of the horns so that the bull never quite touches the cloth. The bull, intent on the cloth, rushes by so close to the man's body that the horns may almost brush the man's legs. At the end of the pass, the bull is carried beyond the cloth by the impetus of his charge and turns to charge again while the man, with only a short step forward, is ready to repeat the maneuver in the opposite direction.

The veronica is the simplest of all passes to execute and the most difficult to do well. It takes its name from the aspect of the bullfighter holding the cape before him with both hands in the same manner that Saint Veronica is represented in religious paintings holding a cloth before the face of Christ.

Watch as the man tries to draw the bull slowly past, first on one side, then on the other. Note the relaxed grace of the man's figure or the lack of it. Watch his feet and note whether or not they are really firmly planted, solid and unmoving as a base, or whether, on the contrary, they move or skip backward uncontrollably each time the bull passes.

Note whether or not the man lowers his hands in the midst of the pass, spreading the cloth like a sail in front of the bull so that the cloth almost sweeps the ground forcing the bull to lower his head and to slow his charge, and whether or not the man is able to regulate the sweep of the cape to the charge of the bull so that the bull appears to be fastened to the cape like a dog on a leash, to be led as the man wishes from one spot to another.

When the man succeeds in controlling the bull's charge in this way and is able to draw him closer in a series of three, four or more passes of this type without having to dodge, step aside, or move in any way, the artistic pretensions of the bullfight become apparent to the most casual observer. For it is in the unbroken rhythm of a series of passes that the matador establishes his domination over the animal, creates the plastic beauty of line and mass and communicates this emotion to the spectator.

Note whether the bullfighter follows through with the pass, sending the bull smoothly away so that he can turn and get set for another pass, or whether he chokes the pass off short so that the bull is always on top of him giving him no time to rest or breathe. Note whether the bullfighter is able to gain the control necessary to lead the bull back and forth past his body in some sort of basic rhythm three, four, or more times, or whether the bull is simply running blindly past at his own pace hardly aware of the man or the movement.

There are two types of veronicas: one in which the man places his feet slightly apart and leans into the pass (*cargando la suerte*), drawing the bull past him with an inclination of his entire body and arms; the second in which the man stands like a statue with both feet together, and by the simple movement of the arms directs the bull's passage past and away from his body.

While both of these types of veronica have their supporters, passes accomplished cargando la suerte are generally considered to be more dramatic and of greater emotional intensity, as well as being of a greater merit because of the greater control and domination exercised over the bull. The second method, however, because of its statuesque economy of movement, is often the more spectacular. In either case the simplicity of the pass calls immediate attention to any trickery on the part of the bullfighter and both are difficult to do well.

When the bullfighter senses that the series of passes must come to end either because the bull is being drawn by so closely that to prolong the series will mean a goring or because the bull will no longer charge, he may cut the bull's charge off short by swinging the cape only half way past his body, at the same time turning against the charge so that the cape winds about his body with a whip-like movement that pulls it away from in front of the bull. This movement so shortens the arc that the bull must follow in his charge, that the bull must halt in order to recover himself. This half pass is called a *media veronica.*

The media veronica is generally performed as the emotional intensity of the series of passes reaches a peak and provides a dramatic period to this opening phase of the bullfight.

In judging the media veronica, note the deliberate intensity with which the man spins against the charge, swinging the cape like a whiplash ahead of the bull and snapping him off short to a dead stop, an action which permits the man to strut casually away, trailing the cape behind him without a backward glance, absolutely master of the situation.

If the man has been unable to gain control of the bull or has been unable to build a series of passes, he will ordinarily not be able to finish with a half veronica, but will rather let the bull simply stop or roam away to be picked up by the cape of one of his men while he does his best to look as if that was the way he had planned it all along.

As the matador steps arrogantly away from the bull after finishing this first series of passes and his first contact with the bull, the president signals for the picadores to enter the ring and the trumpet sounds the opening act in the death of the bull.

The first cape pass. Despite the fact that the bull's charge is still somewhat wild and erratic, the man has managed to center his interest in the cape and is leaning into the pass, teaching him to follow the cloth and at the same time drawing him closer and further under control.

Veronica with the feet together. The man has planted his feet together and is taking the bull past very closely. He is not as elegant as he might be if he held himself a trifle straighter, but the movement of the cape is beautifully tempered to the charge of the bull and the style is otherwise very good.

Veronica with the feet apart, cargando la suerte. The man has stepped forward with his left foot and is leaning far into the pass as the bull sweeps past following the cape. The control over the bull is greater and more complete. Despite the "comfortable" in-curving horns of the bull, the danger to the man is also greater as he hangs poised over the head of the bull throughout the pass.

The same pass done poorly and without style. The man has failed to interest the bull in the cape and has not dared lean into the pass to control the charge. Hesitancy has caused him to alter his position and the bull, attracted by the body movement, is about to hook at him rather than continue to follow the cloth.

The classic veronica. The man has turned almost completely upon himself in a single, smooth, flowing motion. The man's feet are firmly planted in the sand and his body leans far into the pass as he follows through, extending his control beyond all normal bounds without forcing the action in any way. The bull has already turned almost completely around the man's body and is still perfectly controlled by the movement of the cape. The bull is very big and the man's domination is so complete and perfect that the spectators have risen from their seats in delighted admiration.

Media veronica with the feet together. At the end of a series of veronicas, instead of following through, the man swings the cape past his body and then gathers both hands at his hip, snapping the cape away from in front of the bull and bringing him to a halt.

Media veronica with the feet apart. The greater intensity of the same pass made with the feet apart is immediately apparent as the bull winds himself around the man's body in an effort to follow the cloth, while the man stands calm and relaxed in the center of the action.

A graceful finish. As the bull turns sharply at the end of a series of veronicas, the man, in a moment of inspiration, suddenly stands still before him with the cape dangling from his outstretched hand in an elegant gesture of bravado and control.

The unexpected charge. As the man turns away trailing his cape at the end of a series of veronicas, the bull suddenly charges again. Without an instant's hesitation, the man strikes a graceful pose and swings the cape forward past his body, controlling the bull's charge and converting an awkward situation into a further moment of beauty and domination.

11.

THE PICADOR

As the sword went in, his men started forward to turn the bull with their capes but suddenly he stepped back and waved them away. A moment later he turned and walked over to the fence. Everyone thought he was going to get another sword but instead he spoke to his men and they all left the ring. He stood watching the bull for a moment then almost casually, he went over and sat down on the little wooden step that runs around the inside of the fence. Everyone was quiet watching, and when suddenly he called softly to the bull you could hear him all the way up in the top row.

The bull was standing where he had left him out near the center of the ring but when he heard him call he raised his head and looked toward the fence. When he called again the bull turned and started to walk slowly toward him.

It was strange. He didn't move or wave the cloth or raise his voice or anything but, when he called, the bull raised his head and started toward him almost as if he was hypnotized. He sat quietly against the fence, not moving a muscle, watching him come, a step at a time. Finally, just as he was about to reach him, the bull stopped, took a step to one side, hesitated a moment, and then suddenly toppled over dead in the sand at his feet.

They carried him out on their shoulders.

It had been a mediocre fight, but after that they gave him both ears and carried him around the ring and out the big door. It was unbelievable. No one could explain how he had been able to call the bull from the center of the ring or how he could have known that the bull would die just as he reached the fence.

He let them editorialize about it for a week or two then in an exclusive interview he told them how he had done it.

"It was simple," he said with a smile. "During the fight I noticed that the bull

121

had a preference for that area of the fence. When I put in the sword we were directly opposite that spot. I knew the sword had reached him but I could see that he still had a lot of strength left. The important thing was not to excite him. He was already settling down to die when I called to him. He was a brave bull. When he heard my voice it drew him toward the fence. It was only natural that he head for that area to die. My calculation was that he would drop just as he reached the fence. As it worked out I was right. The rest was just theatre."

He was one of the last of the old professionals, one of the last few who still knew all there was to know about bulls.

As the trumpet sounds, a gate in the fence swings open and two picadores ride into the arena.

The action of the picador is not designed to torture or cripple the bull senselessly, but rather to slow and weaken him within certain set limits and, by tiring and injuring the powerful throwing muscle at the base of the neck, to lower his head so that the matador may kill him according to regulations. Without the action of the picador it would be extremely difficult for the matador to kill most of the bulls that enter the ring and impossible for him ever to kill some bulls at all. In addition, it would be practically impossible for the bullfighter to do any of the pretty or graceful things with cape and muleta which have become so fundamental a part of modern bullfighting. As a consequence, with regard to the physical conditioning of the bull, the action of the picador is an absolutely necessary function of the bullfight.

In addition to the essential physical conditioning of the bull, the picadores also provide the bull with the psychological reassurance that there is really something there to fight, something solid to attack, something that can be felt and punished in turn, not just a series of shadows to be chased, a series of movements and cloths that can never be touched. This reassurance is very necessary if the bull is to continue to charge hard and fast in the final phases of the fight and in itself is a major step in refining the bull's charge so that he can be correctly played with the muleta and killed according to the rules.

Finally, the picadores provide the bull with an opportunity to demonstrate his fundamental qualities of strength and bravery against an adversary of equal size; an adversary which returns punishment for punishment, thus simulating the conditions of a real fight between equal forces on the brute level. If the bull is equal to his role, this demonstration serves to forcefully remind the spectator that the bullfight is not only a dance or pageant, not merely a pretty show, but a matter of life and death, of danger and destruction. It reminds the spectator that this animal is a force of nature, capable of destroying everything in its path, certainly capable of destroying the slim figure in silver and gold which comes forward so arrogantly to challenge him. Without the picadores, the fury of the bull remains in doubt, for he is only chasing shadows and perhaps (like any bully) is not worthy of the accolade of brave.

As the picadores ride into the ring they turn to the right and follow around close to the wall outside the larger of the two circles drawn in the sand.

In some rings only the first picador rides around to the right, while the second waits just inside the gate. Each picador is armed with a spearlike pole nearly nine feet long. The end of this pole is garnished with a triangular, pyramid-shaped, steel tip, an inch long, which is fitted into the wooden shaft. Behind this tip the pole is wrapped with cord for a distance of three inches and terminated by a metal cross-piece. The purpose of this cross-piece is to prevent the point from penetrating more than four inches into the bull no matter how much force is applied. The horses are blindfolded so that they cannot see the bull and will not panic, and as a consequence they step gingerly, almost comically, as though walking on eggs. They are protected from the bull's horns by a heavy quilted pad which covers the chest and right side and hangs nearly to the ground. While the pad protects the horses from being gored by the bull the horses are, of course, bruised and otherwise injured by the repeated charges of the bull which sometimes throw both horse and rider to the ground. Repeated rough contact of this sort eventually proves fatal to nearly all of the horses, but very few of them die in the ring, and in this respect the heavy padding is a success.

A third or more of the way around the ring, the bullfighter signals to the leading picador and he stops, turns and faces out, presenting the right front side of the horse to the center of the ring. The second picador remains behind in reserve at a distance further along the fence.

According to the regulation, the picador is not permitted to cross the outer ring toward the center of the arena after the bull, and the bull may not be brought across the inner ring toward the picador until all other attempts at picking the bull have failed. The idea behind this is that the bull is thus given a chance to show his bravery and desire to fight by charging voluntarily from a distance.

The matador or one of the banderilleros draws the bull across the arena to a spot in front of the first picador. The bull is left standing quietly alone inside the inner ring. The picador is outside the larger ring. The bullfighters are strung out along the fence to the left of the picador.

Watch the way the bull is brought to the horse and note whether it is done by the matador himself or by one of his assistants. If the matador does it himself it should be a further demonstration of his control and domination; it should be done gracefully and—ideally—involve a series of linked passes which leave the bull standing exactly in place. In any case, no matter who does it, it should be done smoothly in a professional manner with a minimum of false starts and stops, with a minimum of wild cape waving and cape flopping.

Watch to see whether the bull is brought carefully to a spot opposite and slightly to the front of the horse and whether he is halted inside the smaller of the concentric rings marked in the sand. The bull should be brought to a complete halt and left standing stock still. This not only provides the picador with a clear shot at the bull and an opportunity to place the pic well, but also permits the bull to recognize the challenge and accept or reject it.

The positions of the men and the bull and the horse are also important. The horse should be halted, facing the center between the larger of the concentric rings and the wall, with all the bullfighters and their assistants to his left and the bull halted across the double rings at a distance in front of him.

Note whether there has been a feeling of order and control of the bull throughout the entire operation, or whether the bull has been permitted to run loose or wild. Here, as elsewhere throughout the fight the bull should never be permitted to assume control of the situation.

The attitude of the picador and the manner in which he faces the bull are an indication of his capability. Does he hold the pic choked up a third of the way from the point and angled down at 45 degrees in a position of control and power, or does he hold it far back near the butt end and angled out nearly horizontally like a fishing pole, as far away as possible from the bull in a position from which he can apply no real punishment?

The picador awaits the charge. As the bull charges, the picador leans forward in the saddle and jabs the sharp point of the pic into the heavy muscle at the base of the neck. As the bull smashes forward, the picador leans on the pic, holds the bull as long as he can, then swings the horse to his left and at the same time pushes the bull away toward the bullfighters to be led away to the center of the ring by the quick cape of one of the matadores.

When the pic is well placed and the picador performs his function in accordance with the theory, the action is clean and sharp. The bull forces under the pic, striving and perhaps succeeding in reaching the horse, perhaps even lifting horse and rider into the air and slamming them to the ground, at any rate fighting all the way until finally, after breaking or being led away by the bullfighter, he is led back to renew the attack again.

The bull learns from his encounter with the picador and if he has been picked well comes forth quiet and disciplined, a more wary but more formidable antagonist. He carries his head on a level with his shoulders and is in the state called *parado,* or halted. When the picador corrupts his function either by design or through lack of skill he not only destroys the elemental beauty of this act but often ruins the bull for the rest of the fight as well.

If the bull is reluctant to charge, the picador may provoke a charge by rattling his foot in the stirrup, by shouting, by waving the pic or by spurring the horse back and forth in the area between the outer circle and the fence.

Note whether the picador takes the bull's charge from the front or right front, a position from which he can control the action, or whether he lets the bull hit him broadside or even from the rear at an angle which is all to the bull's advantage. Note too whether the picador leans out of the saddle to meet the charge, shooting the pic in accurately and hard or whether he permits the bull to hit the horse first and then places the point of the pic and by twisting and thrusting forces it in.

Note whether the pic strikes the bull high up on top where the heavy neck muscles join the shoulder or whether it strikes lower down in the shoulder, or, worse, in the ribs or farther back on the spine, injuring the bull unnecessarily and perhaps even crippling him.

Watch how the picador holds the pic and his position toward the bull. Note whether he guides the horse carefully and at the end of sufficient punishment swings the horse to the left, while pushing the bull out to the center of the ring, or whether he swings the horse around to the right, blocking the bull's exit to the center of the ring, meanwhile screwing and gouging the pic into the bull in an operation called the *carioca* which is designed to prevent any escape and to continue the punishment and weaken the bull as much as possible.

Watch how the bull accepts the pic. Does he push under the punishment of the pic and return to charge again, seemingly insensible to pain, or does he back off and refuse the challenge, or charge halfheartedly and refuse to return to charge again once he has been hurt? Does he charge from far out, eagerly, as soon as he sees the horse? Does he follow up, attacking harder the more he is punished, pushing with his hindquarters, in an attempt to throw the horse, or does he simply swing his head futilely, pretending to fight, while trying to dislodge the pic? Worse still, does he turn away at the first touch of the pic, kicking backward with his hooves like some donkey or mule, underlining his lack of bravery for everyone to see?

Does the matador stationed to the left of the horse come forward promptly to take the bull away from the horse with his cape after a reasonable amount of punishment, or does he dawdle and stall, arranging his cape, folding and unfolding it, pretending not to see that the bull is being excessively punished?

Although it is the president who finally decides how many times the bull should be picked, it is the man who is to kill this particular bull who decides how long each pic should last and when he and the others are to go forward to take the bull away from the horse. If you watch carefully after the first *quite,* you will see the bullfighter nudge the second man to go in or more often hold him back as he starts in too soon, to take the bull away in his turn.

Above all it should be remembered that the picador works for and is paid by the matador. As a consequence, he does only what the matador tells him to do. No matter what the bullfighter appears to say or do in the ring, if the bull is being punished excessively, the picador is only obeying orders. The picador may be incompetent, of course, and may not hit the right place, or be unable to handle his horse, but if he is really punishing the bull excessively he is not acting on his own initiative, but only obeying previous instructions.

After a short series of passes which offer the bull an opportunity to breathe and the bullfighter an opportunity to star, the bull is led back to the picador and the process is repeated a second, and after that, a third time.

According to the regulation, each bull should receive three separate and distinct pics. However, if the bull is very small or very weak and the first pics have been very long and very hard, with the bull recharging time and again without a pause, the president may waive the second or third pic and signal for the picadores to leave the arena at the first break in the action. If the pics are of normal length and duration, however, the bull should be permitted to charge freely at the horses three separate times, in order not only that he may be slowed and weakened to the degree necessary, but that he may thoroughly demonstrate his capacity for punishment in what is considered the final measure of his strength and bravery.

Note, then, whether or not the bull receives three pics or two or only one, and how long and hard each of the pics was. If the wild rush of the bull is not calmed sufficiently in this contact with the picador, the bullfighter will not be able to play the bull with the muleta in the later stages of the fight in the way that is expected of him. On the other hand, if the bull is picked too much he may be so weakened that he is unable to stay on his feet, or be unable to charge, and go entirely on the defensive.

Occasionally the bullfighter will request that the president excuse the bull from a second or third pic. He does this by taking off his hat and saluting the presidential box with it. This is a popular gesture with the crowd but, as often as not, after requesting the *cambio* or change he finds himself with a bull he cannot handle. Sometimes the bullfighter will make this request knowing that the president will refuse, simply in order to gain the sympathy of the crowd. Thus it is the president and not the bullfighter who finally decides when the bull has been punished sufficiently. The president can stop the series of pics or continue them as he sees fit. The matador can request that they be stopped; however, it is the president who says yes or no. To a large extent then, the president also is responsible for the condition of the bull as he enters the latter phases of the fight.

Leading the bull to the picadores. The bullfighter has chosen to lead the bull across the ring himself and takes advantage of the occasion to exhibit the extent of his skill and craftsmanship as well as his perfect control.

Setting the bull. As they arrive in front of the picador the man suddenly swings the cape in a graceful overhead flourish which sets the bull perfectly in place for the coming action.

The action. The bull has charged from far out and in a moment will lower his head to strike the horse in the heavy padding below the stirrup. The bull is very big and powerful and will probably throw this horse as he did the one which the ring attendants in the background have not yet been able to bring to its feet. The picador is impressed by the bull's size and is holding the pic well behind the balance hoping to take up some of the shock before the bull hits the horse.

A brave bull. The bull has charged from far out demonstrating his great bravery and desire to fight. He is closing very quickly and in a moment the man will drop the tip of the pic and catch the bull at the point where the swelling neck muscle joins the shoulders. The picador is taking the bull from the front at a good angle, holding the pic decently near the middle for better control. When, as often happens, the men set the bull so close to the horse that the charge becomes a simple push forward, the beauty of the action is obscured and the public is robbed of the chance to evaluate the full extent of the bull's bravery.

A well-placed pic. The man has placed the pic well on top and is holding the bull off by sheer weight and strength of arm. The bull is not very big and is not pushing hard, and if the man wheels the horse to the left as he should, the bull will never make contact with the padding of the horse.

The carioca. Instead of wheeling the horse to the left, thus freeing him to charge again, the man has turned the horse to the right and blocked his exit to the center of the ring, strongly forcing the weight and pressure on the pic and greatly increasing the punishment to the bull. The bull is very big and strong and, despite the punishment, is still charging and trying to lift the horse from the ground.

A hard fall. Despite the heavy padding and the weight of the rider, the bull has lifted the horse completely off the ground and thrown him over backwards against the fence. The man is going to hit the ground first, if he is very lucky, the angle of the fence may prevent him from being crushed under the horse's body. The ring attendant is racing forward with more bravery than prudence to distract the bull from the fallen man.

12.

THE QUITE

After each pic the bullfighters come forward in turn to take the bull away from the horse and lead him out toward the center of the ring in order to permit him to breathe and recover his strength. This action is called a *quite* and usually begins with a simple swing of the cape to attract the bull's attention and lead him away to a distance.

Actually, the word quite really refers to any saving intervention which distracts the bull and lures him away from someone in danger of being gored. Such a saving intervention may be made by anyone at anytime during the fight. In a more limited sense, however, the quite has come to refer particularly to the formal intervention of the matador after each pic, whether there is any danger to anyone or not.

Ordinarily, if the bull turns or is pushed away from the horse, the bullfighter simply comes forward, attracts the bull's attention and leads him away with a casual movement of the cape. However, if the bull is brave and forces under the pic, charging and recharging again, the bullfighter must gauge the punishment the bull is receiving and come forward in time to interrupt this punishment before the bull completely exhausts himself in his fight with the picador. If the bull is really engrossed in his attack the man may have to expose himself considerably in order to attract the bull's attention.

The first quite is always made by the man who is to kill this particular bull. The second quite is made by the man who is to kill the next bull and the third quite is made by the man who is to kill the following bull. If more pics are administered the first man begins again.

If the picador is thrown to the ground or anyone is in danger of being gored, the order of priority in making the quite is of course forgotten and any and all are expected to jump forward to the rescue and take the bull away. This is sometimes the occasion for a display of extreme gallantry as a man may risk a serious goring while trying to distract the bull's attention from a fallen comrade. Even more rarely a man may make a quite under such circumstances and manage to do it both efficiently and gracefully, picking the bull up in the folds of the cape and leading him with a series of passes, smoothly and gracefully, from the scene of danger. Such a quite demonstrating optimum control and presence of mind is extremely rare and is in the finest traditions of the bullfight.

The quite is usually the occasion for an exhibition of artistic capework by the matador.

Often, however, the bullfighter does not feel like extending himself or simply feels that he cannot star with this bull and refuses to make the effort required by a real quite. As a consequence, he foregoes all opportunity and returns the bull to the picador as quickly as possible.

Note then whether the bullfighter takes the bull smoothly away toward the center of the ring after the pic to begin a series of passes or whether he simply turns the bull over to the peones or himself returns the bull directly to the picador for further punishment.

As the bull turns in the free area near the center of the ring, the matador sets himself and begins a series of passes designed to reaffirm his control over the bull. This series of passes may be composed only of veronicas but usually the matador attempts to do something more in order to display a greater part of his repertoire. Among the most popular passes for the quite are the *gaonera* and the *chicuelina.*

If the bullfighter begins a series of passes note which passes are performed, whether the series comes off smoothly and whether the passes are suited to the condition of the bull. Note whether he reaffirms his position with the classical veronicas or whether he rather chooses one of the more colorful and showy passes in order to demonstrate the extent of his repertoire.

In general the condition of the bull influences the type of passes which are attempted, for while the veronica can be performed with any bull which charges at all frankly, the gaonera is especially suited to bulls with a short half-charge, and the chicuelina to bulls which charge with a great deal of energy and clarity.

The gaonera, like nearly all cape passes, begins as a veronica, but instead of continuing the pass the matador flips the cape over his head so that it falls into position behind his back. Then he extends one arm and a segment of the cape to one side. As the bull charges he pivots slowly, drawing him through. When the

bull is past he extends the other arm and repeats the pass in the opposite direction. A series of these gaoneras is usually terminated by an ornamental flourish of the cape called a *serpentina* in which the cape swirls about the man's legs and brings the bull to a dead halt.

As the bull passes the first time note whether the man is able to flip the cape over his head into position smoothly and easily, without giving ground or moving from position, or whether, having missed his opportunity, he must awkwardly resort to passing the cape from one hand to the other behind his back in order to assume the correct position. Note how closely the man cites the bull for the charge and how smoothly he is able to pass the bull first on one side and then the other, and finally with what grace and ease he is able to finish the series and step away.

The chicuelina also begins as a veronica. Instead of drawing the bull through, however, the matador spins slowly on his heels in the direction opposed to the bull's charge and with a snap of the wrists whips the cape away from in front of the bull so that it winds itself around his body in a graceful draped effect while the bull under the impetus of his charge is carried past and away. As the matador turns to face the bull, the cape falls into position again for a repeat of the maneuver.

Occasionally the matador will demonstrate his ability with a zig-zag series of linked chicuelinas finished with a flourish, which take the bull in perfect rhythm from the center of the ring and leave him perfectly placed in front of the horse ready for the next pic.

Note how serenely the man accepts the charge of the bull; how deliberately he spins against the charge; whether or not a light snap of the wrists twists the fold of the cape sharply from under the bull's nose at the same time that it drapes it around the man's figure; or whether the man just rolls up in it without precision or elegance. Note how easily the man recovers his position for the next pass. Whether or not he is at the precise distance to repeat the pass without hurrying, or whether he must hurriedly step aside or backward in order to have sufficient room to accept the next charge. Note whether or not the man is able to finish the series gracefully or simply stops because the bull has been distracted elsewhere or is right on top of him.

If the man performs a linked series of chicuelinas designed to bring the bull in to the picador, note the rhythm and timing, or lack of it, with which the series is performed, as well as the grace and precision of the passes themselves.

After the series of passes the bull is brought back to the picador and left in position for the next pic, while the bullfighter takes his place again with the other matadores at the left of the horse.

The farol. As the man leads the bull away from the horse and out into the ring, he suddenly swings the cape to his left and high over his head in a graceful gesture that brings the bull almost completely around his body. The man is performing the pass perfectly and has the bull well under control. Farols may be performed as a series or may be used to bring the cape into position for the gaonera.

The same pass performed from the kneeling position. The man has dropped to his knees for a more spectacular but less graceful display of his ability. The bull is turning very sharply and, in a moment, the man will be rushed to finish and unable to maintain his position with any dignity.

The gaonera. The man has brought his hands down with the cape behind his back. By extending his arms and the cloth far to the left, he is able to pass the bull past his body. As the bull follows the cloth the man will swing his hands and the cloth behind his back to the right to repeat the pass on the opposite side. The man is leaning forward over the bull's body as he brings him by very closely without either strain or tension.

The same pass out of control. The man has not held his ground and the bull has changed the direction of his charge and is following him as he leaps away. If the man is quick enough he may be able to correct his position, recover control of the bull, and pass him on the left. If he is not quick enough, he will be forced to leap away again as the bull chases him from place to place across the ring.

Ending the series. The man has released the cape with his left hand and is about to pass the cloth from his right hand to the left in a wider, more graceful arc which will turn the bull and bring him to a halt almost directly in front of the picador. The bull is well under control as he follows the folds of the cape, breathlessly close to the man's body.

The same pass without repose. The lack of grace and control, as the man steps backward with a wild swing of the cloth, underlines the basic requirements for repose in everything which is done in the ring.

Citing the bull in the chicuelena. As the bull charges, the man drops his hands and swings the cape slowly past his body. The man is taking the bull well from the front, controlling the charge and guiding the bull with great repose.

Spinning against the charge. The man has raised his hands, snapped the cloth away from in front of the bull and is spinning slowly and elegantly against the charge as he watches the bull pass by.

The bull tries to follow the cloth. As the cloth drapes itself about the man's body, the bull turns sharply trying to follow.

At the end of the pass the man is completely enveloped in the cape. He has not raised his left hand as high as he should for elegance but the pass has otherwise been well performed and the man is still confident and unhurried despite the tremendous size of the horns and the fact that the bull is very close.

13.

THE BANDERILLAS

When the president is satisfied that sufficient pics have been administered he signals with his handkerchief, the trumpets sound, the picadores ride out of the ring, and the man prepares to place the *banderillas.*

The banderillas are simple wooden sticks an inch in diameter and nearly three feet long. They are ornamented with colored paper along their entire length and have a steel, harpoon-like point two inches long protruding from one end. The other end is simply rounded to give a smooth grip. These sticks must be planted in pairs on top of the bull's shoulders at the base of the neck. The number of pairs of banderillas to be placed is left to the discretion of the president, but in practice it is rarely less than two, or more than three.

Banderillas ornamented with black and white colored paper (called *banderillas negras*) are used when, after repeated efforts to get him to do so, the bull still refuses to charge the picadores and accept the punishment of the pic as he should. Aside from their distinctive color and except that the point has a double barb like an arrowhead rather than a single barb like a harpoon, the banderillas negras are otherwise identical to those ordinarily used. The president signals with a red handkerchief when these banderillas are to be used in place of the ordinary kind. Because of the double barb the banderillas negras are supposed to replace the punishment of the pics but in reality the double barb is hardly more than an added annoyance to the bull and is more an insult to the breeder than a punishment to the animal.

The object of placing the banderillas is to provide the bull with a change of pace and a chance to breathe after his encounter with the picadores and to sting him into new strength for the muleta work which is to come.

For the newcomer, the action of placing the banderillas is probably the most easily followed and well-liked part of the entire bullfight. This is due not only to the absolute simplicity of the action, the intent of which is immediately apparent to almost everyone, but to what may be referred to as the athletic or sport aspect of this action, i.e., the man, by his speed and dexterous footwork, outmaneuvers the bull and scores on him without really hurting or injuring him.

To the newcomer this is a familiar action and appears to be the only part of the bullfight during which the bull has an even or better chance at the man. In actual fact this is not the case, however, for if the man is at all fast on his feet and calculates his angle of attack at all well, the bull can never reach him. In other words, barring outlandish accidents in which the man may slip and fall or become flustered for a moment, the mechanics of placing the banderillas in the ordinary routine of the fight are such that the bull offers no danger whatsoever for even the most mediocre hack. It is only when the man, in an effort to outdo himself and place the sticks elegantly, tightens the trajectory of his course and voluntarily permits the bull to approach within a hair's breadth of actual contact that the bull has any real chance of catching him at all, but this of course is true for any phase of the fight and is really what bullfighting is all about.

The matador who is to kill this bull walks over to the fence and hands his cape and his hat to his handlers, takes a glass of water, rinses his mouth, wipes his face with a towel and stands watching as his men bring the bull into position.

Watch the matador as he goes over to the fence. Is he interested in the bull? Does he follow the action in the ring in order to be aware of the physical state of the bull and his response after the pics, or is he more interested in speaking to someone in the stands or arguing with his handlers behind the fence? This is the bullfighter's last opportunity to observe the condition and characteristics of the bull before the total commitment of the muleta work. If the bullfighter is not interested enough to watch the action at this point it is generally a sign that he has no intention of extending himself with this particular bull.

If the matador plans on putting his own banderillas he will wave everyone out of the ring with a theatrical gesture of disdain and take the sticks himself. If not he will nod to his men to go ahead and get the job done.

If the people in the stands begin applauding at this point it is generally because this bullfighter is capable of putting his own banderillas and they want him to do it. Many young bullfighters who are anxious to please and make a name for themselves, and certain older ones, especially those from Mexico or South America, regularly put their own banderillas on all or nearly all the bulls they fight, while most established Spanish fighters omit this action from their repertoire simply because of the additional physical effort and risk involved.

If the matador elects to place them himself he commits himself to doing an elegant and artistic job of it. If he is not skilled in placing banderillas, or if the condition of the bull will not permit him to star, he leaves himself open to the whistles and jeers of the public. Unless they are sure of themselves, therefore, most bullfighters prefer to leave the placing of the banderillas to their foot assistants. These men are not expected to star (although occasionally they do) but simply to do a workman-like job as quickly and efficiently as possible. As a consequence, placing the banderillas is rarely done with much elegance or grace and rarely entails much danger for the man.

One of the assistants retains his cape and plays the bull into position close to the fence while the other two men hand their capes across the fence, receive a pair of banderillas each in return and race out into the center of the ring to challenge the bull.

Since most bulls have a tendency to charge toward the center of the ring, the bull is generally brought in fairly close to the fence and turned to face the center as a preparation for placing the banderillas. This position also provides the banderillero with the greatest possible area in which to maneuver and brings him at the end of his run, at the moment of greatest danger, close in to the safety of the fence.

Note the speed and ease, or the lack of it, with which the bull is brought into position. This should be done with a minimum of useless cape passes and false starts and should leave the bull carefully set, facing the center of the ring, ready for the first pair of banderillas.

Note the efficiency with which the men who are to place the banderillas take their positions and the postures and decision with which they cite or call the bull. Deficiencies include a great deal of insistence upon the exact position of the bull, false starts and other hesitant movements which confuse the action, and any attempt in which the man misjudges the bull's charge and is forced to flee or in which he is only able to place one stick or is unable to place either of them.

The matadores who are not concerned with killing this bull take up strategic positions in the arena in order to protect the banderilleros in case of an accident.

The order and the position these matadores occupy during the placing of the banderillas is prescribed by custom. The matador who is to kill the next bull takes up a position in the far center of the ring behind the banderillero as he challenges the bull, while the remaining matador stands quietly out of the way near the fence in a position from which he can come forward to the rescue should the banderillero be in danger at the end of his run.

Note the physical attitudes of the bullfighters as they stand at their posts. Note whether they are quietly alert and observant of the action, holding their capes gracefully draped before them, ready for any emergency, or whether they are awkward and distracted, with the cape slung under one arm like a dead fish and their attention elsewhere.

There are a number of ways of placing the banderillas but only three ways are commonly seen. These are called *al cuarteo, poder al poder* and *al quiebro*.

The method chosen to place the banderillas depends not only upon the degree of risk the man is willing to assume but upon the condition of the bull as well. In general, the bull must charge extremely well and hard if the man is to be able to place the banderillas al quiebro successfully; he need not be quite so strong and frank in his charge in order to place them poder al poder, and if he can be made to charge at all they can be placed al cuarteo. Sometimes a bull refuses to charge at all and the banderillas are placed by approaching him from the rear and catching him as he turns. This, of course, is simply an expedient and should be used only as a last resort.

Although any method of placing the banderillas can be made as dangerous and difficult as the man chooses, banderillas al quiebro are the most difficult to place well, poder al poder less difficult and al cuarteo the least difficult.

The most common way of placing the banderillas is *al cuarteo,* or quartering. This is the method generally used by the matadores' assistants and consists in citing or calling the bull from a distance in the center of the ring. As the bull charges, the man runs in a wide circle to the right or left. The charge of the bull is slowed as he alters direction to follow the arc, and, as their paths meet and the bull lowers his head to gore, the man rises on tip-toe, his body straight, his arms raised high, and drives the sticks straight down between the shoulders of the bull. He then pivots out from the horns and steps away as the bull hooks into the air at the spot he has just vacated. If the man's judgement of the distance is absolutely correct he can place the banderillas perfectly and step quietly away leaving the bull tossing his head almost at a standstill.

In general the question of whether the banderillas are well-placed or not may be answered at the precise moment when the man and the bull meet. In that instant there must be a definite pause, the man must halt, raise his hands over his head and, with his body held erect, drive the banderillas straight down between the bull's shoulders. The points of the banderillas should be as close together as possible and the banderillas themselves should stand nearly upright as the man steps unhurriedly away.

Points to watch for during the placing of the banderillas are the elegance and ease with which the man cuts and avoids the bull's charge, how high he raises his arms to drive the sticks home, how straight and upright his body is when he does so, whether he is directly in front of and facing the bull at the moment the sticks are placed, the decision and overall elegance with which the act is performed, and how smoothly or unhurriedly he moves out of danger once he has placed the banderillas.

The banderillas may fall out, of course, as the bull moves through the later phases of the fight, but if they have been well placed they will hang for a time in a group like a heavy fan along the bulls shoulders. If they have been badly placed they will jut out at odd angles and trouble the bullfighter as he attempts to pass the bull closer and closer in the muleta faena.

A second method of placing the banderillas is called *poder al poder* or power to power. In this action the man challenges the bull from a shorter distance. As the bull charges, the man races head on to meet him. At the last minute, as the bull lowers his head to gore, the man suddenly alters course to the right or left, drives in the sticks and leaves the bull tossing his head in the air.

Placing the banderillas poder al poder is really only an extreme version of the method al cuarteo and the same general criteria apply. The difference is that the man takes the bull's charge from a shorter distance and counter charges directly in turn, prior to altering direction to the right or left. This of course requires greater speed and timing on the part of the man as well as a bull that charges as he should. Except for a few outstanding exceptions banderillas poder al poder are seldom or never seen unless the matador himself is attempting to star.

The third and most spectacular method of placing the banderillas is called *al quiebro* or swaying. In this method the man stands erect, with his feet together, only a short distance in front of the bull and calls to him, inciting a charge. When the bull rushes forward, the man waits until he is only a yard or two away, then he moves one of his feet slightly to the right or left and sways to that side. As the bull lowers his head and alters his course to follow the movement, the man draws back his foot, straightens to his original position and drives in the banderillas. The momentum of the charge carries the bull away and the man is at liberty to stand as he was to receive the certain applause of the crowd.

Placing banderillas al quiebro requires a cool head, absolute precision and perfect timing on the part of the man as well as a bull that charges frankly and openly without any tendency to hook to either side. To place them well requires these conditions to a superlative degree and always entails the possibility of a serious goring. As a consequence only those trying to make a name for themselves at any cost and a very few of the old masters ever attempt this method of placing the banderillas.

The criteria for judging how well they are placed when they are attempted are the distance from which the man cites the bull, the deliberate rhythm with which he marks the feint to one side, the ease with which he recovers his original position and the deliberate timing with which he places the sticks and steps away to accept the applause of the crowd.

When done correctly the placing of the banderillas becomes one of the most brilliant and spectacular parts of the bullfight and serves to further illustrate the man's domination through grace, skill and intelligence over the bull's power and brute strength. It is the second formal act in the death of the bull.

Short banderillas formed by breaking the normal ones in half are sometimes placed in any of the three ways mentioned above. While this is an impressive and spectacular gesture and insures that the man will expose himself to some degree, it is an artificial way of increasing the danger and is contrary to the spirit of real bullfighting. It is also a more vulgar and less elegant and aesthetically satisfying method, since the man's hands must be lowered and his figure awkwardly hunched forward in order to avoid the horns and reach the spot high upon the bull's shoulder.

Watching the action. The bullfighter watches attentively, noting the condition and conduct of the bull as his men place the banderillas.

Citing the bull from the center of the ring. The matador has taken the banderillas himself and stands alone in the ring facing the bull. The bull's attention is centered on the man and in a moment the bull will charge.

A spectacular pair of banderillas. The matador has raced in a short half-circle to meet the bull. At the last moment he has raised his hands high and left the ground in an act of total commitment which has left him no margin of safety. As he drives in the sticks he will have to pivot upon them to avoid the horn and, should he miss the mark, the bull will surely catch him.

Placing a good pair. The matador's assistant has run in a wide half-circle from the point where the other matador stands in the center of the ring. The banderillero is an experienced man. He has carefully judged his distances so that the bull is almost completely halted as he leans forward directly between the horns to drive in the sticks high up between the shoulders. The man is not a star and has not held his body as straight as he might have, but he has done a good professional job and deserves the round of applause he will receive.

Stepping away. As the bull continues to try to turn, the man releases the sticks and steps away out of range of the charge.

Banderillas al quiebro. From a position with his feet together, the man has moved his left foot and begun to swing his body in the same direction. The bull has not yet begun to follow the movement and the man is intent but not fearful as he judges the distance. If the bull follows correctly, at the last moment he will bring his left foot back to its former position and drive in the sticks as the bull passes under his left arm. The wide, dangerous set of the horns on the bull in the picture add considerably to the merit of the attempt.

A wild spectacular pair al quiebro. In order to increase the spectacular effect, the man has broken the banderillas off short so that they are no more than a few inches long and has called the bull from a position seated in the chair. At the last moment he has leaped to his feet and is beginning to lean far to the left in order to deflect the charge. The man is less confident than in the preceding picture and because of all the movement required, there is less elegance and control in the action. The expressions of the spectators reflect the mixed emotions with which this type of additional flourish is received by the crowd.

The confident challenge. From a position on the estribo (the little step running around inside the fence) the man is calling the bull with absolute confidence. He has edged his way along the estribo from his left to a position directly in front of the bull and in a moment will leap down and forward to race in a short half-circle to his right, place the sticks and escape into the center of the ring. The man's position is extremely dangerous since there is now no escape from the bull except out into the center of the ring.

Another dangerous pair. The man is moving slowly toward the bull, a step at a time, shortening the distance to the absolute limit before making his move. Despite the dangerous position, there is a feeling of absolute control of the situation which is reflected in the intent faces of the spectators and is confirmed by the two well-grouped pairs of banderillas dangling from the bull's shoulder.

The accident. The banderillas are beautifully placed, but in an effort to outdo himself, the man has misjudged the distance and the bull is about to catch him in the thigh with his right horn.

A bad pair of banderillas. The man has misjudged the distance and has almost missed the bull altogether. This is the second pair he has placed badly as evidenced by the banderilla already dangling from the bull's throat and, if he cannot do better than this, he should leave the matter to his assistants.

14.

THE BRINDIS

As the trumpet sounds the banderilleros race to the fence to retrieve their fighting capes and the matador steps out from the fence and gestures to them indicating the section of the arena in which he wishes to start his muleta work. As they run forward to take charge of leading the bull to that section, the other matadores leave the ring.

Watch the bullfighter as he steps out to indicate the spot to which he wishes his assistants to lead the bull. Note his confidence or the lack of it, his command of the situation and his men, whether they pay attention to his orders or ignore him. Note particularly whether it is of any importance to him whether they obey him or not. It is a good rule of thumb that if the bullfighter cannot obtain obedience from his men he will not be able to obtain it from the bull. Conversely if he does not care what his men do, there is no reason to believe he will care what the bull does either.

As the assistants bring the bull across the ring there should be an absolute minimum of unnecessary cape passes and false starts. The bull should be brought smoothly from one spot to another. The men should not be forced to drop their capes or have to run for their lives. They are professionals and are supposed to be able to do a workman-like job. Since there are two or three of them working as a team it should be a smooth, team-like operation. There is no excuse for anything else.

The bull should be brought in close to the fence but should not be permitted to crash into it or into the burladeros, the protected openings through which the men jump to safety. This is easily avoided with a little care, but is sometimes done deliberately, in order to tire the bull further after the pics and the banderillas. This is always bad for the bull and the fight which is to follow, since, even if the bull does not break off or splinter a horn, thus absolutely ruining him for the fight, the action of smashing into an immovable object always tends to stun him and sometimes injures him internally, making him unfit for the action which is to follow.

While his men are bringing the bull into position, the bullfighter turns back to the fence, sips at a glass of water, rinses his mouth and spits into the sand. As he finishes and hands back the glass, his sword handler passes him the *muleta*, which he carefully folds and places in his left hand.

The muleta is nothing more than a piece of red flannel cloth draped over a short wooden stick. The stick is approximately an inch in diameter and generally between a foot and a half and two feet in length. The size of the cloth and the overall size of the muleta are not fixed and may vary considerably depending upon the preference and height of the matador. In general, however, the muleta should not be overly large or the matador will not be able to handle it. The wooden stick is carved to provide a hand-hold along one third of its length, while the cloth is held in place with a set screw which prevents it from coming loose. If the day is windy the man may spread the muleta on the ground and have his men pour water on it to dampen the cloth and make it more manageable.

The bullfighter reaches across and with his right hand draws the sword from a leather sheath his swordhandler offers him. He places the sword in his left hand also and clamps it against the muleta with his thumb holding it in place. Then, still with his right hand, he reaches across the fence again for his hat.

The sword is nearly three feet long and is straight along most of its length with a slight downward curve a few inches from the tip. It is made of heavy, cold-forged steel, has a needle point and both edges are honed razor sharp a good third of the length. The sword weighs several pounds and when held with the muleta in the right hand requires a strong wrist and a considerable effort to handle gracefully.

Because of the weight of the steel sword many bullfighters prefer to work with an aluminum one while performing the muleta work, only taking the steel sword at the end of the faena to actually kill the bull. Theoretically only those bullfighters who have injured their wrists are permitted to do this; however, nearly all bullfighters are able to produce a doctor's certificate attesting some past wrist injury and most of them take advantage of this and the convenience it entails despite the interruption that changing swords imposes when it is time to kill the bull.

You will note that most bullfighters who choose to work with the real sword make a ritual of bending the sword by placing the tip against the fence and pressing with their forearm against the flat of the blade. This is supposed to accentuate the curve of the blade and test the spring of the steel but really has little or no effect on the sword and is simply a reassuring bit of ritual which among other things, informs the public that the men is using the real sword.

With the hat in his right hand, the naked sword and the muleta in his left, he then turns and walks along the fence to a spot directly below the president's box.

Watch the way the bullfighter walks, whether he is interested in what is happening to the bull, whether he comes forward quickly, confidently or slowly, grudgingly, whether he is preoccupied or distracted or eager to begin.

If one of the bullfighters is a novillero who is fighting for the first time as a matador de toros, the senior matador will interrupt the normal order of the fight (with his first bull of the afternoon) at this point and, instead of going toward the president's box, will wait by the fence while the novillero comes out to meet him. While the other matador stands nearby as a witness to the ceremony the senior matador hands the sword and muleta to the novillero who hands his cape to the matador in exchange. During this action the matador may say a few words of encouragement or advice, the men then embrace in the Spanish fashion, placing an arm about each other's shoulders. Finally the novillero turns and walks off alone to kill the bull in place of the senior matador, while the senior matador steps behind the fence out of the ring. This action is called the *alternativa*.

As a result of this ceremony the normal order of the fight is changed. The novillero kills the first and the sixth bulls. The senior matador the second and the fourth bulls and the other matador the third and the fifth bulls.

There are no special requirements for taking the alternativa nor does his performance on the day of the ceremony have any bearing on whether he becomes a matador or not. The man need only to be a registered novillero and know two matadores willing to participate in the ceremony.

The bullfighter stops in front of the presidential box and facing the stands salutes the president, arching back his body, the sword and muleta held out before him, gesturing with the hat in his right hand. This action is called the *brindis* or dedication. As he finishes the brindis the bullfighter turns and throws or hands his hat (the *montera*) back across the fence to his swordhandler for safekeeping.

According to the regulations the bullfighter is obliged to dedicate his first bull of the afternoon to the president; however, if it is the first time that the matador appears in this particular arena or if he feels particularly confident that he will do well with this particular bull, he may turn after a cursory salute to the presidential box and walk to the center of the ring to dedicate the bull to the entire audience. This is a very popular gesture and usually earns him a round of applause. If the brindis is made to the public, the matador drops the montera to the ground rather than passing it across the fence to his swordhandler.

If the bullfighter does decide to dedicate the bull to the crowd, note the way he turns from the fence and with what confidence he strides out to the center of the arena. Note his attitude as he spins slowly on his heel and gestures with his hat to the crowd. Note whether he puts any elegance into it or whether it is a half-hearted gesture lacking confidence and only made in the hope of hearing some small round of applause. Watch as he drops the montera to the ground. Some bullfighters throw it over their shoulder without a backward glance, others place it carefully face down or face up on the sand, still others drop it and then change the way it fell either from face up to face down or vice-versa. The way in which the montera falls really has no significance except that those who pay attention to the way it falls are superstitious, while those who do not are not. Whether any particular bullfighter prefers that the montera be face down or up is simply a reflection of the way the montera fell in some other fight when everything went well and he had a great triumph. Most bullfighters would rationalize this, of course, by the fact that if it does no real good and does not influence what will occur it certainly does no harm and costs nothing.

After the first bull the bullfighter may dedicate the following bull or bulls to anyone he wishes without the obligation to first salute the president. Occasionally the bullfighter will take advantage of this to dedicate the death of the bull to some particular person in the crowd. This may be a friend or some visiting dignitary or anyone he wishes to compliment. If this is the case the bullfighter will walk to a spot below where the person is seated and salute them with his montera. He generally accompanies this gesture with a few appropriate words or phrases. When he has finished he spins on his heel and throws the montera back over his shoulder without looking. The person to whom he has dedicated the bull is supposed to catch the montera and hold it during the fight. After the death of the bull the bullfighter must return to claim his hat, with acclaim if he has done well or with shame if he has done badly. In either case the person receiving the dedication is expected to reply either with a friendly word or a small gift of some kind or other.

Taking the sword and muleta. The man clamps the sword tightly against the furled muleta in his left hand as he carefully takes the hat in his right. The action is ritualized and unusual. The hat is not worn during the muleta faena but is only taken in order to make the brindis, while this is the only moment during the fight that the sword is held in the left hand.

Brindis to the president.

Brindis to the crowd.

Brindis to a friend.

Returning the brindis. At the end of the fight, the person to whom the bull has been dedicated returns the bullfighter's hat with a few complimentary words and a small gift, in this case a fine cigar.

The alternativa. The young man on the right is being promoted to the rank of full matador. He has just received the sword and muleta from the man on the left. He is smiling and happy since, with this simple ceremony, he has taken a major step forward in his career. The man in the background is the official witness to the ceremony.

15.

OPENING MULETA WORK

As he finishes with the brindis, the bullfighter turns and waving everyone from the ring, approaches the bull for the serious business of the opening muleta work.

In the opening muleta work the matador feels out the bull, gauges his state of mind and condition and verifies the distance from which he will charge and the force of the charge itself. Once these things have been established the matador attempts to pick up the bull, to get him interested in the muleta and may begin to improvise in order to demonstrate an ever-ascending control over the bull's action.

The importance of the muleta work or the muleta faena in modern bull-fighting can hardly be overemphasized. This is what most of the people have come to see and the way in which the matador handles the muleta can make or break his reputation. To a large extent, therefore, the way in which the man handles himself and handles the bull during the muleta faena will determine whether this bullfight will be a success or not.

Basically the muleta faena serves to provide the man with an opportunity to exert an intense personal domination and control over the bull. In the process the muleta faena serves to introduce the spectators to every aspect of the bull's personality and to demonstrate what manner of man the bullfighter is and in what intrinsic ways he is equal or superior to the animal before him.

In addition, and theoretically at least, each pass should be performed with the utilitarian object of correcting some defect in the bull's charge or comport-ment so that eventually he may be killed quickly and easily in accordance with the rules of the bullfight. In this respect the bull should be conditioned by the muleta faena to carry his head fairly low and turn to the left at the end of his charge. Generally speaking this can best be accomplished by the use of low, sweeping, left-handed passes. However, if the bull has some inherent defect contrary measures may be necessary. Thus, if the bull carries his head high but hooks naturally to the left, low, sweeping, right-handed passes may be necessary. On the other hand if the bull carries his head very low, higher passes may be necessary to get him to raise it.

As the bullfighter approaches the bull for the opening muleta work, everyone else leaves the ring.

The bullfighter's assistants take up positions behind the fence in order to be ready to come to his aid should there be an accident. The other bullfighters have no responsibility during the muleta faena and generally stand quietly in the narrow passageway behind the fence talking to their sword-handlers and casually watching the action. Should there be an accident they may come to the rescue by flashing a cape or leaping the fence, but they are not really on guard and no formal attention is required of them during this phase of the fight.

As the bullfighter goes toward the bull he unfolds the muleta. Holding it by the wooden stick and letting the folds drape to the ground, he inserts the sword into the cloth in such a way that it spreads the folds to the greatest extent possible.

The muleta may be held in either the right or left hand but the sword must always be held in the right. As a consequence, any passes made with the right hand must involve both the sword and the muleta, while those made with the left hand involve only the muleta. In general, only passes involving both the sword and the muleta are used in the opening muleta work.

Note with what decision, with what confidence the bullfighter approaches the bull. Does he appear sure of himself? Does he seem to have a plan of action? Some definite way of beginning? Or does he come forward hesitantly, thinking already of how to defend himself, of how to escape from the bull, of how to kill him with the least effort?

Although the bullfighter may open the muleta faena in any way he wishes, the seasoned matador generally begins his muleta work either with a series of two-handed passes called *estatuarios*, or else with a series of right-handed passes called *pases de castigo*.

Occasionally a bullfighter will begin in some other more spectacular way such as challenging the bull from the center of the ring with the muleta folded behind his back or from a position seated on the estribo, the little shelf or step that runs around the inside of the fence. These are dangerous crowd-pleasing gambits and add variety to this phase of the action but can only be attempted with very clear and hard-charging bulls, and as a consequence are rarely seen.

The most common method of beginning the muleta work is with pases de castigo. In this action the man approaches the bull easily but cautiously with the muleta spread by the sword in his right hand. As he steps closer the man extends the muleta forward and shakes it to attract the bull's attention. When the bull finally charges, the man swings the muleta ahead of the horns in a wide, low, right-handed pass which maintains the cloth constantly in front of the bull. At the end of the pass, instead of permitting the bull to swing out and turn of his own accord the man maintains the cloth where the bull can see it and steps forward, obliging the bull to turn sharply within his own length in order to follow. As the bull charges again the man repeats the maneuver with a low, wide, back-handed pass in the opposite direction.

If the man begins with pases de castigo, watch the way in which he approaches the bull, the decision with which he shows the bull the muleta, the grace and ease and confidence with which he takes command and brings the bull through the charge time and again. These passes are for difficult bulls, bulls with a strong tendency to hook to either side, bulls of a defensive nature, bulls with a lot of steam and energy which turn quickly and attack constantly. With such bulls it is necessary to double the bull on himself a number of times by passing the muleta smoothly below the horns, turning with the bull and staying with him, keeping the muleta constantly before him so that he follows its slightest movement. These passes exercise an enormous control over the bull and enable the matador from the very beginning to dominate the action and gauge the possibilities of attempting the graceful and artistic work with the muleta which has come to be one of the most important acts in the death of the bull.

If the man chooses to begin with estatuarios he takes up a position in profile to the bull, holding the muleta directly in front of him with both hands like a short fishing rod, the sword extending the cloth, chest-high. Slowly he edges closer, shaking the cloth to attract the bull's attention. As the bull charges, the man holds his body absolutely straight and still but swings the muleta to one side and up and the bull passes beneath it sometimes rearing high in the air to catch the elusive target. As the bull turns and recharges, the man stands just as he was or spins slowly on his heels to repeat the action from the opposite direction.

The estatuario is a very spectacular pass but affords the matador little control over the bull. In general this pass can only be attempted successfully with bulls which charge straight and hard and have little tendency to hook to either side, ie., bulls which are ideal for nearly any form of muleta work. Occasionally the bullfighter will underestimate the condition or difficulty of a particular bull and find himself exposed to a bad tossing or worse before he can change his position.

In judging the estatuario note whether the bullfighter stands with his feet together or slightly apart. If he stands with his feet together note whether he is absolutely quiet and relaxed, his body straight or even arched slightly, stomach out toward the bull, the muleta held chest-high and directly in front of him. Note whether as the bull charges the man is able to retain his position without flinching, swaying, or changing the position of his body in any way. Note whether his feet remain firmly planted in the sand and whether he is able to swing the muleta casually, cooly, up in front of and over the horns of the bull or whether at the last moment his feet twitch or his body bends back out of the way. Note whether he is able to spin slowly on his heels or stand impassively and without moving his feet receive the bull's charge again and again, or whether he finds himself hard-pressed and must give ground continually.

The same pass is sometimes done while standing with the feet slightly apart, in which case as the bull charges the man moves the muleta slightly ahead of the horns and leans into the pass cargando la suerte. This variation affords the man a greater degree of control over the bull but is less spectacular to the casual observer.

If his feet are slightly apart note whether he leans into the pass swinging the muleta ahead of the bull and leading him under control from one point to another, or whether he takes advantage of his wider stance to lean out of the bull's way and without controlling his charge permit him to pass back and forth at will.

The pase de castigo. The man takes the bull from the far right and brings him across to the left in front of his own body. Stepping forward deeply with his left leg, he increases his control and the extent of the arc the bull must follow in seeking the cloth. The bull has already turned more than 180 degrees and, as the man steps forward with his right foot at the end of the pass, the bull will have to turn completely upon himself in order to follow.

The estatuario. The man is absolutely relaxed as he stands like a statue calmly watching the bull charge through beneath the cloth. The bull is not controlled by the cloth, but will turn by himself as the cloth disappears and charge again from the other direction as the man shakes the cloth to attract his attention.

The estatuario. The man is less sure of himself and less relaxed as the bull goes up in the air after the cloth. The bull is very big and powerful, with heavy, dangerously set horns. His charge is short and with little follow-through, and the man is shouting to encourage him to continue and perhaps also to relieve some of his own tension after the tossing which has ripped his suit at the hip.

A spectacular beginning. The man holds the muleta furled in his hand, offering the smallest possible target to the bull. As the bull charges, at the very last moment, the man will release the folds of the cloth and guide the bull away to his left in a long, low, smooth, flowing pass. The bull is big and well armed and the man is calm and confident without any theatrical pose or false bravado.

Lack of Control. The young man has tried to begin the muleta faena with the muleta furled in his left hand as he has seen the big stars do, but as the bull charges he is suddenly unsure of himself and what was to have been a spectacular opening becomes instead a grotesque revelation of his inner panic.

From the kneeling position. The man has edged out from the fence on his knees and has taken the bull in a pass which is neither a pase de castigo nor an estatuario, but something vaguely in between. The bull has come by closer than anticipated and the man has been forced to lean back to avoid being caught, but he is still in control and, with a little luck, will be able to repeat the pass from the other side before being forced to get to his feet.

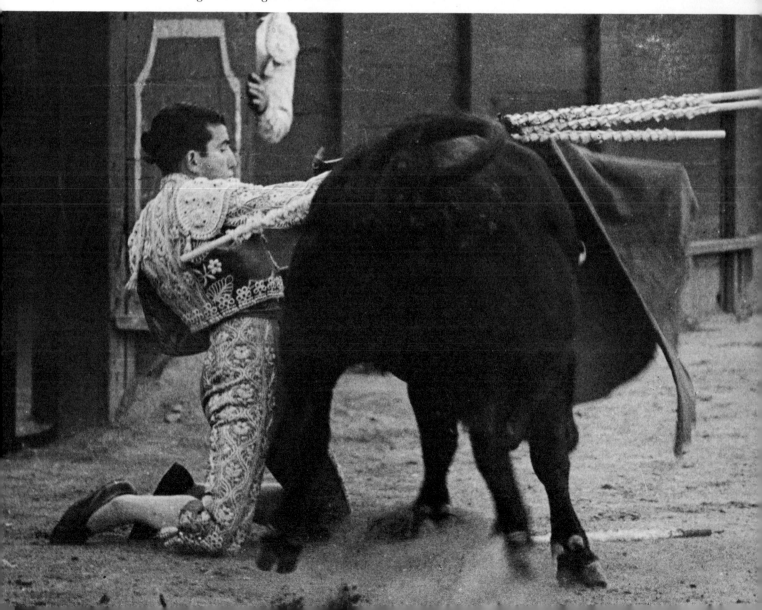

Spectacular control. The man started this pass as though to take the bull across in front from right to left in a regular pase de castigo, but at the last moment he changed his mind and swept the muleta away behind his back, completely changing the direction of the charge. The bull has had to twist into an almost impossible contortion in order to follow the cloth, but the man has maintained his position with absolute calm and has the bull under perfect control as the horn slides by his right side in a hair-raising opening pass which has no name.

16.

BASIC MULETA FAENA

After the opening estatuarios or pases de castigo the bullfighter steps away and strides off a few pases before turning to face the bull again.

Some bullfighters prefer to merge the pases de castigo or estatuarios directly into a short series of right or left-handed passes without a pause, but in general it is a mistake to begin the faena at too high a pitch or there will be nowhere to go except downhill. While there are exceptions to every rule most experienced bullfighters prefer to give both themselves and the bull a breather before moving from the opening muleta work to the more serious and sober right or lefthanded series which are the basis for the artistic muleta faena.

As the man faces the bull he swings the muleta easily into either his right or left hand, throws back his head and shoulders defiantly, and advancing slowly, a step at a time, sweeps the muleta carefully forward and back to attract the bull's attention. As the distance shortens and the man inches closer, he shakes the muleta each time he swings it forward and offers it to the bull. When the man and the muleta finally reach a certain distance the bull will charge.

As the man moves the muleta he calls to the bull, he may even leap into the air or assume some other wild attitude in order to attract the bull's attention, but this is meaningless bravado and serves only to show the temperament of the bullfighter. In any case as he edges closer he watches the bull carefully, gauging the distance and the attitude of the bull, in order to anticipate when he will charge. In this way he slowly gains ground on the bull and does not overstep himself. It is a fundamental error for the man to inch forward without moving the muleta or shaking it periodically, for the only movement the bull will see will be the entire movement of the man and the cloth together and when he charges he may choose to attack the man as readily as the cloth, with disastrous results to the bullfighter.

While the bullfighter has roughly established the distance from which the bull will charge during the opening muleta work, he must refine this judgement almost to the inch if he is to be able to pass the bull successfully in a really close series of linked right or left-handed passes as the terms of modern bullfighting demand.

At the first movement the man sets himself, fixes the bull's charge in the folds of the muleta and swinging it quietly ahead of the horns, leads him from in front, past his own body and away and out again, behind and to the side in one long fluid movement perfectly timed to the bull's charge. At the end of the pass he turns calmly and easily with the muleta before the bull, picks him up again and repeats the movement.

The skill involved in the modern muleta faena consists entirely in distracting the bull from his natural target, which is the man's body while guiding him gracefully from place to place by means of the muleta. The basic tenants of this skill are summarized in the three basic precepts . . . *parar, mandar* and *templar*.

Parar means literally to stop or stand still. In bullfight terminology this is generally used with reference to the bullfighter and refers to his ability to stand quietly without flinching, his feet firmly planted in the sand, while the bull charges close enough to brush his clothing with his horns. This is a skill which transcends bravery and can only be developed by practice, since beyond all question of fear there is an instinctive reaction to step back out of the way of any charging animal which must be overcome. On the other hand, the serenity with which a bullfighter is able to face a full-grown bull intent on killing him is, of course, the result not only of learning this skill but of his inherent courage as well. For it is one thing to overcome the instinctive reaction to step away and another to hold your ground when it may mean a trip to the hospital. The serenity with which the bullfighter is able to face the bull is then one measure of his courage and the seasoned bullfighter who is not able to hold his feet still demonstrates that with this bull at least he has lost his nerve. Parar is absolutely fundamental if the man is to be able to function at all, since if the man makes the slightest movement the bull will be attracted by that movement and charge the man rather than the cloth. If the bull charges the man rather than the cloth the man must, of course, move or he will be caught and thrown. If the man moves he naturally attracts the bull's attention even more, and thus the bullfighter who cannot stand quietly in place must go on the defensive, skipping from place to place in ludicrous fashion, always just a step ahead of the horns, utterly unable to do anything except to try and stay out of the bull's way, and kill him the best way he can. Parar is, then, the first of the basic tenants of bullfighting and the most fundamental, for it is impossible to mandar and templar without having first stood quietly in place.

Mandar means to command. It refers to the attitude of the bullfighter toward the bull. If the bullfighter is confident, positive and aggressive, if he challenges the bull successfully; if he cites well; if he is able to interest the bull in the cloth; if he really controls the action and movements of the bull at all times; if he dominates the situation; he is said to command well. If he is timid, hesitant and unsure of himself or if he permits the bull to run freely as he wishes or to charge when he chooses, if he does not force the bull to fix his attention on the muleta and follow it as he directs, then he is said to be lacking in this quality and in extreme cases the bull may even be said to be commanding him.

Templar means to temper, to moderate, or to be in tune with. In the bullring this refers to the ability of the bullfighter to regulate the swing of the cape or muleta to the bull's charge, sweeping it away in front of the horns in a rhythm so perfect that an illusion of continuity is given as though the bull were being led on a string following the cloth. Ideally the horns of the bull should never touch the cloth, for if they do the bull will immediately toss his head in an attempt to gore and may catch the man or at least require him to give ground to save himself. When this happens, too often the bull begins to anticipate the action, goes on the defensive, and starts to toss his head as soon as he sees the cloth, making it impossible to even attempt to pass him.

Watch the man's feet at the moment the bull charges. Note whether they remain firmly fixed, solidly in place, or whether they skip back a half step at the last minute. Watch the man's body. Note whether at the last moment he sucks in his stomach and pulls back his body, bending forward from the waist in order to avoid the horns only to straighten up again immediately after the horns have passed his body, and perhaps even thrust his stomach forward in an exaggerated movement in order to give the impression that the bull was so close that he brushed him with his shoulder.

While it is not true that all bullfighters who end up with blood on the front of their suit got it by this trick, it is true that a great number of them have done so. On the other hand not all bullfighters who end up with their clothes still spotless are that way because they did not resort to such tricks. Some are clean simply because they never got close to the bull.

In general there is no need for the bullfighter to touch the bull at all with his body or clothes and theoretically he should finish the corrida with his clothes as spotless as when he began it. Some bullfighters, however, have made it a part of their personality and style to end the fight completely disheveled and bloody, but it should always be remembered that the man is not supposed to be caught by the bull; the man is not supposed to be hurt; and the man is not supposed to be wrestling with the bull, opposing force with force, but rather dominating the action by intelligence and skill. Thus when a man ends the corrida in a disheveled condition it is not necessarily an indication of the danger he has been through, or of how close he has worked to the bull's horns, but may only mean either that the man has deliberately permitted the bull to brush him with his shoulder or has been accidentally caught by the bull through some error, or lack of skill, or some odd movement of the animal.

If the bull is particularly slow or uncertain about charging, the man may sometimes be goaded into kicking at the bull's head with his slippered feet or may perhaps slap at his muzzle with the flat of the sword in order to provoke him into doing so. These gestures are in bad taste since they not only tend to demean the bull but detract from the man's dignity as well. By resorting to these expedients the man proclaims his inability to cope with an awkward situation or to discover a more graceful solution to this difficult problem.

If this muleta pass is made to the left it is called a *natural*. If it is made to the right it is called a *derechazo*. These two passes are the basis for all of the artistic muleta work accomplished during the muleta faena.

The basic right-handed pass is sometimes called a right-handed natural since the mechanics of its execution are so exactly similar to the pass with the left hand; however, this terminology is not in general use and the word derechazo continues to be employed almost universally for this basic, right-handed pass.

In the natural the man stands with his feet slightly apart with the sword in his right hand and the muleta in his left. The sword is held at his side or behind his back while he extends his left hand forward presenting the cloth to the bull. As the bull charges the man stands his ground, swings the muleta ahead of the bull's horns and draws him past and away in a long sweeping curve. When the bull turns the man turns with him by taking a step with his right foot and is then in a position to repeat the movement. This should be the beginning of a rhythmic series of passes which draw the bull closer and closer, slowly and ever more slowly about the matador almost as though the bull were a toy led upon a string. When the man feels that the series is about to break, that the bull will no longer follow through, he ends the series with a back-handed pass of the same kind which draws the bull back past his body and liberates him with his head up allowing him to breathe.

Left-handed muleta passes are the most difficult to perform well and consequently have the greatest merit, since with only the muleta in the left hand, the target offered to the bull and used to guide and control his charge is smaller, and the difficulty and danger involved in maintaining control is consequently greater. To appreciate this it should be understood that the cloth hanging undisturbed from the stick must be spread and controlled by the simple wristwork of the bullfighter at the same time that the entire muleta is tempered to the bull's charge by the movement of his arm and body. The skill and delicacy that these simultaneous actions require are considerable and only a few bullfighters ever achieve or demonstrate a fine left hand.

In addition, the left-handed passes condition the bull to turn to the left in his charge and help to correct any tendency he may have to toss his head to the right. Both of these results are, of course, of prime importance later at the time of the kill.

Because of the reduced size of the muleta, if the bull has any marked tendency to hook to the left it will be nearly impossible to pass him in this way and should not be attempted. Occasionally a bullfighter in his desire to triumph will ignore this precept and it will cost him a bad tossing.

There are two ways of performing the natural: the old-fashioned or classic method and the modern or parallel method. These methods differ essentially in the position of the man's feet and the relative positions of the man and the bull at the beginning of the charge.

There are of course a number of variations on these two basic methods depending upon the angle at which the man approaches and takes the bull's charge. In general, the less parallel the man is to the line of charge and the more the charge must be bent or controlled from the very beginning, the greater the difficulty involved and the greater the merit of the pass. The really classic form in which the bull is taken directly from the front is seldom seen at the present time.

In both methods the sword is held in the right hand, either behind the back or vertically parallel with the right leg. It is a fault of execution and detracts from the merit of the pass to prick the point of the sword into the muleta, extending the cloth in order to present a large target to the bull. This is only permissible or acceptable when the wind is strong and the pass could not otherwise be performed without the man being gored. Occasionally the bullfighter may strike a posture indicating the center of the muleta with the point of the sword while performing the pass. This attitude is censured by the purists for aesthetic reasons but does not really detract from the merit of the pass as long as the sword does not extend the cloth from the natural falling lines. The same aesthetic reasons apply to holding the sword out from the body or up in the air or in any other position but vertically parallel with the right leg or diagonally behind the back.

In the old-fashioned or classic natural, the man faces the bull as he approaches him head on from the front. The man's feet are some distance apart and a line drawn between them is perpendicular to the line of the bull's charge. As he steps forward the muleta in his left hand is an extension of this perpen-

dicular line. He reaches forward and offers the cloth to the bull, shakes it and as the bull charges deflects the charge to the muleta, centers the bull's attention in the cloth, guides the bull to the left and around his body to the back in an almost perfect semicircle and sends him away again in essentially the same direction as the original charge. In order to accomplish all this the man must lean into the pass, pivoting on his left foot and guiding the bull with a delicate arm and wrist and body movement that spreads the cloth and withdraws it at an even speed inches in front of the horns, until the bull has been sent on his way.

When accomplished with such elegance, grace and ease that it appears almost effortless, the emotional intensity and plastic beauty of this maneuver are extraordinary. However, the extended domination and control required by the classic natural supposes not only exceptional suppleness and delicacy of movement on the part of the bullfighter, but rare courage and self-control as well in order to face the charge head-on. At the present time only a very few bullfighters even attempt to pass the bull in this fashion and most of those that do either shift their position an instant before the charge or find themselves beyond their depth in a movement they do not dominate.

In the closest modern approximation to the classic form the man approaches more or less in profile to the bull but at the last minute as he brings forward the cloth and offers it to the bull he advances his left foot a half step forward in the direction of the pass thus presenting himself in three-quarter profile to the bull and in a position from which he can lean into the pass cargando la suerte, as the bull charges. Because of the angle at which the charge is taken as well as the fact that the bull's charge must be deflected and controlled from the very beginning, this variation still achieves great plastic beauty and emotional intensity; however, even this variation is seldom seen and even less often perfectly executed.

In the modern manner of accomplishing the natural the bullfighter edges forward with his right side to the bull and his body parallel to the line of charge. The left hand with the muleta is brought forward across the man's body to the right and offered to the bull. The bull charges in a straight line toward the cloth and the man withdraws the cloth ahead of the bull. Once the horns have passed his body, he swings his arm around and away back to the left, really controlling the bull's course only after the horns have passed his body. Performed in this manner the pass requires timing and a certain delicate wrist movement, but does not require the large body movement that the old-fashioned method requires. The pass may be accomplished with the feet together or slightly separated, but there is little or no need to pivot or lean into the pass and as a consequence little or no body control is required.

While any well-executed natural is considered superior to an equally well-executed derechazo because of the additional difficulty involved in handling the unspread cloth, the extreme modern version in which the bull is taken in absolute profile is considered to have real merit only if the man controls the bull's charge from the beginning and demonstrates this by bending the line of charge around him in an arc before sending the bull on his way. If the man only swings the muleta in front of the bull as the bull charges through, without deviating this charge or really controlling it in any way, then the pass is really nothing more than a pretty pose.

In general, all passes in which the bull passes the man without having his course altered, in which the bull moves under his own volition and is not taken from "there" and brought "here" by the bullfighter, are inferior and of little merit except as spice or variations to the basic faena.

In the derechazo the man stands with his feet slightly apart with the sword and the muleta held together in his right hand. His left hand is empty. The sword in his right hand is pricked in the cloth of the muleta in such a way that the cloth is spread and extended, thus presenting a large almost triangular surface for the bull to see and follow. His left hand is held behind his back or at his side or placed on his left hip. The man advances his right hand presenting the cloth to the bull. As the bull charges the man stands his ground, swings the muleta ahead of the bull's horns and draws him past and away in a long, sweeping curve. As the bull turns the man turns with him by taking a step forward with his left foot, and endeavors to link up a rhythmic series of three, four, or more passes of the same kind. When the man feels that the series is almost about to break, that the bull will no longer follow through, he may terminate this series with a back-handed pass of the same kind with the right hand or, by crossing his hands behind his back, transfer the muleta to the left hand and with the sword in his right terminate with a back-handed pass of the left hand.

The right-handed passes are considered of lesser merit than those performed with the left, since with the sword pricked in the cloth of the muleta, the size of the target that the bull follows is larger. As a consequence there is a larger margin for error and the bull need not pass as close to the man's body unless the man really so desires it.

The weight of the sword and the muleta in the right hand also limit the lightness and the delicacy of the right-handed pass and the sword pricked in the cloth adds a certain rigidity to the movement which cannot be avoided even by the most gifted.

Finally, while some bulls need right-handed passes to straighten out an erratic charge or an exaggerated tendency to hook to the left, the right-handed passes are fundamentally illogical in the sense that they are designed to accustom the bull to turn to the right, which is not only generally undesirable but may be dangerous later at the time of the kill when a bull accustomed to turn to the right may catch the man with his horn.

There are two ways of performing the derechazo; the old-fashioned or classical method and the modern or parallel manner. The distinction between the two depends upon the position of the man's feet and the relative positions of the man and the bull.

In general the same criteria with regard to merit that apply to the natural apply to the derechazo as well, i.e. the less parallel the man is to the line of charge and the more the charge must be bent or controlled from the very beginning, the greater the difficulty involved and the greater the merit of the pass. The really basic form in which the bull is taken almost directly from the front is, of course, rarely seen.

In both methods the sword and the muleta are held together in the right hand with the sword pricked in the muleta extending the cloth. With the sword spreading the muleta, the cloth is extended to its maximum. It is a fault to guide the course of the bull with the point of the muleta formed by the point of the sword rather than centering the horns well within the spread of the cloth since with his attention fixed on this point the horns of the bull must necessarily pass at a more than adequately safe distance from the body of the man and all real danger and emotion are excluded from the action.

The left hand may be placed on the left hip or held behind the back or at the left side throughout the pass. Postures in which the man extends his left hand out to the side or up into the air for balance are criticized for aesthetic reasons but do not really detract from the merit of the pass as long as the hand is not extended before the man's body in such a way that it could be used to ward off the bull in the event he did not follow the cloth. A distinction should be made between this fault and the adorno, in which the man edges forward to touch the bull's horn lightly with his left hand before the bull charges. This gesture is acceptable if the man is able to do it lightly and gracefully, to demonstrate how close he is to the bull, and his absolute domination of the situation. It is unacceptable when the man maintains his hold on the horn as the bull charges under the pretext of guiding him through, thus excluding all danger of the bull goring him by being able to spring away at the first false movement. A similar fault is for the man to put his left arm across the shoulders of the bull once the horns are past and, while holding his body tightly against the body of the bull, swing the muleta ahead of the horns so that the bull will move in a circle around his body. In this position it is of course impossible for the bull to gore the man no matter how little control the man may have. As a consequence such a pass is meaningless. On the other hand the authentic variation of this technique is one of the most impressive passes in modern bull-fighting. In this version the man maintains his position with his left hand behind his back or at his side and with the muleta floating just ahead of the horns guides the bull in a complete circle about his body. While this circular pass is often criticized by purists on the basis that once the horns have passed his body the man is really beyond all danger, it should be recognized that the man is able to maintain this position beyond danger only on the basis of his ability to stand his ground, command the bull and temper the swing of the muleta exactly to the rhythm of the bull's charge. In other words, unless he cheats by using his left arm to bind himself to the bull, the bullfighter is able to accomplish this pass only in so far as he adheres to the basic precepts of bullfighting, e.g., parar, mandar and templar.

In the old-fashioned or classic derechazo the man faces the bull as he approaches him from the front. The man's feet are slightly apart and a line drawn between them is perpendicular to the line of the bull's charge. As he steps forward the sword and muleta in his right hand are an extension of this perpendicular line. He reaches forward and offers the cloth to the bull, shakes it and as the bull charges the man deflects the charge to the muleta, centers the bull's attention on the cloth, guides the bull to the right and around his body to the back in an almost perfect semicircle and sends him away again in essentially the same direction as the original charge. To accomplish this the man must lean into the pass pivoting on his right foot cargando la suerte, while his arm, wrist and body guide the muleta at an even speed inches ahead of the horns.

The old-fashioned, really classic, derechazo in which the bull is taken almost directly from the front is seldom attempted anymore. Variations which approximate the classic derechazo in which the bull is taken more from the front than from the side, are attempted more often than they are with the natural, however, since the larger target offered by the sword in the muleta provides greater control and permits the bullfighter to limit the proximity of the charge and the consequent danger with greater ease. In the closest modern approximation to the classic form the man approaches more or less in profile to the bull but at the last minute as he brings the cloth forward and offers it to the bull he advances his right foot a half step forward in the direction of the pass, thus presenting himself in three-quarter profile to the bull and in a position from which he can lean into the pass cargando la suerte as the bull charges.

In the modern manner of accomplishing the derechazo the bullfighter edges forward with his left side to the bull and his body in profile parallel to the line of charge. The right hand with the muleta is brought forward across the man's body to the left and offered to the bull. The bull charges in a straight line toward

the cloth and the man withdraws the cloth ahead of the bull. Once the horns have passed his body he swings his right arm around and away back to the left really controlling the bull's course only after the horns have passed his body. This method requires skill and timing but does not require the large body movement that the old-fashioned method requires. The pass may be accomplished with the feet together or slightly separated but there is no need to lean into the pass and no real body control accompanies the pass.

The extreme modern derechazo in which the bull is taken in absolute profile and the bull's course only deviated slightly, if at all, is really of little or no real merit, although any such pass requires a certain skill to accomplish it. In judging the derechazo, the degree to which the bull's course and charge is deviated from a straight line and bent or controlled by the man must be the deciding factor. The man can, of course, control the proximity of the bull's charge much more easily with the extended muleta. If he takes advantage of this to pass the bull consistently at a safe distance the merit of the pass diminishes. If he permits the bull to pass closer and closer, then the merit of the pass increases.

The pase de pecho (or chest pass) is a type of back-handed pass used to finish off a series of naturales or a series of derechazos. It is in fact a sort of back-handed or reverse natural, and, while it may really be accomplished with either hand, it is generally performed (by switching the muleta behind the back) with the left hand even when finishing off a series of right-handed passes.

By its very nature the pase de pecho is the logical ending for a series of naturales or derechazos, since the beginning position is essentially the position the man is in after sending the bull on his way at the end of these passes. As a consequence, the bullfighter is able to continue and end such a series without the slightest wasted effort or the slightest break in the rhythm.

Normally the pase de pecho should occur as a single pass at the end of a series of naturales or derechazos. When the pase de pecho is performed in this way as one continuous motion out and away and then back again with the bull following almost as though he were tied to the cloth, it is of more value than when it requires laborious preparation. Often it is the graceful solution to the problem of the bull which turns very quickly or charges unexpectedly at the end of a series of these passes. The pase de pecho permits the man to escape from this awkward situation without giving ground while continuing to dominate the bull and illustrate his control. Sometimes a bullfighter will link two or three pases de pecho in a series, but unless they mount in emotional intensity this is generally less aesthetically satisfying than a single pass at the end of a series of naturales or derechazos.

Together with the natural and the derechazo, the pase de pecho is one of the fundamental elements of every muleta faena. It is important because at the moment when the man has drawn the bull as close as he possibly can pass him without being caught, the back-handed pass completely reverses the direction of the bull's charge, giving the man distance and room in which to recover and prepare for a new series and a new approach. The pase de pecho is important with respect to the bull as well, since after an intense series of low, sweeping passes it draws him through and leaves him with his head up and erect, providing him with a pause in which to breathe deeply and recover for the next series of passes.

The basic tenets of parar, mandar and templar apply to the pase de pecho as they do for all other passes made with cape and muleta. Thus the pase de pecho, in which the man holds his ground awaiting the bull's charge quietly without the slightest movement of his feet or body, in which he challenges or calls the bull and controls or bends his line of charge, and in which he tempers the swing of the cloth inches in front of the horns so that the bull almost goes up in the air after it, is of an entirely different degree of merit from one in which the muleta is merely shown to the bull, or in which the bull is permitted to charge through in a straight line underneath it, or in which the bull's horns touch the cloth, or one in which all of these things occur together.

In the left-handed pase de pecho the man stands more or less in profile with his left side to the bull. The muleta is held in his left hand and extended out and far back to the left. The sword is held in the right hand parallel or nearly parallel with the right leg. The left leg is extended backward and the right extended forward, forming a solid base as the man edges sideways and backwards extending the muleta into the range of the bull's vision. As the bull surges forward charging the muleta, the man draws the muleta forward ahead of the horns past his own leg and his body and around to the right until at the limit of his reach he rises on tip-toes with his left foot and raises his left arm higher and higher so that the bull can charge through beneath it while the muleta flutters up and back over the length of the bull's body.

The left-handed pase de pecho is more difficult to perform well and is of greater merit than that with the right since the muleta held alone in the left hand offers a smaller target to the bull and the difficulty and the danger involved in maintaining control is consequently greater. In judging the pase de pecho note the angle at which the man takes the charge. In general the bull's charge should be almost directly from the man's rear. The bull should be brought past the man's left side and the bull's charge controlled and bent around and to the opposite side past the man's chest. Note whether the bull is brought by close to the man's body or farther out. Whether the charge is bent around past the man's chest or whether the bull is simply sent straight through on his way. Note whether the bull is permitted to touch the cloth with consequent unavoidable head tossing and whether the man is obliged to step or dance away in the midst of the pass to escape a goring because of this.

In the right-handed pase de pecho the man stands in profile with his right side to the bull. The sword and the muleta are held in his right hand and the sword is pricked in the muleta in such a way that the cloth is spread and extended by the sword, thus presenting a larger surface to the bull to see and follow; the muleta is extended out and back to the right. The right leg is extended backward and the left extended forward as the man edges sideways and backwards extending the muleta into the range of the bull's vision. As the bull charges, the man draws the muleta forward ahead of the bull's horns past his leg and his body and round to his own left until at the limit of his reach he rises on tip-toe with his right foot and raises his arm higher and higher so that the bull can charge through beneath it while the muleta flutters up and back over the length of the bull's body.

The right-handed pases de pecho are of lesser merit than those performed with the left, since with the sword pricked in the cloth the size of the target is nearly doubled and the difficulty and danger involved in controlling the bull's charge is consequently lessened.

While the right-handed pase de pecho is the logical ending for a series of derechazos, occasionally, in order to add variety and difficulty to the faena, the bullfighter will switch the muleta from his right hand to his left behind his back and finish a series of derechazos with a left-handed pase de pecho which draws the bull in one continuous movement completely around his body. In this pase he switches only the muleta and maintaining the sword in his right hand goes on to perform the pass as he would any left-handed pase de pecho.

The natural and the derechazo with the corresponding pase de pecho are the basic passes of the muleta faena . . . the framework on which all the artistic action is built. Like any framework they require some decoration, some ornament, to give them body, and to relieve the stark severity of their outline. In the muleta faena such ornament is provided by the decorative passes.

In judging the right-handed pase de pecho note the angle from which the man takes the charge. Normally this charge should be almost directly from the man's rear. The bull should be brought past the man's right side and the bull's charge controlled and bent around to the opposite side past the man's chest. Note particularly whether the bull's attention is centered well within the spread of the cloth or whether on the contrary the bull's attention is fixed on the point of the muleta so that he passes at a more than adequate distance eliminating all danger from the action. Note whether the bull is permitted to touch the cloth with the consequent horn tossing and whether the man is obliged to step or dance away in the midst of the pass to escape a goring because of this. In the event that the man switches the muleta behind his back, note the ease with which this change is made and the smoothness with which the bull is brought past on the left side.

The classic natural. The man has stepped forward with his left foot into the bull's charge and is drawing the bull past and around his body with only the simple, straight-falling folds of the cloth in his left hand. He is holding the muleta well toward the middle and is taking the bull very closely in an easy, natural gesture that controls and dominates the animal completely.

The modern natural. The man stands with his feet together as he draws the bull past his body with the straight-falling folds of the cloth. The man's position is very good, but not particularly elegant. He is holding the muleta well toward the middle and is taking the bull very closely, but he is only just beginning to control the course of the bull's charge and with his feet together is unable to lean into the pass as far as he should.

The modern natural. As the man stands like a statute with his feet together, the bull charges past his body following the flaring muleta in a wide arc. The bull is under control, but the man is holding the muleta by the very tip and taking advantage of the greater sweep of the cloth thus obtained to pass the bull at a more comfortable distance.

Using the sword to control the cloth. The man has tried to pass the bull in a modern natural, but has hesitated to rely entirely upon his skill with the muleta. He has brought the sword around to maintain the cloth at a greater distance from his body throughout the pass. In doing so, he has sacrificed much of the beauty of the pass and some of his control over the bull. Use of the sword in this way is sometimes a necessity if there is much wind to disturb the cloth or the bull is particularly unmanageable on the left.

Lack of control. The man has tried to pass the bull in a modern natural, but the bull has failed to follow the cloth correctly and the man has been forced to alter his position dramatically to avoid being gored. He has been able to hold his feet still, but has had to finish the pass any way he could. If he permits the same thing to happen a second or third time, he may soon find himself completely on the defensive and unable to do anything with the bull.

The classic derechazo. The man has stepped forward with his right foot and is leaning far into the pass as he guides the bull around his body. Despite the fact that the sword extends the cloth making a larger target, the man is taking the bull very closely. The cloth is perfectly tempered to the bull's charge and the man is relaxed and in absolute control.

The modern derechazo. The man stands quietly with his feet together as the bull charges past in an almost straight line. There is great repose in the static figure of the man, and the contrast with the charging figure of the bull is impressive. There is less control over the bull when the pass is performed in this manner, however, since the bull is merely passing by rather than being brought from one spot to another.

The same pass performed with less control and less repose. The man has not tempered the swing of the muleta and the bull is hardly following the cloth at all. The man is unsure of himself and has instinctively drawn in his stomach to avoid the horn, while his left hand reflects all the tension he is otherwise trying to hide.

A poor derechazo. The bull is not charging as he should and the man has tried to use the tip of the muleta to take him by at a distance. The bull is already almost out of control and, although the man is trying to hold his ground, the position of his body as well as the left hand high in the air reveal his tension. The bull is very small and has been heavily picked, which may account for his failure to follow through, although the cause may simply be that the man has failed to interest him in the cloth.

The modern derechazo with the feet apart. As the bull charges past in a straight line, the man stands in profile with his feet apart. Although the man is taking advantage of the full extent of the open muleta to guide the bull with the fluttering tip, the cloth is beautifully tempered to the charge of he bull. The man is completely relaxed and, because of his open stance, is better able to follow through or lean into the pass. His control of the bull is only just beginning to change the direction of the charge, but he does have control and will bring the bull around far to the right in a partial arc before sending him away.

The circular pass. The man has placed himself with his feet apart and his back to the bull and has reached far around to his left with the muleta in an attempt to draw the bull in a long derachazo completely around his body. The position is an artificial one but, if the man is able to temper the cloth properly to the charge in one smooth, flowing gesture, the result will be impressive. The man is very calm and assured despite the size of the bull and the length of the horns, and has the bull well under control as he begins his charge.

Cheating. In the midst of the derechazo, the man has stepped forward with his left foot and pressed himself up against the bull's body. As he holds himself in this position behind the horns, he swings the cloth ahead of the bull in an attempt to turn him in a complete circle. There is no merit in the pass since the man is in no danger whatsoever and exerts no real control over the bull. At the end of the pass the man's suit will be covered with blood as though he had passed the bull dangerously close, but the action is only a cheat.

Changing hands. At the end of a series of derechazos, in an action reminiscent of the media veronica, the man swings the muleta past his right hip behind his back. His left hand (see the shadow in the picture) reaches behind from the opposite side to take it and, as the bull turns to follow the cloth, the man will step forward with his right foot and pass the bull from the rear under his left arm in a single un- broken movement.

The pase de pecho. The man has stepped forward with his right foot and is drawing the bull forward under his left arm and around his body. The bull is under
perfect control and the cloth perfectly tempered to the charge as the man leans far
into the pass.

The pase de pecho. As the bull nears the limit of the man's reach, the man raises
the muleta above the horns and sends the bull away. The man's position is elegant
and graceful and the sword in his right hand is held as it should be, close to his
leg.

The same pass without elegance or control. With the sword held high in the air and the muleta held far from the center, the figure of the man loses all grace and elegance as the bull charges through.

Lack of control. In the midst of the pase de pecho the man has lost control. Instead of following the cloth the bull has raised his head and hooked at the man. The bull is very well armed and the man has had to leap away to save himself from a nasty wound in the stomach or chest.

The right-handed pase de pecho. Instead of changing the muleta to his left hand at the end of a series of derechazos, the man has simply stepped forward and passed the bull forward under his right arm. The sword extends the folds of the cloth and the man is taking advantage of this fact to pass the bull at a slightly more comfortable distance than would be possible on the left. The execution of the pass is very good and the figure of the man is quietly relaxed with the bull well under control.

The same pass in an exaggerated form. The man has taken the bull at the same angle and has him well under control, but he has carried the pass far beyond his normal reach. Because of this, he has been forced to raise his left arm and contort his body in order to maintain his balance and much of the natural beauty and elegance of the action has been lost.

17.

DECORATIVE PASSES

After a series of basic passes with either the right or left hand the bull-fighter generally inserts some variation into the muleta faena with one of the decorative passes in his repertoire.

The decorative passes can be spectacular variations of the basic passes or different passes altogether. In either case the emphasis is upon technique and flourish rather than upon domination and control of the bull. Those decorative passes which maintain some semblance of control are of course of greater merit than those which do not. Such passes are not necessarily the most spectacular or pleasing to the casual observer, but are deeply appreciated by the real enthusiast and differentiate the real maestro from the ordinary bullfighter.

In the artistic construction of any muleta faena the decorative passes are absolutely necessary, and the experienced matador always employs some of them no matter how few or how sparingly, for while they contribute little or nothing to the control or domination of the bull they add variety to the muleta work and provide relief from the stark severity of the basic passes. They are the sauce and the spice, the seasoning and sometimes the fancy dessert of the muleta faena. As such they are indispensable.

The decorative passes generally come as a series at the end of the muleta faena after the man has amply demonstrated his domination and control of the bull with the basic passes. Certain bullfighters, however, prefer to insert some of these flourishes into every series of basic passes they perform, thus giving a lighter, more care-free, effect to their style of fighting. Either approach to the decoration of the muleta faena is acceptable, although the more serious style is generally considered the more profound and the most difficult to do well.

The decorative passes do not replace and cannot be substituted for the basic passes since they do not control or dominate the bull but merely pass him in spectacular fashion to one side or the other. In modern bullfighting, however, a number of young bullfighters have tried to build a reputation by substituting these passes for the basic passes, but while such a procedure generally succeeds to some extent with the small bulls fought at the beginning of their careers, it has invariably failed when attempted with full-grown animals of real temperament. It is of course a fundamentally unsound approach to bullfighting and may be compared to the young artist who starts working with oils before he has learned to draw.

Among the most commonly seen decorative passes at the present time are the *molinete*, the *abanico*, the *pase de bandera*, the *manoletina* and the *espaldina*.

Like fashions in clothes and automobiles, the fashion in decorative passes changes from time to time and decorative passes which may have been in vogue yesterday are out of fashion tomorrow.

Most of these passes can be accomplished with either the right or left hand and all of them can be accomplished from either the standing or kneeling position. In general, unless the bull is quite small or the man quite tall, it is extremely difficult to accomplish any pass elegantly from the kneeling position and passes from this position are generally only attempted by very young fighters intent upon demonstrating the extent of their courage or foolhardiness.

In the molinete the man cites the bull in much the same manner as he does for the pase de pecho, although the bull is generally taken more from the side than from the rear. As the bull charges, the man swings the muleta across his own body in front of the bull, but rather than continuing to raise the muleta above the bull's head, the man maintains it at waist level and spins his own body in the opposite direction so that the cloth is snapped briskly away from in front of the bull and winds gracefully around the man's body much as the cape does in the pass called the chicuelina.

Like the pase de pecho the molinete develops naturally out of a series of right or left-handed passes and is often used either to terminate such a series or to add variation to it. The molinete can be executed with either the right or left hand. In the right-handed version the sword spreads the cloth so that it covers most of the man's body as he spins, while when accomplished with the left hand the muleta winds around the man's waist and the sword at his side in the right hand like a bright red sash.

Timing, grace and elegance of execution are of prime importance in accomplishing the molinete. Because of the body movement involved it is extremely difficult to accomplish this pass successfully from the kneeling position. Attempts to do so generally result in an awkward lunge which is more dangerous than elegant and has more the character of a desplante than a decorative pase.

Although the molinete does not exercise a great deal of control over the bull it does maintain the continuity of the faena and is generally neither forced nor awkward. Among the decorative passes it is one of the oldest and one of the most difficult to do well.

In the abanico the man moves away directly in front of the bull. As the bull charges the man swings the extended muleta back and forth from left to right alternately in front of the bull's horns almost as if fanning him with the cloth. The bull presented with this shifting target swings his head back and forth trying to make up his mind which way to charge until finally the man with a flourish ends the series, turns his back and quietly walks away leaving the bull at a standstill.

If the abanico is accomplished with the right hand, the sword helps to extend the cloth and maintains it in a vertical position; however, when accomplished with the left hand a delicate wrist movement is necessary in order to maintain the extension of the cloth and prevent the bull from fixing his attention on the man in front of him. As a consequence the abanico performed with the left hand is more difficult and of greater merit than that performed with the right.

The abanico has the great merit of blending into and providing an ending to any series of right- or left-handed passes. While not a real pass in the sense that the bull does not really pass the man's body in a full charge, the abanico exercises considerable control over the bull's movement and in many cases helps to dominate him completely.

The pase de bandera begins as though the man intended to perform an ordinary derechazo. Instead of drawing the bull through and sending him on his way in the usual manner however the man raises the sword and muleta above the bull's horns half way through the pass and at the same time spins slowly on his heels in the opposite direction so that the extended muleta flutters away above the bull's head and back the length of the bull's body like a flag. At the end of the pass as the bull turns to charge again, the man is again facing him and in a position to repeat the pass.

The pase de bandera is always performed as a right-handed pass with the sword extending and spreading the cloth. While the pase de bandera exerts little or no real control over the bull it develops naturally out of any series of ordinary right-handed passes and imposes no break in the continuity of the faena. The difficulty and degree of danger involved in the pass can be controlled by the way in which the man holds the muleta. When the muleta is held at arm's length the difficulty and danger involved are, of course, reduced to a minimum. However, when the man holds the muleta with his elbow locked close to his right side the bull may pass close enough to strip the decoration from the man's suit with his horns.

In judging the pase de bandera note how straight the man stands and how slowly, gracefully and elegantly the pass is accomplished as well as how easily the man recovers after the pass and places himself in position to repeat the action.

In the manoletina the man stands with his feet together, more or less facing the bull which is to his left. As in the pase de bandera he holds the muleta in his right hand with the sword pricked into the folds extending the cloth; however, his left hand is passed behind his back and holds the lower inside edge of the muleta limiting the distance the muleta can be moved away from his body. With the muleta in this position the man edges forward shaking the cloth. As the bull charges and lowers his head to gore the man raises the cloth above the horns and spins slowly on his heels against the charge. The impetus of the charge carries the bull through while the muleta flutters down the length of his back. As the bull turns the man is again facing him and is in a position to repeat the action.

The manoletina is probably the most popular of all the decorative passes and is utilized by bullfighters of every degree of experience. The manoletina is always performed as a right-handed pass with the sword extending the cloth and while it is a very spectacular pass it is not nearly as dangerous as it appears, since the bull charges the movement of the cloth and the man need only stand absolutely still to avoid the danger. It exercises no control whatsoever over the bull nor does it develop naturally from any of the basic passes. It is accomplished from an artificial and awkward position and generally breaks the continuity of any well-built faena. Despite its popularity both with the spectators and the bullfighters it is a pass of little real merit even when done well. When done without elegance, grace, or timing it is little more than a vulgar flourish. Manoletinas are generally done in a series of three, four or even more at the end of the faena as a kind of dessert or frosting just prior to killing the bull. They are seldom or never interspersed in the muleta faena itself. In judging the manoletina note the serenity of the bullfighter, how straight and quietly he stands, the angle at which he takes the bull and the elegance, grace and timing with which he raises the muleta above the horns as well as the ease with which he spins and recovers his position in front of the bull.

In the espaldina the man stands with his feet together and his back to the bull with the muleta extended out to the side at arm's length. As the man edges backward toward the bull he looks back over his shoulder and shakes the muleta.

When the bull charges and lowers his head to gore, the man raises the muleta over the horns and spins around against the charge. As the bull turns to charge again the man is in position to repeat the action.

In the espaldina the man makes no effort to control the bull whatsoever, but simply raises the muleta above the horns letting the bull charge through under his arm. The espaldina may be performed with either the right or the left hand. In the right-handed pass the sword extends the cloth presenting a larger target, while in the left-handed version the cloth hangs naturally in place. In either version the bull may be taken from a variety of angles from the rear depending upon the audacity of the bullfighter. This pass is only rarely attempted from the kneeling position, since the man runs the risk of having the bull step on his legs as well as the usual risk of being gored. The espaldina develops naturally out of any series of right or lefthanded passes and consequently does not break the continuity of the muleta faena but, since it exerts no control over the bull, it is of little more merit than the manoletina. Unless the bull is taken at an extremely sharp angle and passed very close to the man's body it is really little more than a trick and the danger so slight that even the newcomer is hardly impressed. *Note:* A series of espaldina should not be confused with a series of pases de pecho. The difference is, of course, that in the pase de pecho the man guides the entire course of the bull, while in the espaldina the bull simply flips by underneath.

The molinete. The man has drawn the bull across in front of his body and is spinning against the charge, while the cloth flares up and around his left side and shoulder. The pass exerts little control over the bull but the man is accomplishing it quite elegantly despite the large body movement involved and the fact that he is on his knees.

The abanico. At the end of a series of flourishes, with the muleta in his right hand, the man passes the cloth almost vertically around to the right and behind his back into his left hand in a gesture that spreads the cloth like an open fan.

The pase de bandera. Although the bull is very big and well armed, the man has taken him past well in the center of the muleta. The figure of the man is so composed and the execution of the pass so calmly arrogant that the action is charged with much emotion, even though the pass really provides little control over the bull.

The same pass performed from the knees. Despite the perfect execution of the pass and the increased danger involved in fighting from the kneeling position, there is less emotional impact and less art in this version of the pase de bandera.

The manoletina. The bull charges by under the cloth so closely that the horns almost graze the man's body. The man is perfectly relaxed and unmoving as he maintains his position to the last possible moment before turning to repeat the pass. The apparatus on the man's right leg is a brace to support his ankle which was injured earlier in the season and has not healed properly.

The same pass without repose. The bull is very big and instead of charging through has gone high up in the air after the cloth. The man, fearful of having taken the bull too closely, has already altered his position and is stepping away to save himself.

The arrucina. The man has crossed his right hand with the sword and muleta behind his back so that only the tip of the cloth extends beyond his left hip. As the
bull charges, he spins in the opposite direction and is in a position to repeat the
pass. The pass exerts no control over the bull and is really a type of highly spectacular manoletina to the left. The left hand does not touch the cloth but is raised
high in the air to prevent its being struck by the bull's horns.

The same pass performed badly. The bull has not charged through as he should. As the man instinctively moves away to save himself, he is drawing the bull after him with the movement of the cloth. In another moment the bull will be on him and the man will have to be very quick to save himself from a bad goring.

The espaldina. The man has edged backward and sideways toward the bull with the muleta extended out behind him in his right hand. As the bull charges, the man lifts the cloth above the horns. Since the man is not looking at the bull, there is no real control and the pass is only a flourish.

The espaldina. In this variant the man is holding the muleta at the inner edge without spreading the cloth with the sword. The bull has not yet reached the cloth and the man is standing stock still, watching the charge out of the corner of his eye. The bull is charging in a straight line and there is no control over him whatsoever.

18.

DESPLANTES AND ADORNOS

Besides the decorative passes, the bullfighter may strike certain attitudes or indulge in certain highly spectacular gestures during the muleta faena in order to show his absolute control of the situation and domination of the bull. Such attitudes and gestures are called *desplantes* or *adornos* and are pure decoration.

In general all desplantes or adornos are a form of bravado and a concession to the public demand for something more. The hard-core enthusiast recognizes that they are a circus trick and has little patience with them. However when done within the limits of good taste they add a certain flourish to the muleta faena and are in the great flamboyant tradition of bullfighting. When overdone or badly timed they are meaningless nonsense no matter how risky or dangerous.

Although the words are sometimes used interchangeably, a distinction should be made between desplantes and adornos. In general the desplante may be defined as being a mere gesture having nothing to do with controlling or moving the bull at all but rather demonstrating that the bull is already thoroughly dominated and completely under control, while an adorno is a flourish added to any basic or decorative pass in order to make it more difficult or more dangerous to do.

Desplantes vary widely depending on the situation, the imagination and the good taste of the bullfighter. They include such things as reaching forward to touch the bull's horns or his head, hanging a hat on the bull's horn, kissing the bull or placing the horn tip in the mouth, turning one's back on the bull while only inches away and looking up at the stands, kneeling in front of the bull with the elbow propped on the forehead of the bull, and even throwing the muleta and sword to one side and kneeling with one's back to the bull, edging closer and closer to the horns so that the slightest recovery on the part of the bull means an almost certain goring.

Adornos include passing the bull while looking away or up at the stands, or with the feet tucked into the montera, or while standing upon a handkerchief. They also include passing the bull with a handkerchief or a hat in place of a muleta, or any other action which can make a basic pass more difficult. A famous adorno of this type consists of the man plucking the banderillas from the bull's shoulders with one hand while passing the bull with the other, first to the right and then to the left.

Strictly speaking, the decorative passes themselves may also be considered adornos since the purpose is to add variety to the faena and demonstrate the control of the bullfighter. But this is a fine point and open to some discussion.

Desplantes are usually performed at the end of a series of passes during which the bullfighter has established his domination over the bull and judges him well enough under control to risk placing himself in such a dangerous situation with some chance of success. To attempt a desplante with a bull which has not been thoroughly dominated is the sign of a rank amateur.

In performing a desplante the man takes advantage of the fact that at the end of any particularly successful series of right or left-handed passes the bull is in a more or less complete state of domination. As he is brought up short, squared away and stands breathing heavily, the man has a few seconds during which he may be reasonably sure that the bull will not move no matter what the man does. This state of immobility will continue for an undetermined length of time depending upon the temperament of this particular bull and the extent of the man's domination of him. It is the man's judgment of the length of time which the bull will require to recover himself before he is capable of charging again which is demonstrated by the desplante. By the same token it is the nonchalance with which the man is able to prolong the desplante beyond all reasonable limits more than the particular gesture itself which is of real value.

In judging the desplante it must be remembered that while disdain for danger or death and gestures portraying this are legitimate, any gesture which ridicules or belittles the bull or tends to humiliate him, such as spitting or kicking at him, is not only undignified, but rebounds on the man who merely cheapens his own actions by demeaning the bull.

Basically, then, the gauge of all desplantes, no matter how blatantly vulgar or in what bad taste, is the ease and grace with which the bullfighter is able to pull them off. If his timing is right he should be able to move into the desplante and out again smoothly, unhurriedly and with perfect ease. If he must rush, hurry, or leap to save himself at the last moment then the desplante is a failure and of no value.

Adornos may be added to any pass at any time, but these flourishes are usually included toward the end of the muleta faena when the attention of the bull has been well centered in the cloth and the man is confident that the bull will follow and not be easily distracted. Among the exceptions to this rule is the adorno in which the man begins the muleta faena by performing a series of estatuarios while standing on a handkerchief or with his feet tucked into his montera. Such an adorno, of course, is not attempted unless the bull is exceptionally straight-forward and open in his charge and man is quite sure from his previous actions that he will not deviate from the cloth.

In judging any adorno, the size and difficulty of the bull as well as the ease and grace with which the man is able to incorporate these frills into the action without interrupting the continuity of the faena are matters of primary consideration. If the flourish appears forced or added rather than an integral part of the action or if the bull is small and docile rather than strong and dangerous, the effect and the merit of the flourish are obviously less than if the opposite were true.

Desplante and adorno. Once the man has the bull well under control, he may begin a second series of passes by citing the bull from a position so close that it seems the bull can catch him with a simple toss of the head. Citing the bull in this fashion is really only a flourish to demonstrate the extent of the man's courage and domination. The merit of the gesture lies in whether the man is able to judge the distance and condition of the bull precisely and bring the cloth forward in time to take him away in a smooth-flowing pass to the right.

Kicking the bull. The bull refused to charge and the man is kicking at him to provoke the action. The gesture is ugly and meaningless and only serves to underline the small size and lack of bravery of the bull.

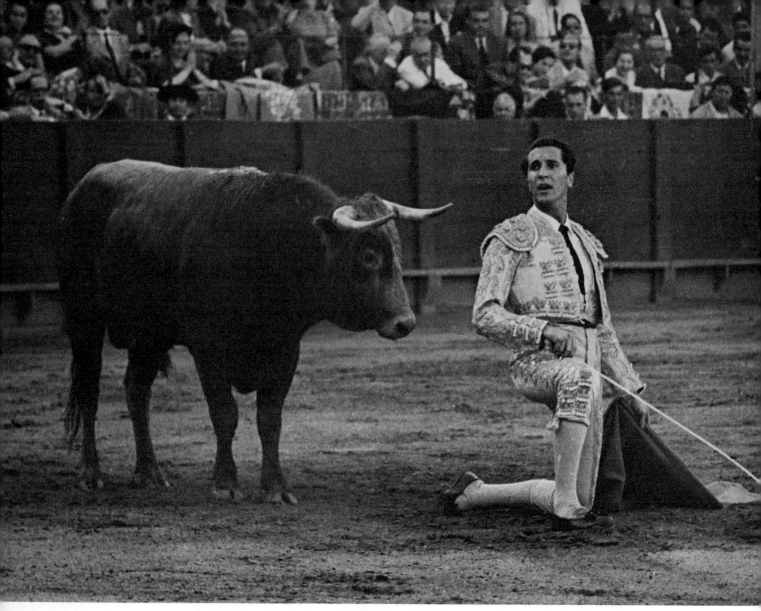

A cool gesture of disdain. At the end of a series of passes the man has dropped to one knee with his back only inches from the bull in a gesture designed to show his absolute domination of the situation. With the muleta at his side, the man is defenseless for the moment and, should the bull unexpectedly charge, the man would almost surely be tossed.

The telefono. In this desplante, the man edges forward first to touch the bull's head with his hand and then closer still to rest his elbow on the bull's forehead in a position which literally places his head between the bull's horns.

A graceful adorno. With the bull thoroughly dominated the man has dropped to his knees to make a right-handed pass more difficult. To demonstrate his control, he has reached out to touch the bull's horn and start the charge. The bull is very big and the horns are impressive, but the man is very calm and sure of what he is doing.

19.

THE KILL

In theory at least the muleta faena is the final preparation for the most important single act of the bullfight . . . the killing of the bull.

If the muleta work has adhered to the theory, every pass and every sequence of passes has been conceived and executed not only for its grace and artistic merit but for its effectiveness in preparing the bull for this final action. In bullring parlance this moment is called *la hora de la verdad,* which is sometimes translated as "the moment of truth." In plain language it is nothing more than the supreme test of the matador's mastery and domination over the bull.

More than this, however, the kill is the bullfighter's final exhibition of control and domination not only of the bull but of himself as well. It is his final statement of confidence in his ability and in his luck; of his conviction that nothing can harm him; of his immortality; that he will triumph.

To kill well requires a special type of courage in a bullfighter. It is one thing to await the bull's charge knowing that there is a certain margin for error; that with enough skill it is possible to deflect and control the charge or, by flinching, escape it. It is another thing entirely to launch oneself directly into the face of danger in a total commitment from which there is no retreat, knowing that everything hinges not only on split-second timing but to a large extent on sheer luck as well. For in any real attempt to kill well there is no turning back and there is no margin for error. The slightest mistiming, mistake, or even a slow reaction on the part of the bull in following the cloth may mean a terrible goring in a particularly vital spot. During the muleta faena the man may pass the bull incredibly close to his own body, but this is generally only accomplished through a series of passes which bring the bull closer and closer increasing the danger gradually in the midst of action. The kill is always accomplished after a pause, as a separate single act, in cold blood. The man has time to look at and see the horns. Above all he has to think and weigh the danger.

In every muleta faena there comes a time when the bull is ready to be killed. This is a matter of intuition for the matador but sometimes it is so obvious that even the non-professionals among the spectators may recognize it and begin to call out to him to kill the bull. When this moment arrives the matador begins to adjust the bull for the coming action. with as much care as a photographer arranging a subject for a portrait.

The moment when the bull should be killed generally occurs at the end of a particularly intense series of passes in which the bullfighter has succeeded in achieving almost complete domination and control over the bull and the bull in turning too sharply has been brought to a dead halt and stands facing the man with no further desire to attack.

It is a fundamental error for the matador to ignore this moment when, in effect, the bull is almost literally asking to be killed. However, while many young bullfighters fail to recognize this moment because of their ignorance or inexperience, fullfledged matadors ignore it nearly as often for other reasons entirely. This generally occurs when the matador is trying too hard for a successful muleta faena and not succeeding or when he is so carried away by a successful faena that he wishes to prolong it indefinitely. In either case he goes on when he should stop and the bull begins to go to pieces, his charge becomes shorter, he is easily distracted and finally he goes completely on the defensive and becomes almost impossible to handle and difficult to kill correctly or at all.

When the man is ready to kill the bull he generally brings him in fairly close to the fence with a series of short, effective passes and lines him up parallel with it so that the bull's left side is toward the center of the ring and the bull is standing stock still, all four feet squared away, each pair side by side and fairly close but not too close together. The bull's head should be on a level with or slightly lower than his shoulders but not carried too low or too far forward. Above all the bull's attention should be fixed intently on the muleta to the exclusion of everything else in the ring.

Ideally the man has anticipated the moment when the bull should be killed and has brought the bull in close to the fence during the artistic muleta faena so that there is no need to move him into position. However, more often than not, the man must draw the bull into some more desirable location and position him as described.

. This is particularly true and the break in continuity particularly marked when the man is using a light aluminum sword to spread the cloth throughout the muleta faena and must go over to the fence to exchange it for a regular steel sword with which to kill the bull.

A well-placed sword must enter one of four tiny openings on top of the bull's shoulders which are formed by the junction of the third and fourth ribs, his shoulder blades and the spinal column. The blade should drive down at an angle of approximately 45 degrees. Contrary to popular belief, such a sword rarely or never touches the heart of the bull, which is lodged well forward and deep inside his chest. Rather than the heart the blade usually cuts either a large artery or a giant vein, both of which pass close under the spinal column and are exposed to the thrust. When either of these two major blood vessels is cut the bull dies within a matter of seconds from an internal hemorrhage.

If the bull's feet are too far apart the tops of his shoulder blades will press together and the sword will not be able to enter. If the feet are too close together the bottoms of the shoulder blades will tilt inward and the sword will only penetrate a few inches. If one foot is farther forward than the other the position of the shoulders is distorted and the same thing will occur. If the bull carries his head too high the man will not be able to reach over the horn to place the sword; on the other hand, if the head is too low the neck will be stretched unnaturally and the position of the shoulder blades affected. If the bull is distracted or no longer follows the muleta for any reason the chances of the man being caught are so greatly increased as to be almost certain. For this reason most bullfighters insist that everyone leave the ring once they begin to line the bull up for the kill.

The bull's left side should be toward the center of the ring, since most bulls have a tendency to turn toward the center of the ring at the end of their charge and the man can take advantage of this fact to lessen the danger involved in attacking along the bull's right flank close to the fence.

Once the bull has been placed in position the matador takes his position in front of him at a distance of from six to ten feet. In his left hand he holds the muleta. In his right hand the sword. He profiles to the bull, exposing his left side, raises the sword across his chest in his right hand parallel to the ground, attracts the bull's attention to the muleta and then, either calling the bull or racing head-on toward him, performs a sort of backhanded pass with the muleta in his left hand, at the same time that he reaches over the bull's horns and drives the sword deep into a spot directly between the bull's shoulders.

Since it is almost impossible to discern from the outside the precise spot between the shoulders at which the sword should penetrate, the manner in which the matador attacks is of greater importance than the effect produced by the sword. If the man enters well, crosses perfectly, leans over the horns and drives forward with the sword as prescribed, the merit of the attempt is his, even though the sword strikes bone and rebounds into the air with no injury to the bull. If on a second attempt, however, he has no better luck the crowd will begin to be impatient no matter how well he enters and an unsuccessful third attempt means that he has failed and implies that there is something fundamentally wrong with his technique. While this is not necessarily true, it is true often enough to form a good rule-of-thumb in almost every instance.

Occasionally the bull will bleed slightly at the nose and mouth from a perfectly executed thrust due to the fact that the sword has grazed a lung. This should not be confused with the violent and excessive visible bleeding caused by a badly placed sword which has gone under the shoulder or into the neck to pierce the lungs or throat and which produces the violent hemorrhage and bloody vomit from the nose and mouth, which is one of the ugliest and most painful spectacles in the bullring. While such a thrust may kill the bull very quickly and sometimes fools a majority of the public into believing that the man has done well, it is really an action of no merit whatsoever since the man has avoided all danger and has assassinated the bull in the most cowardly fashion without coming within reach of the bull's horns or offering him the slightest opportunity to retaliate.

In general, the action of how well the sword is placed can best be checked when the bullfighter and the bull are lined up in the spectator's line of vision. From such a vantage point, any deviation from the direct line of attack is immediately apparent as the man drives in to place the sword. If the man and the bull are not lined up in the spectator's line of vision, however, it is often difficult to tell if the man has really entered well, particularly if the action is viewed from the opposite side of the ring. In such a case, the only way to judge the honesty of the attempt is by the position of the sword in the bull's body, since it is impossible to place the sword well without having entered at least reasonably well.

Defectively placed swords can be recognized once the action of placing them has been completed by the position and angle of the sword which is left in the bull's body. If the sword is positioned down to the side in either the right or the left shoulder rather than directly between the shoulders, if it is too far forward of the spot where the base of the neck joins the shoulders, or if it is directly between the shoulders but the point juts out through the side of the bull rather than down into his body, and, of course, if the sword is just shoved in anywhere into the neck or throat or the side of the bull the sword is badly placed no matter what the effect may be.

Of the many ways in which the bull is sometimes killed there are only two basic methods recognized by precedent and tradition. The first way is called

recibiendo or "receiving!" The second is the *volapie* or "with flying feet." In the former the bull is brought to the sword. In the latter the sword is taken to the bull.

In judging the kill it should be understood that trickery, dishonesty and outright cowardice on the part of the matador are more common than the casual observer generally suspects, and that the great majority of all bulls are killed badly or worse than badly. Thus, out of six bulls killed in any corrida the chances of seeing more than one or two killed decently or well are extremely light.

The receiving method is the more difficult of the two ways of killing the bull. Formerly it was the only accepted way of killing the bull; however, despite a revival among the top matadors several years ago it is rarely seen in modern bull-fighting. To perform this maneuver the man stands directly in front of the bull in profile with his left side to the bull, with the sword in his right hand at chest level and the furled muleta in his left hand held low and forward. When the matador is ready, he calls the bull by tapping his left foot and moving the cloth. As the bull charges, the man stands quietly in place and directs the bull through past his body to the right with the muleta. As the bull lowers his head to gore at the cloth, the matador leans over the horns and drives the sword into the precise spot between the shoulders. The force of the bull's charge drives the sword home while the momentum carries him past the man and away. The matador, with the muleta still in his left hand, remains standing as he was. The bull with the sword between his shoulders takes several steps, turns, and, if the sword has reached home, drops dead in the sand.

The difficulty in killing the bull recibiendo lies in the fact that the matador is thrusting at a fast-moving target and that consequently the chance of striking the precise opening between the bull's shoulders is greatly reduced. Moreover, the bull must be brought past the man's body very closely and in a straight line if the sword is to penetrate correctly. This requires a dexterity, coolness and control in performing the necessary back-handed pass, while at the same time placing the sword, which is beyond the ability of most men. Needless to say these difficulties increase the danger to the matador tenfold and are the main reason this method is so rarely practiced today.

The receiving method of killing is so rarely seen that no real standards currently exist for judging it. However, since it is occasionally attempted, certain distinctions should be made if only to distinguish the real thing from a poor imitation. To qualify as "recibiendo" it must be obvious that the man has attempted to kill the bull by this method. In other words there must be no doubt that the man has really called the bull by tapping his foot and shaking the muleta. Once he has called the bull, the man must retain his original position without leaping aside or shifting his feet. He must await the charge of the bull quietly and, as he crosses with the left hand and drives the sword in with the right, he must remain standing quietly as he was while the bull charges past with the sword between his shoulders. Occasionally it happens that the man is taken unaware by the bull charging as he is preparing to go in for the volapie. As a defensive measure the man may make a type of back-handed pass and seeing an opportunity drive in the sword, thus killing the bull without moving from his original position in an action resembling the recibiendo. Despite the fact that such a kill has much merit and displays coolness and presence of mind, it is not really considered to fall into the category of recibiendo and is distinguished from it since the man did not prepare or control the action but only took advantage of an accidental situation.

For the spectator the visual effect of a well-accomplished kill recibiendo is extraordinary since the bull literally impales himself on the sword. The action by the man who stands godlike and serene is reduced to an absolute minimum in a perfect demonstration of the effortless mastery of intelligence and skill over brute strength and force, which is the very essence of bullfighting. However, since killing recibiendo not only requires the very highest combination of skill and courage on the part of the bullfighter but also leaves so much to sheer luck in the matter of placing the sword, most modern bullfighters prefer to rely on taking the sword to the bull rather than bringing the bull to the sword. In addition, and in defense of modern bullfighters, it should be mentioned that the recibiendo can only be successfully accomplished with a bull which still has sufficient energy left to charge straight and hard. In present day bullfighting with the emphasis on long muleta faenas, the bull is played so long that he arrives at the kill in no condition to charge in the straight, long line that is necessary if this action is to be performed correctly.

With a few rare exceptions each season, the volapie or some variation of it is the only method of killing the bull ordinarily seen in modern bullfighting. In this method the man stands directly in front of the bull in profile with his left side to the bull, with the sword in his right hand at chest level and the furled muleta in his left hand held low and forward. When the matador is ready he suddenly launches himself straight at the bull. At the same time he moves his left hand with the muleta across his own body to the right as far as he can, while with his right hand he plunges the sword straight forward into the precise spot between the shoulders of the bull. The force of the thrust is enough to drive the sword home while the impetus of the man's attack carries him forward past the horns along the bull's right flank to safety. The bull with the sword between his shoulders takes several steps, turns and if the sword has reached home drops dead in the sand.

In order to qualify as a true volapie the man must drive the sword into the bull before the bull has a chance to charge or move forward. This means that the man must profile and attack from close in with great speed and impetus in a straight line. It is a very powerful, dramatic and effective way of killing the bull and often topples him dead in his tracks. In order to get past the right horn which is in his way, the man must cause the bull to turn his head slightly to the left, which he does in one smooth movement with the muleta in his left hand. At the same time that the bull's head turns aside and the way is clear, the man drives straight forward from the shoulder with the sword in his right hand, driving it deeply into the spot between the shoulders. As the man's momentum carries him forward to safety, the bull's head swings back into position closing the gate again. The bull may lunge forward a step or two in retarded reflex action but generally stands still in his tracks hardly aware that the sword has touched him until he drops dead.

The simultaneous action of placing the sword with the right hand and deflecting the right horn with the muleta in the left is called the cruz or cross and is absolutely fundamental to the action. The secret of the successful volapie lies in the perfect syncronization of these two separate and difficult movements. If something goes wrong in the midst of this direct frontal attack the man is terribly exposed to a bad goring in the chest or stomach. For this reason, and because of the strength, timing and speed required of the matador, the classic volapie is nearly as rare as the deliberate recibiendo.

In order to control or dissemble the peculiar fear involved in attacking and killing the bull, some bullfighters have developed the preparation for the volapie into an elaborately stylized series of actions. These men take their position almost mechanically, carefully furl and place the tip of the muleta before the bull, raise the sword, profile, turn, bounce on tiptoe once, twice, or even three times and then launch themselves like an arrow from a bow. None of this elaborate preparation is really necessary or important. The important thing is that the man cross well with the muleta in order to turn the right horn to the left out of the way, that the man attack in a straight line and that he reach well forward to place the sword directly between the shoulder blades at the correct angle. Other preparations may add a certain style to the performance but these are the essntials.

The most common method of cheating in the volapie is for the matador to attack the bull by running around in front of him in a short half-circle, much as banderilleros place banderillas al cuarteo, rather than meeting him head-on in a straight line. As a result of this action, the man can thrust the sword into the throat or into the chest in front of the right shoulder rather than placing it high up between the shoulders as is required. Such a procedure permits the man to place the sword with little or no danger to himself since he never comes within range of the horns. It is comparable to stabbing the bull in the back since the bull is killed beyond the range of his defenses. Curiously the effect of such a thrust is sometimes far more rapid than a well-placed sword. However, even though the bull may drop dead almost immediately, there is no honor or merit for the man in such an action and a knowledgeable crowd will whistle and jeer.

The easiest single check in judging the volapie is to note whether the man, driven by the momentum of his attack, goes by the length of the bull's body and is carried out past the hindquarters in a single straight line.

Other methods of cheating include draping the muleta over the bull's head before attacking so that he cannot see, pushing on the sword after the horns have passed, and stabbing at the bull from a safe distance in front without ever attacking at all.

The usual way of killing is generally some compromise between the volapie and recibiendo, in which both man and bull in motion meet head-on.

Just as any kill accomplished while the man remains more or less as he was and the bull charges past him is called recibiendo, any kill in which the man attacks while the bull is more or less stationary is called a volapie, even though the bull may also be moving as the man places the sword.

Real enthusiasts distinguish between the volapie arrancando, in which the bull surges forward just as the man places the sword, the volapie a un tiempo in which both man and bull charge at the same time and meet halfway, and the volapie al encuentro in which the bull charges the man who at the last minute steps forward to meet him but these are fine distinctions and for the vast majority of the spectators all bulls are killed either recibiendo or volapie.

As long as the man attacks in a straight line, meets the bull head-on, reaches over the horns and places the sword in the precise spot between the shoulders, any of these variations is acceptable although generally less effective or aesthetically satisfying.

While such a kill may entail great risk and be accomplished with complete honesty and complete commitment on the part of the bullfighter, it obviously does not reflect the skill, control and domination shown in either the true recibiendo or volapie and should be distinguished from them.

Bringing the bull across the ring. With the muleta in his left hand, the man moves backward across the ring, guiding the bull in a smooth zigzag that prevents him from developing a charge but carries him smoothly to the fence.

Adjusting the bull for the kill. The man moves the muleta back and forth trying to fix the bull in the proper position for the kill. The front feet are not quite right and the rear feet are so far out of position that the man will probably turn the bull upon himself and start all over again.

Squared away. The man has dropped to one knee to verify the position of the back feet of the bull that is well squared away and ready to be killed.

Driving forward for the kill. With the muleta held low and to the front, the man starts his drive straight forward toward the bull. The man has started from rather far out but the bull has not yet reacted to the movement. The man appears to know what he is doing and is attacking with style and decision, directly from the front.

Running to the side. Instead of attacking in a direct line, the man has started around the bull in a half-circle. He has not crossed with the muleta but is only holding it out in front of him as a shield. He will not be able to reach the correct spot with the sword and has already dropped the point for a lower side thrust.

The action. The man has tried to attack correctly but has not crossed sufficiently with his left hand and the bull has followed him so closely that the right horn has nearly caught him in the thigh. The man is a hair's breadth from a nasty wound, but he has gotten the sword in although it is low in front of the shoulder and not on top as it should be.

Assassination. The man has managed to get the sword in without coming within reach of the bull at all.

Against the fence. The bull has gone on the defensive with his back to the wall and the man has had to try to kill him from this position. The bull has tossed the muleta aside and is watching the man who cannot get far enough past the horn to push in the sword and will have to try again.

Fearful desperation. Sometimes a man simply cannot muster the courage to face the horns and in fearful desperation he will hurl himself at the bull with his eyes closed and his face turned away in a wild effort to kill the bull at any cost.

A perfect sword. The man stands with his hand up watching the bull. The sword is perfectly placed and the man is signaling to his men not to interfere or distract the bull in any way, but rather to leave them alone together.

Going down. The bull fights to maintain his balance, but the sword high up between the shoulders has reached some vital spot and his hind legs begin to buckle as the man watches intently.

The dramatic moment. The hind legs suddenly give way and the huge bulk of the animal towers over the man as the bull, still fighting for balance, crashes over dead at the man's feet.

.The long walk. Occasionally, despite a well-placed sword, the bull will turn and walk along the fence. At such times, he moves with great dignity and the men follow quietly, respecting the moment and the final effort he is making.

An ugly spectacle. The man has thrust the sword forward through the neck and into the lungs and stands grimly, watching now as the blood pours from the mouth and nose of the bull in one of the ugliest spectacles of the bullfight.

Removing the sword. The man reaches forward over the horns of the dying bull to remove the sword. This is not necessarily a compassionate gesture. The purpose is to let air enter the open wound to kill the bull more quickly. The man is very close to the horns, but the touch of blood in the bull's mouth means that he is already dying and the man is almost positive the bull will no longer charge. The sword is well placed and the bleeding from the mouth is slight.

20

THE DESCABELLO

If the first sword does not kill the bull the matador may have his men remove it and place another and another until he reaches a vital spot.

The first sword must be removed before an attempt is made to place a second. This is generally done by throwing a cape over the bull's back so that the cloth will entangle the hilt and the sword can be pulled out by pulling on the cape. Sometimes the bull will be brought in close to the fence and an attempt will be made to remove a sword by snatching at the hilt from the other side. This is seldom effective and is generally a waste of time. Even more rarely a man may race up behind a wounded bull and attempt to snatch out a defective sword in the open ring. This is a risky business however and should never be attempted unless the bull is very sluggish and heavy on his feet.

When a sword has been placed which does not kill the bull immediately the bullfighter's assistants race forward and spin the bull round and round against the angle of the thrust in an effort to insure that some major blood vessel will be cut and that the bull will die. Although this action is expressly forbidden by the regulation it has become so common that it is no longer seriously protested by anyone. If this action of spinning the bull is unsuccessful, a second or a third sword may have to be placed to kill the bull.

Occasionally the sword may be so placed that it is or appears to be impossible to remove it. In such a case an inexperienced matador, in desperation, may attempt to place a second sword without removing the first one. This is inexcusable even for an absolute novice.

If the second sword does not kill the bull, the man may place a third or even a fourth or fifth, but in each case he must remove the sword already in the bull before placing another. Placing more than a second or third sword indicates defective technique and should be judged accordingly.

If after having placed one or more swords the bull goes completely on the defensive, or carries his head too low, or the man simply prefers not to risk another complete attack, he may resort to an instrument called the *descabello* in order to kill the bull.

The descabello is an instrument similar in appearance to a regular sword except that a cross piece has been attached to the blade about six inches from the tip so that the blade cannot enter beyond this point. Some descabellos are regular swords which have been adapted with a removable crosspiece and serve both purposes. On the other hand many are tailor-made to individual specifications and in some cases are no more than long daggers which the man can handle with great precision.

The regulation provides that the man must have placed at least one regular sword before attempting to kill the bull with the descabello. This rule is seldom violated altogether; however, many bullfighters who hate to expose themselves in the regular method of killing, often place a first sword any way they can and go on immediately to the descabello.

When the man decides to kill the bull in this way he approaches the bull cautiously from the front with the descabello in his right hand, and the muleta in his left. After a few chopping passes to right and left to center the bull's attention and lower his head even further, the man holds the muleta still and close to the ground so that the bull's head will be lowered as far as possible. He raises the descabello in his right hand so that the point is poised at the base of the bull's skull. In one sharp movement he thrusts downward so that the point enters between the first and second vertebrae, cutting the spinal cord and dropping the bull in his tracks, killing him instantly.

In order for the descabello to be successful, the bull's head must hang as close to the ground as possible. To accomplish this as quickly as possible, once the first sword has been placed, the matador and his men swing muleta and capes alternately to right and left in an effort to tire the neck muscles and bring down the bull's head to an abnormally low position. This cape flopping also tends to put the bull solidly on the defensive, preferably with his back to the barrera in a position from which he will not be likely to charge unexpectedly. In this position the bull is completely at bay and can no longer be killed with the regular sword, since he no longer follows the cloth. Occasionally a bull in this defensive position will carry his head quite low but the head will be laid back in a position which closes the spaces between the vertebras and makes it impossible for the point of the descabello to enter. This position of the head must be changed by further muleta and cape passes before the man can hope to succeed with the descabello.

In recent years much importance has been given to skill in accomplishing the descabello. This is not an authorized, alternate way of killing the bull, however, but simply an expedient method of dispatching a badly wounded animal as quickly and painlessly as possible. It is a relief to everyone if the man is able to accomplish this task coolly and efficiently, but even an excellent descabello demonstrates no control of the bull, requires no real courage on the part of the man, and is a technique more closely related to the slaughterhouse than the bullring. As a consequence, whether or not the man kills the bull on the first try has nothing to do with how well the man has fought and previously attempted to kill the bull. On the other hand if the man stands jabbing time after time at the bull's head in an unsuccessful attempt to finish with him, the public understandably tends to forget all that has gone before no matter how exceptional it may have been and may whistle him out of the arena in disgust.

If before or during the descabello the bull goes to his knees from the effects of the sword or swords previously placed by the matador, the man's obligation to kill the bull is at an end. In such a case a subordinate called the puntillero comes forward, with a dagger in his hand approaches the bull from behind and administers a coup de grace to the wounded animal, severing the spinal cord and killing him instantly exactly as the matador might have done with the descabello.

Occasionally the bull will go to his knees and the puntillero will attempt to kill him but the bull will get up again. In such a case the bull again becomes the bullfighter's responsibility and the man must begin again to try to kill the bull either with the sword or the descabello.

If the man cannot kill the bull either with the sword or the descabello at the end of fifteen minutes from the time he made the first muleta pass, he must retire from the ring and tame steers will be sent in to take the bull out alive to be slaughtered in the corrales.

Ten minutes after the first muleta pass is made the trumpets sound the first aviso or warning. Three minutes later they sound a second warning and two minutes after that a third warning, at which time everyone is obliged to leave the arena and the trained steers enter to remove the bull.

The bull does not earn a pardon by staying the limit, however, and is inevitably slaughtered in the corrales to insure that he is not fought a second time elsewhere.

Trying to get the head down. If the man cannot kill the bull with the straight sword and wishes to use the descabello, he must first get the bull into position with his head down, close to the ground. If the bull is still strong or the men are particularly incompetent, this can be a messy affair with capes scattered about on the ground and everyone working at cross purposes. The men in the picture are beginning to settle down, but the bull's head is still very high and he is not yet ready to be killed.

Coordinated effort. The bull stands with his head well down, his attention fixed on the muleta, while the man raises the descabello for the downward thrust. One of the man's assistants stands behind him with a cape thrown well forward to help fix the bull's attention and keep his head low.

The descabello. The man has driven the sword down with a sharp thrust which has severed the vertebrae at the base of the bull's skull and killed him even before his body has touched the ground.

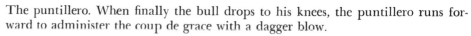

The puntillero. When finally the bull drops to his knees, the puntillero runs forward to administer the coup de grace with a dagger blow.

21.

APPLAUSE AND REWARDS

When the bull is dead the matador turns and walks back to a spot in front of the president's box, salutes and returns to the section of the barrera where his men are waiting. As he passes the sword and muleta across the fence and receives a towel in order to wipe the sweat from his face and hands, a team of horses is brought in to drag out the dead bull.

If the fight has been a good one the spectators will begin to applaud or they may stand up and begin to wave their handkerchiefs violently back and forth. The handkerchief is a recognized petition to the president to grant the matador the ear of the bull as a trophy. If there are enough handkerchiefs the president will signal to the alguaciles to cut the ear from the bull. If there are a great many handkerchiefs and they continue to wave, he may signal for the other ear to be cut as well. According to the regulation, the president must conform to the petition of the public in awarding the first ear but the second ear is awarded solely at his own discretion. In provincial rings if the matador has been triumphant the crowd will often insist on the tail and sometimes, despite the regulation which prohibits it, a hoof as well as the ears. This slaughterhouse type of butchering is considered a disgusting and vulgar practice in Madrid and Sevilla where the standards of good fighting are considerably higher.

In theory, at least, the awards granted the matador correspond approximately to the following: two ears . . . exceptional or outstanding; one ear . . . excellent; vuelta (a trip around the ring) . . . very good; ovation . . . good; applause . . . fair; silence . . . mediocre; whistles and jeers . . . poor. In practice, except for Madrid and to a lesser extent Sevilla, these standards are rarely kept, so that reports of ears and tails cut in the provinces give no valid reflection of the matador's performance. As a good rule-of-thumb two ears elsewhere generally correspond to less than one in Madrid.

The horses are yoked to the horns of the bull and with a great cracking of whips and cries from the drivers the dead bull is dragged from the ring.

If the bull has been brave and noble the crowd will applaud in homage to these qualities as he is dragged from the ring. If he was cowardly or vicious they will speed his exit with whistles and jeers. On rare occasions when the bull has been exceptionally brave he may be dragged slowly around the periphery of the ring to the accompaniment of an ovation from the crowd.

When the bull has been dragged from the ring the attention of the crowd is directed to the matador, who steps out into the ring to acknowledge the applause if he has done well or back behind the fence if he has done badly.

If the man has done badly the crowd manifests its displeasure by whistles and jeers and the matador is glad to retire from the ring and blend into the crowd behind the fence. On the other hand if he has done well an ovation begins and the matador may step out to the tercio line to acknowledge the applause and if the ovation continues or if he has been granted the ear or ears of the bull, he may be encouraged to walk around the periphery. During this triumphal circuit the spectators may throw hats, coats, shawls, cigars, flowers and other objects into the ring. In the general enthusiasm shoes, purses, cameras and other valuable accessories sometimes follow. The matador is expected to return the valuable objects but he may keep the flowers and cigars. This is when the man takes his bows and it is interesting to note the way in which different men acknowledge the applause. Some are sober and unsmiling, others are earnest and glad, some are exuberant, still others triumphant, many are happy, while a few seem almost sad. Once he has completed the circuit the matador may bow from the tercio line or even from the center of the ring. He is then expected to retire to the barrera, the ring is cleared and the trumpet sounds the entrance of the next bull.

Sometimes, if the man has had an outstanding afternoon, enthusiasts in the stands may leap down into the ring after the fight is over and carry the man around the ring on their shoulders. If the man has really been exceptional and cut at least two ears, he may be carried out through the main door of the plaza and sometimes all the way back through the streets to his hotel.

Cutting the ear. The man's assistants cut the ear from the bull. The stick and twigs resting against the bull's body form a rustic broom which is used to smooth the sand after the bull is dragged from the ring.

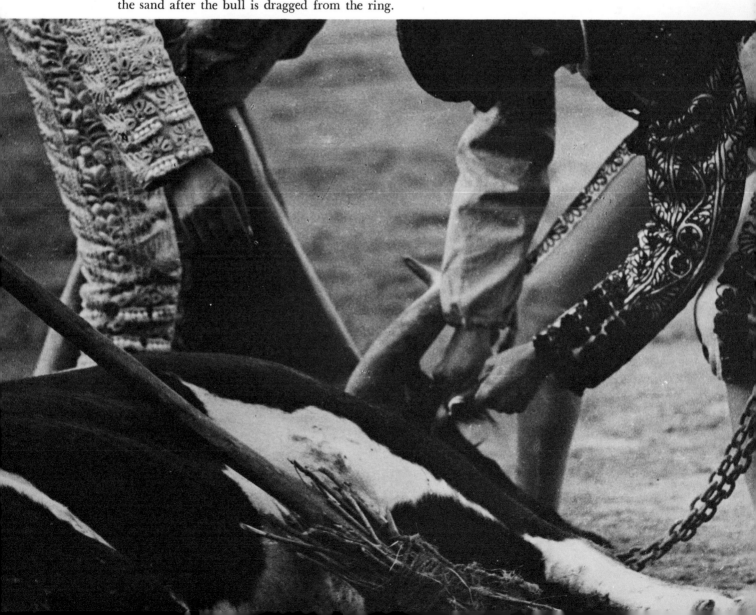

Hooking up the mules. A team of mules is driven in to drag out the dead body of the bull. The man loops a length of chain around the horns and fastens it to the harness with a large hook. The entire operation takes only a few moments.

Dragging the bull from the ring. Ordinarily the body of the dead bull is dragged straight out across the ring at a gallop, but if the bull has been a particularly brave one the president may order that he be given a tour of the ring. In this case, the mules are driven at a walk around the ring as the people stand in homage.

Smoothing the arena. Almost before the bull is dead, the ring attendants leap into
the ring and begin to smooth the sand to provide solid footing for the next fight.

Presenting the awards. The alquacil congratulates the matador after a successful fight and presents him with the ears of the bull he has just killed.

Saluting the president. The man salutes the president with his trophies before beginning a triumphant tour of the ring.

A tour of the ring. The man is happy and smiling as he accepts the gifts and applause of the crowd during his tour of the ring.

Out the big door. Sometimes the bullfight is so perfect and the man's triumph so great that a tour of the ring is not enough. Then in a burst of wild enthusiasm the spectators pour into the ring and carry the man triumphantly out the big door.

All the way to the hotel. And sometimes the crowd cannot bear to let him go and so they carry him all the way through the streets, back to his hotel.

Leaving the ring in disgrace. After a bad afternoon the man crosses the ring, alone with his assistants, ignored by the spectators who are applauding those who did well.

22.

LEAVING THE RING

When the last bull has been killed the bullfighters are free to leave the ring.

While the last man is busy killing the last bull of the afternoon, the matador's helpers are busy folding capes and packing other equipment away so that, by the time the bull has been killed, everything is ready for the matadores and their banderilleros to leave the ring.

As the man who has killed the last bull salutes the president, the other matadores recover their dress capes from the stands and, with these draped casually over their left arm, leave the ring.

There is no protocol or order in leaving the ring, although the two senior matadores generally try to start out before the last man steps forward to take his bow.

If the matadores have had a triumph they may be carried around the ring on the shoulders of the enthusiasts. If they have had a good afternoon they may walk back out across the ring, each man with his banderilleros, nodding to the crowd and acknowledging a round of applause. If they have had a bad afternoon they may cross the ring to a chorus of whistles and jeers or, in an effort to avoid this, they may follow the passageway around behind the fence to the door, and try to slip out unobserved among the helpers and the men with the capes and other equipment. In any event, once outside of the ring, they are driven back to their hotel where they shower and dress and try to relax and unwind after the tension they have undergone. If they are supposed to fight the next day, they may only have time for a quick meal before they are on the road again traveling to the next city or town and the next bullring.

As soon as the bullfighters have left the ring, the spectators begin to push toward the exits.

If you do not happen to have seats directly in front of one of the exits so that you can leave without difficulty, it is generally a good idea to wait until most of the people have left the stands before trying to make your way out of the bullring. It is really only a question of a few minutes more or less, and the time saved is hardly worth the effort involved in fighting the crowd.

In order to avoid the press of the crowd, if the last fight is not particularly satisfying, many spectators will start for the exits in the midst of the muleta faena. Aside from the fact that this is prohibited by the regulation and is therefore a civil offense, it is also an annoying distraction to the rest of the spectators and a conscious insult to the man in the ring.

Try not to be the last to leave the stands.

The moment when the stands begin to empty is a poignant one, with the empty ring, and the shadows, and the diminishing murmur of the crowd, where only a few moments before there was light, and life, and the roar of massed voices. It is a poignant moment, and one worth savoring, but do not spend too much time at it, for the ring attendants are anxious to close up and go home and if you wait too long, you may find the nearest exit closed and be obliged to hurry around under the stands looking for a way out. Should this happen, it is worth knowing that one of the last doors open is the door through which the dead bull was dragged out of the ring. Beyond this door, under the stands, is the butcher shop where the dead bull is cleaned and quartered. Most bullrings permit people to watch or at least, look in on this operation. If you have never seen it, and if such things do not bother you, it is an interesting operation, for the men are skilled in their trade and take pride in their work.

Once the bull is butchered the meat is weighed and taken to the market where it is sold. The money from the sale of the meat goes to the promoter who has provided the animals for the fight. The meat is good to eat but is stronger than domestic beef and has a wild game flavor. It is normally marinated before cooking the way venison is.

In the larger cities do not count on finding a taxi or on being able to use other public transportation right after the fight.

Immediately after the fight, the crowd is too much for the normal transportation system. If you have driven, it is a wise move to wait a little in order to avoid the worst of the traffic. If you are afoot, a leisurely stroll not only comes as a welcome change after having been seated so long, but is really the only answer unless you are prepared to fight for a place on the bus or in the subway. In either case, an effective solution to the problem of what to do is a glass of something and a snack at some nearby bar or cafe. Pick a quiet spot, preferably outside, at some sidewalk cafe where you can sit and relax while you discuss the details and remember moments of the afternoon in a post mortem which, if you are with friends, may last through dinner and well into the night.

As you leave the bullring and begin to relax you will probably suddenly feel very tired.

After a good fight you will feel tired as a result of your identification with the fighter and his triumph and the emotional tension inherent in this situation. If the fight has been a bad one, the reaction will be the result of intense boredom or disgust sustained for an extended period of time. If you are a newcomer, your reaction will probably be definitive and will determine your future attitude to the bullfight forever after. No matter what your reaction however, the bullfight is over, the bulls have demonstrated the extent of their bravery, nobility and strength, and are dead; the men have demonstrated the extent of their courage, integrity and art and are alive; the order of our universe has been reaffirmed and a moment of some significance has ended.

APPENDIX I

THE REJONEADOR

Occasionally, and as a special attraction or entertainment before a regular bullfight, a single bull is killed by a mounted horseman called a *rejoneador*. For the regular bullfight enthusiast this method of killing bulls has little or nothing to do with the serious business of bullfighting. For the average spectator, however, it is an agreeable diversion especially if the rejoneador is a good rider and accomplishes his task quickly and well.

Historically the rejoneador is a throwback to the very earliest days of bull-fighting. The modern version of this entertainment differs little from the version practiced hundreds of years ago when bullfighting was in its infancy and was regarded as the sport of kings. The basis of the entire spectacle is the horses. These are the finest thoroughbreds available. They are strikingly beautiful, superbly fast and well-trained. Under the direction of their fine riders they prance, bow, leap, and perform other precise evolutions which are a pleasure to watch. The riders are generally equal to their mounts and the whole exhibition of their skill is often spectacular and well worthy of the applause they earn.

In theory, at least, the action of the rejoneador in killing the bull is divided into three parts; the placing of the rejónes, the placing of the banderillas and the killing of the bull. In actual fact these three parts generally blend into one continuous exhibition of masterful riding on the part of the rejoneador. The horses wear no protection of any kind but since their speed is greater than that of the bulls and since the bull's horns are deliberately blunted for the occasion the horses are rarely injured. Barring accidents, there is no danger whatsoever for the rider.

The *rejón* is a lance about five feet long, with a wooden staff and a leaf-shaped steel blade about six inches long and two inches wide. The rider holds the rejón by the end of the wooden shaft like a long dagger. As the bull charges he races his horse forward, leans from the saddle and drives the lance down into the shoulders at the base of the neck. The shaft of the lance is weakened at the head and snaps leaving the head of the lance planted in the bull's shoulders. This maneuver is repeated three times and derives its merit from the neatness and precision with which it is performed and from the angle at which the rider places the weapon.

The banderillas are placed in the same manner as the rejónes. They are usually placed together held in one hand but the finest rejoneadores habitually place them with one held in each hand leaning far out of the saddle and guiding the horse during the maneuver only with their legs. The banderillas used are the standard ones of the regular bullfight and are sometimes broken off short to make the maneuver more difficult. The killing of the bull is done with a *rejón de muerte.* This is a lance with a shorter staff and a longer blade and is placed in the manner already described for the ordinary rejónes. The longer blade, if it is well-placed, drops the bull into the sand. If the bull does not die immediately the rider may dismount and kill the bull in the usual way with sword and muleta. Many prefer to leave the sometimes messy job of killing to a young apprentice who is paid for that purpose.

Both the public and the president are generally quite lenient in judging the performance of the rejoneador and the ears of the bull are awarded with great facility even in the big rings of Madrid and Sevilla.

Two styles of dress. The rejoneador on the white horse is dressed in the Spanish style, the "traje corto" of Andalucia. The other man is wearing the 16th century finery of a Portuguese nobleman. In Spain the rejoneadors generally wear the Spanish costume although the Portuguese costume is occasionally seen.

A magnificent flourish. As the horse rears high in the air, the man stands straight in the stirrups holding him calmly under control.

Placing the rejon. The man is placing a rejon de muerte or killing lance. Ordinary rejones are slightly shorter but are placed in exactly the same way. The style is very good, but the man has taken the bull at an "easy" angle rather than from the front as he should.

Placing banderillas. The man has charged the bull almost directly from the front at a dangerous angle. As he leans out of the saddle to place the banderillas, his left hand swings the horse out of reach of the horns.

Riding without hands. With the reins attached to his belt, the man is leaning far out with both hands to place a difficult pair of short banderillas. The riding is superb as the man guides the horse with the shift of his weight and the pressure of his legs.

APPENDIX II
NINE OUTSTANDING VETERANS AND
FIVE YOUNG MEN OF PROMISE

The following is a list of nine veterans, all of whom are outstanding, active figures in the world of Spanish bullfighting. Every effort has been made to describe them objectively in terms of their actual capability and reputation in the world of bullfighting. Where criticism has been stated or implied it is the generally accepted criticism of informed enthusiasts and is not intended to belittle their real talent. It goes without saying that they are outstanding not because of their defects but in spite of them.

The fact that one of these men is fighting on any particular day is no guarantee that the fight will be outstanding. It simply means that at least one of the men in the ring that day is really capable of an outstanding performance. Whether or not he will realize such a performance on any given day is dependent upon many factors beyond prediction or analysis.

EL CORDOBES

Born Manuel Benítez Pérez in Puebla del Río, Córdoba on 10 December 1937, took his alternativa in Córdoba 25 May 1963. He is a fairly tall, roughly handsome and extremely attractive man with an awkward, strongly built body. He wears his hair long and moves with a flatfooted swagger which often makes him appear uncouth and unelegant even when he is passing the bull perfectly. He is an extraordinary personality both in and out of the ring and is in the great tradition of bullfighting. Flamboyant, dynamic, colorful, with a raw courage which is seemingly without limits and apparently almost without thought, he has risen from the poorest of family beginnings as an orphan and day laborer to the position of millionaire landowner on the basis of his personality and talents and is undeniably the greatest popular figure in bullfighting since Manolete. He has been terribly gored by the bulls many times and has been on the brink of death more than once, but none of this has affected his enthusiasm for bullfighting. He is deficient with the cape, mediocre with the sword and no longer puts his own banderillas, although he did so spectacularly but never elegantly as a novillero. With the muleta, however, he is unique and incomparable, with a style all his own. He has developed an entirely unorthodox approach to the problem of dominating bulls which is based upon his enormous courage and consists in standing stock still while passing the bull with the muleta, so that the bull has the impression that his body is a post or some such solid extension from the ground. In order to maintain this bodily rigidity he has had to sacrifice the coordinated body and arm movement which provides the classic control of the muleta, and instead accomplishes this control with an arm and wrist movement which none has been able to duplicate. Through this technique he is able to play the bull closer and from angles which previously were considered impossible. He has been sharply criticized for his lack of elegance and departure from the classic standard of bullfighting, and there is no doubt that he has had to sacrifice much of the languid grace and beauty of the passes in order to fight the way he does, however the fact remains that he fights all kinds of bulls throughout a long season, and consistently dominates and controls them as no other bullfighter has succeeded in doing during the last twenty years. A major operation was performed on his right shoulder at the end of the 1965 season which threatened to leave him without the use of his right arm. This arm has responded to treatment, however, and at the present time there is no reason to suppose that he will not continue to fight as often as he pleases at the price he cares to name until he is ready to retire.

PACO CAMINO

Born Francisco Camino Sánchez in Camas, Sevilla on 19 December 1941, took his alternativa in Valencia, 17 April 1960. He is a small, slightly built young man with delicate, rather pretty features and an extremely supple body which compensates for his lack of height and reach in leaning into the pass. Despite his fragile appearance, he is a hot tempered and fiercely proud competitor and has maintained his position among the top matadores ever since he took the alternativa. He is an exquisite stylist with both the cape and the muleta and can be quite competent with the sword when he feels like it. He is an outstanding example of the profile style of fighting at its best but is capable of fighting in the classic manner as well. His talent is enhanced by his tremendous intuitive knowledge of bulls and their habits which permits him to perform with great assurance and ease no matter how difficult the bull may be. He has plenty of courage and more than enough art but until recently lacked a certain fundamental honesty and enthusiasm which prevented him from being the outstanding figure he is otherwise qualified to be. During the 1966 season he surprised everyone by throwing off the apathy and cynicism which afflicted him and promptly established himself as one of the two or three very best matadores in Spain.

JAIME OSTOS

Born Jaime Ostos Carmona in Ecija, 8 April 1933, took the alternativa in Zaragoza on 13 October 1956. He is tall, square-shouldered and handsome in a flamboyant, old-fashioned sort of way. His reputation is based on his exceptional courage and his profound sense of personal honor which together give a peculiar intensity to his style of fighting and classify him as a very masculine type of fighter with a highly emotional impact. He consistently prefers to take the bull from the front in the classic line but despite this there is always a touch of flamboyance in his performance that is unique. He is extremely capable with both cape and muleta without being a stylist with either but is really outstanding with the sword. He is probably one of the two or three consistently good killers in Spain. He likes his bulls strong and prefers not to pic them too much, but sometimes overdoes this and finds himself with a bull which cannot be fought smoothly. He was terribly gored at the end of the 1964 season and for a time it was thought that he would not live or would lose one of his legs through amputation but he has recovered and come back to take his place again among the very best.

EL VITI

Born Santiago Martín Sánchez in Vitigudino, Salamanca on 18 July 1938, took his alternativa in Madrid, 13 May 1961. He is a very honest, very brave, very scientific bullfighter and is one of the two or three really good killers currently fighting in Spain. Physically he is a rather plain looking, undistinguished man with a sad face and a long neck which gives him a naked and rather fragile appearance in the ring. He is very serious and never smiles even in the midst of his greatest triumphs. On the other hand he has a great sense of personal honor and responsibility toward the public and always does his very best. There is something a little cold, almost mechanical, about his style of fighting which is in the classic tradition and he is often criticized for having little or no emotion in his fighting. He seems to approach the bull as a problem to be solved. Sometimes he does not find the solution, of course, but even when he does he often does not move the public. He is extremely capable with the cape, the muleta and the sword. He has a considerable knowledge of bulls and dominates them easily. At his best he is a sober, serious, deep type of fighter and has consistently been among the best in Spain since his alternativa.

ANTONIO ORDONEZ

Born Antonio Ordonez Araujo in Ronda, 6 February 1932, took the alternativa 28 June 1951. He is a fairly tall, rather well built man whose father Niño de la Palma, was the model for the bullfighter in *The Sun Also Rises*. While the Niño de la Palma was really undistinguished as a bullfighter his son Antonio is considered one of the very best in Spain and the epitome of the sober, classic, Ronda school of bullfighting. In the full maturity of his powers, he is exceptionally brilliant with both the cape and muleta and extremely capable with the sword when he feels like trying. He is often criticized for not extending himself with all the bulls he fights and is sometimes considered a cynical bullfighter, capable of extraordinary effects but satisfied with (for him) second-rate performances. He retired in 1963 but came out of retirement in 1965 to re-establish his position as one of the very best. He has been plagued by wounds which would not heal correctly and the beginning of his 1966 season was spoiled by special treatment which kept him from fighting. He is considered one of the real masters of modern bullfighting but now limits his performances to the larger, more important fairs where a knowledgeable public knows how to evaluate his performance.

CURRO ROMERO

Born Francisco Romero López in Camas, Sevilla 1 December 1935, took his alternativa 13 March 1959. A handsome, rather wooden faced man with a very deliberate way of walking and holding himself, he is an exquisite stylist with both the cape and the muleta. On his good afternoons he fights in the classic bullfighting style, cargando la suerte, stepping into the pass with a particular gypsy grace and emotional intensity that no other active bullfighter is able to equal. On such afternoons all things are possible and the majesty and ease with which he is able to dominate and control the bulls is unbelievable. He is a highly unreliable fighter, however, who is often so utterly carried away by fear that he is hardly able to function in the ring and appears to know absolutely nothing about bullfighting. On such afternoons, which are unfortunately the majority, it is impossible to believe that he has ever triumphed or to understand why anyone would bother to go and see him perform. Although, when he is good, he is incomparable with both cape and muleta, he is always extremely limited with the sword. His poor killing has ruined many triumphs and his fear has ruined others. The few times a year, however, when he feels invincible and triumphs, are such enormous triumphs that he continues to fight a substantial number of times each season on the strength of them.

DIEGO PUERTA

Born Diego Puerta Diane in Sevilla, 28 May 1941. Took the alternativa in Sevilla, 29 September 1958. He is a small, undistinguished looking young man with a bright, open face that might belong to a bank clerk or a bond salesman. He has been terribly punished by the bulls and has received at least one serious wound and sometimes more every season since he took the alternativa. He has always returned to bullfighting with his enthusiasm undiminished. He has constantly developed and improved his knowledge of bulls and bullfighting and continues to maintain a position among the very best. He is outstanding with both the cape and the muleta although a trifle less exquisite as a stylist than Paco Camino with whom he is often compared. While he generally kills well he is not exceptional with the sword or particularly noted for his work with it. He is a happy fighter with great courage, honesty and art. In addition, he has an enormous enthusiasm and desire to triumph and please and does his best to fight all the bulls he faces. He is very popular with the public because of this and because of his real merit as a bullfighter, but he still lacks a certain maturity which manifests itself in a lack of restraint. He often gets carried away by his enthusiasm and has a tendency to prolong the muleta faena too long which sometimes spoils both the bull and the fight. He continues to improve however with each coming year and gives promise of developing into a real master of the profession.

MONDENO

Born Juan Garciá Gimeńez in Puerto Real, Cádiz, 7 January 1934, took the alternativa in Sevilla, 29 March 1959. He is an extreme example of the profile style of fighting. He fights with his elbows close to his body in a way that permits him very little control over the course of the bull but which brings the bull past very close. Despite this lack of control, the extreme calm and post-like quiet of his figure in the ring is extremely impressive and gives a peculiar intensity to his work. He is a tall, handsome, graying, distinguished young man and was in the first rank of bullfighters until his retirement in 1964 when he entered a Dominican seminary with the intention of becoming a priest. His health broke down under the intensive study, however, and on the advice of his superiors he finally left the seminary and returned to bullfighting at the beginning of 1966. He is extremely competent with both the cape and the muleta within the profile style of fighting but is only fair with the sword which more than once has prevented him from obtaining the triumphs he otherwise had earned.

JULIO APARICIO

Born Julio Aparicio y Martínez in Madrid, 13 February 1932, took his alternativa 12 October 1950. He is an openfaced lank-haired man with a great intuitive knowledge of bulls and is an outstanding example of the profile style of fighting. At his best he is extremely capable with the cape, outstanding with the banderillas and inspired with the muleta. With the sword however, he is deficient and has spoiled many triumphs bcause he could not kill the bull cleanly and quickly. He is a highly temperamental bullfighter and extremely aware of and dependent upon the attitude of the crowd. Their reaction to him and what he is doing in the ring is often more important to him than the bull he is fighting. He often gets carried away by his reaction to the crowd or his feeling of impending triumph or the excitement of the fight and loses track of the reality of the bull so that he appears to forget all he knows and do things which are fundamentally unsound and unworthy of a man of his experience and talents. He came out of retirement in 1965 to start again but has probably passed the high point of his career.

None of the five young men of promise listed below have more than a year or two as full matadores. Most of them has less. As a consequence it is difficult to assess their real ability or their real worth. All of them have talent, all show great promise and all of them are fighting for a place in the first rank. Only time will tell whether they will be able to maintain the pace and establish themselves solidly among the veterans. Meanwhile their names on the program mean enthusiasm and a desire to triumph at almost any cost.

PALOMO LINARES
Born Sebastian Palomo Martinez in Linares, Jaen, 15 September 1948, took his alternativa 19 May 1966.

PAQUIRRI
Born Francisco Rivera Perez in Zahara de los Atunes, Cadiz, 24 March 1948, took his alternativa 11 August 1966.

PEDRO BENJUMEA
Born Pedro Benjumea Duran in Palma del Rio, Cordoba, 29 November 1945, took his alternativa 27 February 1967.

ANGEL TERUEL
Born Angel Teruel Penalver in Madrid, 20 February 1950, took his alternativa 30 June 1967.

MIGUEL MARQUEZ
Born Miguel Marquez Sanchez, in Fuengirola, Malaga, 5 May 1946, took his alternativa 3 March 1968.

APPENDIX III

TEN POPULAR RANCHES AND

FOUR FAMOUS NAMES

There are over 250 ranches which breed fighting bulls in Spain. Some of these produce only a few animals each year while others ship and sell 50 or a 100 or more. Generally speaking, the ranches which furnish the most bulls do so because they have bred them to the requirements of the established bullfighters who are to face them in the ring. Since the established bullfighters are able to specify the ranch of their choice when they sign their contracts to fight, and since they are understandably reluctant to select animals which will not permit them to start, there has been a general tendency on the part of the ranch owners to breed out all traits which might interfere with this result. Some ranches have come closer to producing the bullfighter's ideal animal than others and these are the most popular with the big stars.

The following is a list of ten of the most popular ranches in Spain.

Fermín Bohorquez   Atanasio Fernández
Juan Pedro Domecq   A. Pérez de S. Fernando
Marqués de Domecq   Carlos Urquijo
Carlos Núñez   Joaquín Buendía
María Montalvo   Alvaro Domecq

When these animals are being fought by established stars it is a worthwhile indication that the bullfight will be an artistic success although the bulls may sometimes be small, with unpretentious horns and little real force, and the action may be wanting in emotion because of this.

Among the less popular ranches are those which are frankly bad and those

273

which have maintained some different standard or ideal of what a fighting bull should be. Concerning those which are bad there is nothing to be said except that the animals are seriously lacking in one or more of the fundamental characteristics of the fighting bull and are unacceptable to the established bullfighters for his reason. As for those ranches which have maintained a different standard or ideal of what a fighting bull should be, some have bred for fire and temperament, others for length of horn, others for disproportionate size and strength while still others have tried to obtain all of these.

The following is a list of four famous ranches of this type which have built their reputation on the magnificence of the animals they produce.

> Eduardo Miura
> Pablo Romero
> Tulio e Isaias Vazquez
> Palha

Bulls from these ranches are fought only a few times each year and rarely by any of the stars. The name of one of these ranches on the program means that the fight will probably not be an artistic success. It is, however, often an unparalleled opportunity to observe the fighting bull at his very finest. On the rare occasions when bulls from these ranches are fought by an established star, the chances of seeing bullfighting at its serious best are greatly enhanced. An opportunity to see such a fight should not be overlooked, although it is unreasonable to expect the star to be able to perform in his accustomed way or to do "pretty" things with bulls of this type and difficulty.

APPENDIX IV

A SCHEDULE OF MAJOR BULLFIGHTS

Bullfights are held in almost every city or town in Spain on special occasions throughout the season. These special occasions usually coincide with the feast day of the patron saint of that city or town. The fights are often the high point of the entertainment scheduled for this yearly holiday and the accompanying fair which may last several days or a week or more.

The following is a list of major bullfights (*corridas de toros*) held during the year in Spain. The dates given are those of the 1966 season and do not necessarily apply *exactly* to any other season. The most important fairs are marked with an asterisk for quick reference.

Besides these major fights (corridas de toros) there are many minor fights (*corridas de novillos or novilladas*) held throughout the country as well.

In Madrid, Barcelona and Seville there is a fight of some kind almost every Sunday during the season and sometimes in Madrid and Barcelona there is a fight every Thursday as well. The men who are to fight in these places on these odd dates are not designated until the date approaches and the names are often not known more than a week in advance.

For a complete list of all the scheduled bullfights at any given moment during the season, the Spanish weekly newspaper *Dígame,* on sale at any Spanish newsstand, has the most complete list which includes the date, the town, the bullfighters and the bulls to be fought.

Note: It is important to double check the time and date of all bullfights whenever possible since cancellations occur and feast days vary from year to year.

January	*March*
Elche 9	Alcaniz 19

Algeciras 19
Castellon de la Plana 13
Huelva 19
Malaga 19
Murcia 29
*Valencia   17, 18, 19, 20
Villacarrillo 13

April
Alcala de Henares 2
Alicante 3
Andujar 24
Barcelona   10, 11, 17, 24
Cadiz 10
Castellon de la Plana 24
Egea de los Caballeros 17
Madrid (Ventas)   3, 10, 17, 24
Madrid (Vista Alegre)   3, 14
Malaga 10
Marbella   3, 17, 24
Murcia 10
Oviedo 19
Palma de Mallorca   3, 24
Pamplona 17
Sanlucar de Barrameda 10
*Sevilla   10, 16, 17, 18, 19, 20, 21, 22, 23,
            24
Toledo 3
Tudela 1
Zaragoza 10

May
Alcala de Henares 5
Alicante 1
Aranjuez   1, 30
Baeza 8
Barcelona   1, 8, 15, 22, 29, 30
Burgos 8
Caceres 31
Castellon de la Plana 8
*Cordoba   1, 8, 25, 26, 27, 28
Ecija 8
Figueras 8
Jerez de la Frontera   1, 2, 15
La Carolina 13
Leride 8
*Madrid (Ventas)   1, 14, 15, 16, 17, 18,

19, 20, 21, 22, 23, 24, 25, 26, 27, 28
Malaga 19
Madrid (Vista Alegre)   8, 15, 22
Marbella   1, 15, 22
Palma de Mallorca   1, 8, 15, 22, 29
Pamplona   1, 15
Puerto de Santa Maria 7
Puertollano 4
San Feliu de Guixols 29
Santa Cruz de Tenerife 1
Santisteban del Puerto 29
Sevilla 19
Talavera de la Reina   15, 16
Tudela 1
Valencia 22
Valladolid 19
Zaragoza   19, 22

June
Algeciras 25
*Alicante   23, 24, 26, 29
Antequera 1
Badajoz   24, 25, 26
Barcelona   5, 9, 12, 16, 19, 23, 26, 30
Bilbao   18, 19
Brihuega 12
Burgos   29, 30
Cabrea 26
Caceres 1
Cadiz 9
Chiclana 12
Ciudad Real 29
Granada   9, 10, 11, 12
Huelva 9
Jaen 11
Leon   24, 26
Linares 5
Madrid (Ventas)   16, 26
Madrid (Vista Alegre)   5, 12, 19
Madrid (San Sebastian de los Reyes)
            7
Malaga   9, 29
Marbella   12, 26
Munguia 29
Ondora 5
Palma de Mallorca   5, 12, 19, 26
Plasencia   9, 10, 11
Quintanar de la Orden 12

Ronda   19
Segovia   29
Sevilla   9, 19
Tarragona   19
Toledo   9, 26
Tolosa   26
Trujillo   5
Villanueva y Gelton   19
Vinaroz   26
Zamora   29

July

Alicante   24
Barcelona   3, 7, 14, 17, 18, 21, 24, 25, 28, 31
Barco de Avila   25
Benidorm   18, 25, 31
Brihuega   17
Burgos   2, 3
Calahorra   31
Castellon de la Plana   3, 16
Ecija   17
Figueras   3, 10, 17, 24, 31
Gerona   17, 24, 31
Ibiza   18
Jerez de la Frontera   30
La Coruna   31
La Linea de la Concepcion   17, 18
Lloret del Mar   17, 25, 31
Madrid (Ventas)   3, 7, 10, 17, 24, 31
Madrid (Vista Alegre)   3, 10
Malaga   3, 31
Marbella   10
Palma de Mallorca   3, 10, 18, 24, 31
*Pamplona   7, 8, 9, 10, 11, 12, 13, 14
Puerto de Santa Maria   10, 31
San Feliu de Guixols   3, 10, 17, 24, 31
*Santander   23, 24, 25
Sevilla   18
Soria   3
Tarragona   17
Teruel   6, 9
Tudela   24, 25
*Valencia   24, 25, 26, 27, 28, 29, 30, 31
Valladolid   18
Villanueva y Gelton   10
Vinaroz   17
Vitoria   25

August

Alcala de Guadaira   20
Alcala de Henares   25
Alicante   5, 14, 20
Almendralejo   16
*Almeria   22, 23, 24, 25, 26, 27
Antequera   21
Arenas de San Pablo   29
Aviles   28
Baeza   15
Barcelona   4, 7, 11, 14, 15, 18, 21, 25, 28
Benidorm   7, 11, 15, 21, 28
*Bilbao   21, 22, 23, 24, 25, 26, 28
Brihuega   17
Burgo de Osuna   15
Cadiz   13
Calahorra   31
Castellon de la Plana   14
Castro Urdiales   7, 14
Cazalla de la Sierra   15
Cieza   21
Ciudad Real   17, 18, 25
Colmenar Viejo   27, 28
Cuenca   22
El Escorial   10
Estella   7
Figueras   7, 14, 21, 28
Gerona   7, 14, 21, 28
*Gijon   12, 13, 14, 15
Huelva   3
Huesca   10, 15
Ibiza   5
La Coruna   4, 7
*Linares   28, 29, 30, 31
Lloret del Mar   7, 14, 21, 28
Loja   29
*Malaga   1, 2, 3, 4, 5, 6, 7
Madrid (Ventas)   7, 14, 21, 28
Manzanares   9
Marbella   13, 14, 20, 21, 27
Martos   25
Ondara   14, 20
Palma de Mallorca   7, 15, 21, 28
Pontevedra   14, 16
Puerto de Santa Maria   15, 28
Quintanar de la Orden   18
Sabiote   24

San Clemente 21
San Feliu de Guixols 7, 14, 21, 28
Sanlucar de Barrameda 14
*San Sebastian 13, 14, 15, 16, 17, 18, 19, 20, 21, 28
Santander 7, 13, 14, 26
Tafalla 15
Tarazona de Aragon 28
Tarragona 7, 21
Toledo 15, 19
Tomelloso 30
Valdepenas 2, 17
Valencia 15
Villarrobledo 15
Vinaroz 7, 14
Vitoria 5, 6, 7, 8, 9

September

Abaran 27
*Albacete 10, 11, 12, 13, 14, 15
Alcaniz 10
Alcazar de San Juan 7
Alicante 3
Andorra 8
Andujar 12
Aranda del Duero 12
Aranjuez 5
Ayamonte 8
Barbastro 8
Barcelona 8, 11, 15, 18, 22, 24, 25
Barco de Avila 4
Baza 10
Benidorm 4, 11
Berja 11
Cadiz 2
Caceres 30
Calasparra 29
Calatayud 9, 11
Carinena 17
Cehegin 11
Consuegra 25
Cordoba 25, 26
Corella 28
Ecija 21
Egea de los Caballeros 11
Figueras 4
Fuensalida 18

Gerona 4
Granada 25
Grijuelo 6
Jerez de la Frontera 10, 13
La Coruna 10
*Logrono 21, 22, 23, 24, 25
Lorca 18
Los Yebenes 14
Madrid 4, 30
Madrid (Vista Alegre) 18, 22, 25
Madrid (San Sebastian de los Reyes) 11
Madridejos 15
Malaga 4, 11, 25
Marbella 17
Medina del Campo 4
Merida 3, 4
*Murcia 6, 7, 8, 9
Olivenza 18
Ondara 5, 19
Oviedo 21
Palencia 24
Palma de Mallorca 4, 8, 11, 18, 25
Pozomlanco 27
Puerto de Santa Maria 18
Ronda 9
*Salamanca 13, 14, 15, 16
San Feliu de Guixols 4, 11, 18
San Martin de Valdeiglesias 9, 12
Santona 8
Segovia 15
Sevilla 4, 29
Talavera de la Reina 23
Valencia de Don Juan 14
*Valladolid 18, 19, 20, 25
Vera 25
Villacarillo 16
Villamayor de Santiago 6
Villena 7
Vitoria 4
Zamora 11

October

Barcelona 2, 9, 16, 23
Cadiz 12
Ecija 12
Fuengirola 9
Hellin 22

Huercal-Overa 23
Madrid 12, 16, 23
Madrid (San Sebastian de los Reyes) 2
Madrid (Vista Alegre) 30
Marbella 2
Merida 9
Motril 16

Orihuela 2
Palma de Mallorca 2, 9, 16, 23, 30
Salamanca 9
Sevilla 1, 12
Toledo 12
Villena 30
*Zaragoza 12, 13, 14, 15, 16

APPENDIX V

THE OFFICIAL BULLFIGHT REGULATION

BULLFIGHTING CODE

G O N I
Benito de Castro, 5
Madrid 2

BULLFIGHTING CODE

DECREE of March 15, 1962, Official Bulletin of the State No. 68 of March 20, 1962, by which is approved the revised text of the New Code of Bullfighting. With the correction of *errata* of the said *DECREE,* Official Bulletin of the State No. 71 of March 23, 1962.

Madrid

CONTENTS

1.

THE BULLRING

Article 1. Permission for the construction of new bullrings must be solicited from the Mayor of the town in a petition signed by the owner of the structure, or by his legal representative, accompanied with three copies of the final plan, drawn up by the specialists who determine the Laws or provisions in force at the time of submission.

Another copy will be sent for approval to the Director General of Security or the civil Governor of the province, according to the particular case, who will hear the case presented by the appropriate Advisory Committee for Public Spectacles, which may propose modifications it considers useful to the plan, in accordance with the precepts of this code. Construction or remodelling will not begin until the said approval is obtained.

The plans must be on a scale of a centimeter to a meter, except that of the site, which shall be on a smaller scale with all the necessary dimensions.

The materials which are to be used and the wiring to be installed must be specified in the Memorandum which accompanies the plan.

When the builder of the bullring in question is actually the City Government, it will be necessary to guarantee before the Director General of Security or the appropriate Civil Governor that it has all its obligations duly covered, particularly those which concern National Education.

Article 2. When it is a matter of alterations or repairs in a building already constructed, permission must be solicited in the same manner set forth in the preceding article.

Article 3. Bullrings must be situated in places of easy access and provided with the necessary means of communication with urban centers. They must have frontage on public thoroughfares.

283

Article 4. The size of bullrings must be in relation to the public thorough-fares, in the proportion of 200 spectators to each meter of width of the said thoroughfares.

Article 5. The entrance gates to bullrings must be in the proportion of one meter of unobstructed width per 400 estimated spectators, and their minimum width must be a clear meter and a half.

If vehicle entrances are provided, they must be independent of those intended for pedestrians.

The stands shall be provided with ample exits, with smooth stairs or ramps a meter and a half in width per each 200 spectators, and of a number in proportion to the size of the stands.

The stairways to the upper levels must be, as a minimum, a meter and a half wide. For each 450 spectators, there must be a stairway leading directly to the outside or to independent passageways.

Article 6. The seats in all bullrings, whatever their category, must be marked off and numbered, arranged in rows 0.80 meters wide, of which 0.40 meters will be reserved for the seat itself, and the other 0.40 for the aisle, the seat having a width of 0.50 meters.

The main and intermediate aisles will be at least one meter wide and the aisles giving access to the seats will be eighty centimeters wide.

The galleries or hallways must be a meter and a half for each 300 spectators, with an increase of 0.25 meters per each 100 more or fraction thereof.

The number of seats in a row between two aisles, cannot exceed 25 in the first row of Grandstand, Galleries, and Upper Galleries.

The seats will be laid out with the necessary gradient and other specifications, so that from any one of them, when the bullring is filled to capacity, the ring may be seen in its entirety.

Each group of 400 Grandstand and Gallery spectators must dispose of an aisle one meter wide.

In rings which have terraces where the public may remain standing, they will be measured at the rate of half a square meter per spectator, at a depth of a meter and a half at the end which faces on the ring.

Waterclosets and urinals will be provided and distributed according to seating sections, in hygenic and decent conditions.

Both facilities will be enclosed and those of each sex will be independent of each other. For each 500 spectators there will be a watercloset, of which one-third will be for ladies, and for each 150 spectators there will be one urinal. All of them must be provided with wash-basins.

Article 7. The arena fences (barreras) and coverts (burladeros) must be smooth on the side facing the arena, and the posts and inevitable projections must have their edges rounded, with the exception of the vaulting step (estribos).

For the greater safety of the fighters, there must be provided coverts of a permanent nature in the arena fences, which will permit the fighters to enter the ring passageway, or alley, under appropriate safety conditions, it being absolutely prohibited for the fighters, with the exceptions of the participating matadors and the alternating *banderilleros,* to stop or stay behind them.

In those present-day bullrings which do not have a passageway (callejon), nor consequently coverts, there shall be installed in the arena a covert for each of the teams of assistants (cuadrillas), in a proper state of safety and solidity.

Article 8. Between the lower part of the ringside section and the supporting wall of the grandstand (which wall will be 2 meters, 20 centimeters high, topped with the necessary posts for stringing the rope or safety cable for the protection of the spectators), there must be a passageway from one and a half to two meters wide, in which shall be installed, in the proper safety conditions and sufficiently comfortable, coverts to be occupied by the official delegate of the authorities, Chiefs and officers of the service forces of the bullring, Veterinaries, Ring Empresario, *cuadrillas,* picadors, chief herders, muledrivers, stable-boys; as well as four more coverts distributed around the quadrants of the arena, of sufficient capacity for a pair of service force members in each one.

In addition, another covert of adequate width must be installed for the medical personnel, as close as possible to the entrance of the infirmary and easily accessible, built in a shady place and with the requisite conditions of safety and comfort.

Without detriment to the previously mentioned coverts, others may be installed which the Governing Authority considers convenient.

Article 9. The dimensions of bullring arenas, whatever their category, must not be of a diameter greater than sixty meters nor less than forty-five, and the fence which encloses them must be of wood, one meter 60 centimeters high, and equipped with four large gates, three meters wide and in two sections; the latter, on the side facing the ring, will be exactly like the rest of the fence, and on the inside will be fitted with bolts and locks, easily manipulated and of the necessary strength to withstand, without deterioration, the mishaps and vicissitudes of the fight. Of these four gates, one will correspond to the *cuadrilla*'s gate, and the other to the gate through which the dead bull is dragged out.

Article 10. Bullrings must have at least three corrals, connected by gates; they shall have the minimum dimensions of 20 by 14 meters, and they shall be enclosed by a wall one meter fifty high, serving as a fence or barricade, with trapdoors one-half meter wide to facilitate the safe examination of the bulls. One of the corrals shall have direct access to the passageway communicating with the place where the bullpens are.

There must also be another corral for the purpose of loading and unloading the bulls, with a direct entrance from the street and of sufficient width for easy manouvering of trucks.

Article 11. No less than ten bullpens shall be constructed, with the dimensions of 2 meters, 10 centimeters wide, three meters long, and two meters high, all inter-connected. Their gates, which must all open outwards, must be of metal and sufficient strength, and may be braced on the inner side with easily replaceable wood, to avoid the bruising and scratching of the bulls on splinters or jagged edges, and equipped with easily manipulated bolts, to be moved by ropes from a convenient spot.

At the same time, there must also be installed an enclosure for veterinary treatment, duly equipped within for killing with the short dagger those bulls returned from the ring, for practicing in it the necessary operations or treatments, and for filing the horns and tipping them with balls, according to the type of bullfight being held.

Article 12. Bullrings must have two large patios with entrances from the street and direct communication with the ring; one of them called the *patio de caballos* (patio of the horses) and the other the *patio de arrastre* (patio for dragging out, or removal, of the bulls), in which, if their capacity permits it, the vehicles of the officials, the bullfighters, and their assistants may be parked.

Article 13. In the *patio de caballos* shall be installed the stables, the tack-room, and any other necessary structures.

Article 14. There must be three stables, independent of each other: one with capacity for 12 horses, well-ventilated and lighted, with mangers, a drinking-trough with running water, a waterproof but not slippery floor, sloping adequately towards the three drains with which it should be equipped; another, to be used as an infirmary for the horses, with three stalls; and the third, with six stalls, reserved for the horses used by the *rejoneadores* (mounted bullfighters); both in hygenic-sanitary conditions analogous to those established for the first stable.

The tack-room must be of adequate size for its purpose, and in it there must be a scales for the weighing of the protective padding for the horses' chests.

Article 15. In the *patio de arrastre,* there shall be an alcove set aside for the butchering of bulls killed in the fight or slaughtered afterwards.

This alcove must be of adequate dimensions to handle easily eight bulls at a time, and it must have an abundant supply of running water, a waterproof floor sloping on all sides towards the center, and a large drain permitting easy cleaning, by hosing or washing down with buckets of water; the walls must be tiled or covered with some waterproof material, easy to wash and disinfect, with a minimum height of one meter, 80; adequate ventilation and lighting.

It must have a washbasin with running water, and the necessary instruments for the Ring Veterinaries to perform the necessary *post mortem* inspections with complete cleanliness, as well as at least two troughs, with ample drainage, for washing the viscera thoroughly.

This alcove must be equipped with a pulley for the easy hanging and quartering of the bulls: at least 34 hooks, distributed along the walls, and attached in such a way that the quartered parts may be hung from them, and it will be provided with the necessary equipment for the workers to carry out the task to completion. For the weighing of the meat, there will be a scales, so installed that it will not interfere with the slaughtering tasks.

Article 16. In all bullrings of a permanent character, whatever their category, there shall be set aside for a chapel a spacious room, easily accessible to the bullfighters upon their arrival at the bullring, which must be decorated with appropriate respect, and equipped with an alter so that Holy Mass can be celebrated at any given moment.

Article 17. The installation of canteens or refreshment stands in the corridors leading to the seating sections is hereby authorized, provided that the size of the corridors permits it without in any way decreasing the minimum width required in such corridors, and that they be supplied with filtered, running water, which must empty into special deposits of the general drainage system.

Article 18. All bullrings, whatever their category, must necessarily have two ticket-windows for the sale of tickets to the public, completely independent of each other and operated by the personnel necessary to handle the volume of tickets which are to be sold; they should be open for at least five hours before the spectacle begins, or two when it is held in the morning.

TEMPORARY BULLRINGS

Article 19. Those places which are arranged in a makeshift way in order to hold bullfights are to be completely enclosed by wooden planks, it being absolutely forbidden to use for that purpose wagons, carts, or other kinds of materials not expressly outlined in this article.

In the part intended for the ring, a barricade-fence or coverts shall be set up in the manner set forth in the last paragraph of Article 7 of this Code.

In the construction of the bleachers, or grandstands, neither rope nor cord may be used, the planks being solidly fastened down with nails, and in such a way that the bulls cannot leap over them, nor the spectators take part in the fight.

The same safety precautions are to be adopted in the installations intended for bullpens and/or release-pens (*toriles*), the doors of which must be guarded in such a way that the bulls cannot get out until the proper moment.

They shall have at least one large corral connected to the passageway leading to the bullpens and equipped with coverts, all with the safety guarantees necessary for the perfect safekeeping of the livestock and their examination by the veterinary personnel.

Makeshift bullrings which are set up must meet the necessary safety conditions, taking into consideration their proportions and sites.

Article 20. The conditions set forth in the previous article must be accredited before the Governing Authorities specified in this Code by the organizers of the spectacle, by means of a certificate issued by an architect or building supervisor with a professional license, who will answer for the solidity and safety of the stands, structures and installations, a certificate which must be issued each time a portable ring is set up.

Article 21. In temporary bullrings, bullfights of all kinds may be held, provided that the fight is managed by professional bullfighters.

Article 22. Bullrings are divided in three categories.

They are: first-class bullrings: Barcelona (Monumental and Arenas), Bilbao, Madrid (Monumental); San Sebastián, Sevilla, Valencia, and Zaragoza.

Second-class: All the remaining bullrings in provincial capitals which have not been classified as first-class, including that of Carabanchel (Madrid), in addition to: Algeciras, Aranjuez, Cartagena, Gijon, Jerez de la Frontera, Linares, Merida, and Puerto de Santa Maria.

Third-class: the remaining bullrings, including temporary and makeshift rings.

The preceding classification shall never be the object of any interpretation whatsoever, existing in all its force whatever the type of bullfight being held.

Bullrings of new construction will be classified by the Main Advisory Committee for Public Spectacles.

Article 23. In all first and second-class bullrings there must be installed a clock in perfect working condition, visible from the President's box.

BULLFIGHTING SCHOOLS

Article 24. Establishments intended for instruction in bullfighting may not be set up without prior authorization by the Director General of Security in Madrid, and by the Civil Governors in the other provinces, who will order the inspection of said establishments for safety and other conditions appropriate to the purpose for which they are intended, by an Architect; and as for the infirmary installations which must form a part of said building, by the subdelegate of Medicine of the District in which the school is set up.

Article 25. If mechanical devices are used for instruction in place of bulls, their designs are to be presented to the above-mentioned authorities, who shall order them to be tested before the person or persons designated for the purpose, it being obligatory to prohibit the use of those which might produce lesions or injuries.

If bulls are used, they must be inspected once a month by the Veterinary appointed for the purpose by the Governing Authority from the nomination of the Provincial Department of Sanitation, which must only authorize the fighting of yearling calves or heifers, with blunted or capped horns, in the requisite state of health, ordering the substitution of those which, because of their frequent use, make the fight dangerous. The charge to be made by the Veterinary who conducts these examinations will be 100 pesetas per bull.

Article 26. During the practical lessons, a professional or recognized competence must act as director of the fighting, the infirmary facilities being attended to by the corresponding professional person, the owner of the school being obliged to communicate the appointment of both, with a description of their personal circumstances and addresses, to the authority which has granted the operating permit.

No paying members of the public will be allowed in these schools during the lessons, nor is it permitted to charge any amount other than that stipulated for instruction.

Failure to comply with these regulations will be punished with a fine of from 1000 to 2500 pesetas, imposed on the proprietor of the school and, in case of repetition of the offense, with closure for the time determined by the Authorities.

INFIRMARIES

Article 27. *Their classification.*—Bullring infirmaries are to be situated near the arena; if at all possible, with direct and independent access; and in all which may concern the technical personnel assigned to them as well as all that pertains to the conditions of the physical plant and the medical supplies with which they must be provided, will be divided into three categories:

In the first class will be all those infirmaries of bullrings of first- and second-class, according to the classification referred to in Article 22 of this Code.

In the second class will be all the infirmaries of those remaining bullrings, temporary or permanent, in which bullfights or *novilladas* (fights with young bulls) with picadors are held.

In the third class will be all those of bullrings which do not hold bullfights or *novilladas* with picadors.

Concerning the Physical Plant.—The first-class infirmary will consist of two parts, one for carrying out whatever treatment and surgical interventions may be necessary, and another for the hospitalization of the injured until they may be removed without any danger to their lives.

The first part will consist of a room for examination of injuries and treatment of minor injuries; it will be an area of four by five meters, three and a half meters high. Adjoining this room and easily accessible to it will be the room reserved for serious operations, which will have minimum dimensions of five by six meters, and three and a half meters high. Both rooms will have direct ventilation, and must also be equipped with adequate electrical lighting. The floors and the walls must be tiled throughout. The part of the infirmary reserved for hospitalization of the injured will be next to the operating-room, but independent of it, and it must be a room ten by four meters wide and three and a half meters high, in which shall be installed four beds with the corresponding supply of mattresses, sheets, blankets, etc.

In second- and third-class infirmaries, the examining-room may be eliminated, the infirmary thereby consisting of the operating-room and convalescent ward, of the dimensions already mentioned, and in the third-class infirmary, the beds may be reduced to two.

In all infirmaries there must be installed an emergency lighting system, battery-powered, in order to be able perform operations in case of power shortage or failure.

Medical Equipment:—First- and second-class infirmaries must be equipped with:

A steam-pressure sterilizer for the sterilization of instruments used in treatment, and for washing by the surgeons; it must have a minimum capacity of 1.30 cubic meters, and the tanks of sterilized water must hold approximately 40 liters. Two washbasins, with faucets for the sterilized water from the tanks, with a direct drainage outlet. An enclosed case for surgical instruments. An operating-table flexible enough to be able to place the injured person in position for surgery on the perineum, and in the Trendelenbourg position. A gas, alcohol, or electric boiler, 60 by 30. Two side-tables for setting out the surgical instruments.

Third-class infirmaries require, as a minimum:

An operating-table of the same specifications already mentioned. A boiler, 50 by 20. A side-table. An enclosed instrument-case. A washbasin and a tank for sterilized water, of a minimum capacity of 20 liters, which may be portable.

Concerning surgical supplies.—First- and second-class infirmaries must have:

Two sterilized containers, 40 by 25, for sheets and hospital gowns. Two containers, 25 by 15, for sterilized cloths. Four containers, 20 by 15, for linen and rubber gloves. They must contain, as a minimum, 4 gowns, 3 surgical masks, 4 large sheets, 18 large gauze dressings, 18 abdominal dressings, 6 pairs of gloves, strips of gauze, cotton; all duly sterilized.

Third-class infirmaries must have:

One container 40 by 25. Two containers 25 by 15. One container 15 by 15. They must contain, as a minimum, 12 gauze dressings a meter square, 2 hospital gowns, 4 pairs of gloves, gauze and cotton, all duly sterilized. Two drip-apparatuses for the administration of fluids and medications for the lower limbs, one drip-apparatus for upper limbs; Grammer splints of different sizes.

Instruments.—First- and second-class infirmaries must have:

Four scalpels, 4 scissors—straight and curved, 2 dissecting forceps with teeth, 2 without teeth, 18 kocher forceps and 12 Pean forceps, 6 heavy forceps of the Le Fort type, 6 field forceps, 2 Farabeuf dividers, 2 dividers with handles—one Gosset, one Finochietto, an abdominal valve, one Periosteotome, one costotome, 2 gouging forceps, a hand-trepan, a hammer, 2 surgical chisels, 2 straight clamps, 2 curved clamps, 2 needle-holders, 12 Hagedor needles, 12 intestinal needles—straight and curved, an aspirator for body cavities, a controlled-anesthesia appliance for gases, with gauges, rotating gauges for oxygen and protoxide of nitrogen, and an ether vaporizer, with all their accessories and with a closed-circuit anesthesia mechanism; 2 cylinders of protoxide of nitrogen, 2 cylinders of oxygen, with their corresponding knobs and outlets; for the oxygen, a complete inhalor apparatus, with its corresponding sets of catheters of rubber or of plastic, for tracheobronchial aspiration. One set of rubber masks (adult, adolescent, and children's), a metallic mask of the Schimmelbusch type, a set of Guedel catheters (rubber pharyngeal tubes) in 3 sizes. One tongue-depressor, one Magill forceps, one complete set of rubber endotracheal catheters, a complete set of endotracheal catheters for maintaining respiratory airways, a set of metal connecting-tubes for the catheters (of the Cobb type), for aspiration through them, 4 or 5 sizes; a brass probe, a McIntosh-type laryngoscope with 2 sizes of guides for it, and light-bulbs and a spare set of batteries; one stethoscope, and a machine for measuring blood-pressure (aneroid, with a long, rubber tube), 2 Smarch compressors, 2 tracheotomy tubes of different sizes; a universal type, 3-gauge, metal wrench; 4 drip-apparatuses for the limbs, assorted Grammer splints; one Guyon tube, assorted catheters, syringes, assorted injection needles, for intravenous and hypodermic injections, rubber draining tubes of various sizes; 12 tubes of catgut, of various sizes; 4 skeins of silk, 24 Cambrioge bandages, of various sizes. An apparatus for drop by drop infusions.

Third-class infirmaries must have as a minimum:

Two scalpels, 2 scissors—straight and curved, 2 grooved catheters, 2 dissecting forceps, 12 Kocher forceps, 12 Pean forceps, 6 field forceps, 2 Farabeuf dividers. One Gosset divider, an abdominal valve, 2 straight intestinal clamps, 2 curved intestinal clamps, 12 Hagedor needles, 12 intestinal needles, 2/10 cc. syringes, two 2 cc. syringes, and two with 20 needles for intravenous and hypodermic injections, assorted. Two Smarch compressors, 10 Cambrioge bandages, of different sizes. Draining-tubes. Catgut, of varying calibres. Assorted silk. A simple apparatus for anesthesia by ether vaporization (Omo Oxford-type or Ombredane-type), two pharyngeal tubes, Guedel-type, of different sizes; 2 needles for spinal puncture, 2 needles for local or regional anesthesia, a tongue depressor, a forceps for the tongue, and a tank of oxygen with a knob (for opening and closing the outlet) .

Medicines.—Bullring infirmaries, whatever their category, must be equipped with a medicine-chest composed of the following medicines:

Ten ampules of novocaine, at 1 per 100, without adrenalin; 250 cc. of sterilized solution of sodic-citrate, 1000 cc. of blood. An equal quantity of plasma. Six 300 cc. ampules of glucose serum. Six ampules of anti-tetanus serum. Six ampules of anesthetic ether. Six 300 cc. ampules of physiological serum. One hundred cubic centimeters of tincture of iodine. Four liters of alcohol of 90 degrees, 500 grams of sulphuric ether. An assortment of fluids for injection, of stimulants: cardiac, peripheral, sedative, hypnotic, and hemostatic. Antiseptics and antibiotics, both powdered and liquid. Sterilized vaseline.

First- and second-class infirmaries must have, besides, 12 ampules of one gram each, of extra-fast-acting barbiturates, 24 ampules of 20 cc. of twice-distilled water. Four boxes of muscular relaxants; 10 vials of depolarizing muscular relaxants; 3 boxes of 6 anti-relaxant ampules, 3 boxes of antihistaminic agents; 3 boxes of cortical hormones; 2 packages of soda-salt. A box of ampules of injectable vagal blocking agents.

Third-class infirmaries must have 2 boxes of ampules of spinal anesthetic.

All the supplies mentioned must be in the infirmary, available for use, four hours before the bullfight is held.

Article 28. Concerning the medical personnel.—Medical staffs for first-class infirmaries must be composed of:

A Surgeon-in-Chief, directly responsible for the service. An assistant surgeon, who will be able to exercise the functions of the Chief Surgeon during absences and illness. An assistant doctor. A doctor specialized in transfusions. A specialist in anesthesiology. A practical-doctor (*practicante*) , and an operating-room attendant.

Second-class infirmary staffs will be composed of the same personnel.

Third-class infirmaries will have the following staff:

A local doctor, who will act as Staff Chief; an assistant doctor, appointed by him from among the residents of the same or nearest town, in case there are no other licensed doctors there; a practical-doctor and a nurse from the Citizens' Public Welfare, if there is a branch in the town, and if there are several qualified persons, the Staff Chief will appoint them at his discretion.

On the appointment of personnel.—The Bullfighters' Fund (*Montepio*) will inform the Council of Medical Colleges of each vacancy existing or which may arise, so that the Council, in turn, may communicate it to the proper Provincial College, so that once the vacancy is announced on the college premises, and allowing a term for acceptance of applications not greater than two weeks, the Board of Directors may form a list of three candidates from those applicants who, in its judgment and in consideration of their professional files, have the necessary qualifications and surgical training for the position which they are to fill.

For the composition of the above-mentioned candidacy list, the Health Department, having been informed by their National Council, must draw up a resumé, which it will send to the proper Medical College, so that, basing its judgments on the said resumé, it may qualify and propose the appropriate candidacy list. This list will be forwarded to the Bullfighters' Fund, which will choose the licensed doctor, extending to him the appointment in question, stamped by the President of the Medical College and by the Provincial Inspector of Health. The personnel of the staff will be named by its chief, who will inform the Bullfighters' Fund of the name of the assistant surgeon, so that the Fund may make the appointment, which will not go into effect if so requested by the chief of staff.

Transfusion specialists.—Their appointment will be made by the chief of the surgical staff of the bullring infirmary, and should go to a doctor having this title, granted by some official body, or department in charge of this discipline, or to one who has practiced the said specialty previous to the promulgation of the present Code.

The said Chief may coordinate the service with the Institutes of Hematology and Hemotherapy, if he considers it suitable. In any event, the transfusion specialist must have adequate supplies at his disposal, and necessary blood and plasma for a hemotherapeutic intervention of any nature, the cost of blood and plasma used being at the expense of the Ring Management.

In order to facilitate the work of this staff member, fighters must all wear a medal or carry an identity-card with their blood group and Rh Factor, thus preventing any cases of sensitization of the latter.

Article 29. It is the responsibility of the Bullring Management to maintain infirmaries in the proper condition and to keep them supplied with the means of treatment defined in the previous articles, as well as to replace the equipment and supplies used and/or no longer serviceable.

It is also the duty of the Management to pay the medical personnel attached to the service of its infirmaries the fees due them for their attendance at the same, which will be:

Bullfights, novilladas and festivales (minor fights) with picadors

	Pesetas		Pesetas
First-class infirmaries	5,000	Third-class infirmaries	2,250
Second-class infirmaries	3,000		

Fights with young bulls without picadors

	Pesetas		Pesetas
First-class infirmaries	3,000	Third-class infirmaries	1,500
Second-class infirmaries	2,000		

Minor fights without picadors, becerradas (amateur calf-fights) and comic bullfighting

First-class infirmaries	1,500	Third-class infirmaries	600
Second-class infirmaries	1,000		

These fees will be paid per individual fight, and will be distributed among the medical staff according to the following percentages:

First- and second-class bullrings:

Chief Surgeon, 50% of the total amount.	Transfusion specialist, 9%.
First assistant doctor, 18%.	Anesthetist, 9%.
Second assistant doctor, 10%.	Practical-doctor, 4%.

The operating-room attendant will be paid separately by the Management, as a bullring employee.

Third-class infirmaries:

Chief of Staff, 50% of the total amount.	Practical-doctor, 12%.
Assistant doctor, 30%.	Nurse, 8%.

In case of illness, absence, or for any other reason, staff members may name a substitute, with the authorization of the Staff Chief, allowing 50% of the corresponding fees to be paid to the person substituting.

In the event that the spectacle should be suspended, and if the medical personnel are present at the bullring, the management must honor 50% of the medical fees.

For spectacles held in bullrings, of a private character, such as the shooting of films, etc., the organizing Empresarios will contract freely with the chief of the infirmary services; medical personnel will receive fees equivalent to double those set for fullfledged bullfights, provided that the spectacle does not last longer than two hours, and if it should exceed this amount of time, the fees will go up 40%.

Article 30. If the professional performance of the Chief of Services of a given infirmary should give cause for complaints or claims, these must be made to the Bullfighters' Fund, which, if it considers them important, must request that three doctors, one named by the Medical College of the province corresponding to the denounced infirmary, another by the Bullfighters' Fund, and a third—to act as President—by the Council of Colleges, examine the legally formulated denunciation and, after interviewing the interested party, they shall determine if there is any shortcoming and the seriousness of it, informing the College to which the offender belongs. This tribunal is authorized to propose dismissal from employment to the Bullfighters' Fund. The legal proceedings will take place in Madrid, and the expenses occasioned by the transportation and stay of the Doctor who comes to act as Official Representative will be charged to the account of the Bullfighters' Fund.

When an unfortunate accident occurs in the bullfight, the delegate of the authorities in charge will arrange for the agents under his command to establish the appropriate service to keep the public from crowding around the vicinity of the accident and the gates, and to prevent unconcerned parties from entering the infirmary. It is left to the judgment of the Staff Chief to permit the entrance and stay in the infirmary of some member of the family or close friend of the injured person.

When the injured person has been treated, the doctor in charge will fill out the medical report in quadruplicate: one copy for the Authority presiding over the bullfight, another for the judiciary authority, if the doctor has any reservations in his prognosis; a third for the Management and, lastly, one for the injured party. In it he will give an account of the injuries sustained, his medical analysis, and an opinion on whether or not the fight can be continued.

If it is determined in the medical report that the fighter is not in condition to go on with his work, the delegate of the authorities and his aides must prevent it at all costs.

The infirmary will dispense first aid to whichever spectator or Management employee needs it.

So that the injured may be attended with the greatest possible speed, one of the doctors or assistants must be on the premises of the infirmary at all times, the others occupying a covert, which is provided for in the second paragraph of Article 8 of the Code.

Article 31. The conditions of the premises of the infirmary as well as its equipment of instruments and medical supplies, will be duly inspected every year before the beginning of the season by the Provincial Health Inspector, or by the District Sub-Delegate of Medicine.

Notwithstanding this inspection, the Bullfighters' Fund may arrange at any time for a medical professor to check the state of the premises referred to, reporting on whatever shortcomings he may observe to the Provincial Health Department.

2.

CONCERNING THE GENERAL STAFF

Article 32. Under the title of General Staff, we include those groups of employees who, with a specific task, are employed in all kinds of bullfights. They are: porters, ushers, ringsweepers, carpenters, kettle-drummers, grooms in charge of horses, pics, and *banderillas;* constables, bullpen keepers, bull-tenders, and refreshment vendors.

All of them shall wear uniforms, bearing a badge with the corresponding number in large figures, which will be analogous to the number of their license registered in the bullring administration.

The Management will have the total responsibility for maintaining these uniforms in a perfect condition of cleanliness and repair for all bullfights held, whatever their nature.

Article 33. During the bullfight, there shall be, in each of the quadrants of the ring, inside the arena alley, a container of sand and a pair of sweepers, with two full buckets and two empty ones, the full ones to be used to cover immediately the blood shed by bulls and horses, and the empty ones, lined with oil cloth, to gather up with all speed and care possible, the offal of the animals, utilizing a 50 centimeter-long stick with a double iron hook in the butt in order to place it in the pails. They shall also have ready four ropes with slip-knots for dragging out the dead bulls and horses, which must be done by two traces of mules, the bulls being taken out first.

In those bullrings not having a ringside fence, and consequently, no alleyway, the equipment mentioned in the previous paragraph will be kept inside, as close as possible to the arena entrances.

These same workers will, after each bull is dragged out, be responsible for cleaning the ring, and smoothing out and levelling the sand stirred up during the fighting.

Article 34. An adequate number of grooms must be assigned to helping the picadors mount, adjusting their stirrups, taking away injured horses, removing saddles and bridles from dead horses, and leading to the stables, with the greatest haste, those horses which have been rendered useless for fighting but can still leave the ring under their own power.

Also, said personnel must be careful to lift, not drag, the saddles and trappings and not to remove bridles from horses until they have died.

The said grooms are forbidden to stop the bull, to attract the attention of the bull in any way, except when it is a matter of drawing-away the bull from a bull-fighter in danger, and to lead horses by the bit in order to place them in action; two grooms are required to go behind each picador in order to be at his disposition; they may remain in the ring only during the action of the picador, in which they are involved, afterwards being required to stay behind the covert assigned to them in Article 8.

Infraction of the above-established stipulations will be punished the first time by a fine of 50 pesetas, the second time, by 100, and the third, with disqualification from working in the ring for the number of fights decided at the discretion of the authorities.

Article 35. At each gate of the arena fence, there must be two carpenters, to open the gates when necessary; they should not enter the ring except when they have to repair some damage to the fence, which done, they must return to their posts.

Article 36. In the area of the bull-enclosures in those bullrings where there is one, there shall be no personnel other than the Chief Herder and those employees necessary for placing the bullranch colors and passing the bulls from one bullpen to another. The openings through which this operation is effected must be made in such a way that they offer no risk of accident.

Article 37. The drummer and the two clarinetists in charge of announcing the changing phases of the fight, and the other decisions of the President, will be placed facing the President's box.

Article 38. The band will be placed in a spot as far away from the bullpens as possible, and furthermore, they may perform during the fighting as well as in the intermissions, according to the custom of the bullring.

Article 39. The boys who lead the mule-teams for the dragging-out, will occupy a covert, built in the alleyway to the left side of the gate through which they perform their function; persons not connected with this service may not utilize this covert.

When the bull is dragged out, the chief of this operation must keep an eye on the President's box, in case the bull should be awarded a turn around the ring. In case the turn should be made without the President having ordered it, the chief of the operation will be punished with a fine of 500 pesetas, and in case the offense is repeated, with disqualification for the time considered suitable by the Authorities; and the muleteers will be regulated by the same rules as the grooms, as established in Article 34 of this Code.

Article 40. The *toril*-keepers and the *baderilleros'* assistants, there being at least one in every bullring, will be in charge, respectively, of opening the bullpen door for the entrance of the bull into the ring, and handing the *banderillas* to the fighters, as well as picking up those banderillas which have fallen into the ring, at the moment determined in Article 102.

These employees may wear the suit of lights or some badge to indicate their function.

Article 41. In the stands there must be a sufficient staff of ushers, perfectly instructed and trained, to take care of the spectators, and should any usher behave incorrectly, the agents of the authorities will be asked to help discipline him, enforce compliance, or proceed to his detention.

Article 42. The Management will be obliged to post in the passageways and doorways leading to the stands, and in a place where they can be seen clearly, posters stating the precepts elaborated in Article 60, and the punishments which will likewise be imposed on those who, protecting the violators, attempt to hide them, help them get away, or frustrate the efforts of the authorities' agents to carry out their duties.

The employees of the Management who, out of negligence or benevolence, do not abide by this rule will be corrected in the manner prescribed for grooms in Article 34.

Article 43. Vendors of fruit, flowers, refreshments, etc., may not circulate except before the fight and during the dragging-out of each bull, and only in places where they do not disturb the public; they are not permitted to toss their wares from one side of the bullring to the other.

Article 44. Maintenance and cleaning in the arena alley, and clearing the way on horseback will be performed by two constables, who will communicate to the fighters and the employees, the President's orders, to the end that they may be complied with, without overstepping their authority and maintaining the tone of circumspection and respectfulness required by the job.

3.

THE ORGANIZATION OF THE SPECTACLE

Article 45. No kind of bullfight spectacle may be announced to the public or held without its program of events and participants being duly authorized by the General Director of Security, in Madrid, and by the Civil Governor, in the other provinces.

Article 46. Bullfighting spectacles, as mentioned in the previous article, are classified accordingly:

a) Bullfights (*corridas de toros*)
b) Fights with young bulls with picadors (*Corridas de novillos con picadores*)
c) Fights with young bulls without picadors (*corridas de novillos sin picadores*)
d) Festivals
e) Amateur calf-fights (*becerradas*), and comic bullfighting (*toreo cómico*)

The Managements in charge of the organization of these spectacles must communicate to the appropriate Governing Authority their names and addresses and, when a legal representative is designated, his name and address also, the said authorities being obliged to deal directly with him, and both the Managements and their legal representatives being required to inform the authorities of any changes of name and address that may occur.

The General Director of Security, in Madrid, and the Civil Governors in the other provinces, shall arrange that bullfighting entertainments be attended by officials of the General Police Corps, the forces of the Armed Police, the Civil Guard, or the Municipal Guard, whichever they deem necessary. All of them, as well as the Delegate of the Authorities, will be under the command of the President.

It is absolutely forbidden to run bulls or calves, tied or loose, freely through the streets and squares of towns. Mayors are under the strictest responsibility to enforce this prohibition.

The General Director of Security, or the civil Governors, depending on the situation, will order those safety measures adopted which they consider necessary to avoid accidents.

The fighting of bulls which do not meet the requirements strictly pointed out in this Code is absolutely forbidden.

Article 47. The request for permission for the celebration of any bullfighting entertainment, subscribed to by the Entity, Management, or individual organizer, and directed to the General Director of Security, in Madrid, or to the civil Governors in the other provinces, should be accompanied by the following documentation:

a) Certification by the Architect or building inspector stamped by the respective College, in which it is stated strictly that the bullring, whatever its class, meets the safety conditions set forth in Article 21.

b) Certification by the Provincial Health Director, the District Subdelegate of Medicine or, if there is none, the resident Public Welfare doctor, according to the place in question, in which it must be stated that the Infirmary meets the necessary conditions for its purposes, and that it is equipped with all the supplies specified in this Code.

c) Certification by the Provincial Veterinary Health Inspector, stating that the corrals and bullpens, as well as the horse-stables, the installations related to the livestock, and the slaughtering facilities, meet the hygienic-sanitary conditions prescribed by the Code.

The certifications referred to in sections *a, b,* and *c* will be presented annually by the Management when it requests permission to open and operate the permanent *plaza,* notwithstanding the inspection visits made by the members of the Committee for Spectacles. Nevertheless, the governing Authorities may, at some time during the season, demand those certificates when it considers it suitable.

d) Certification by the Mayor, the Management, or the individual organizer of the spectacle, in which it is stated that all the bullfighters and assistants who are to take part in the fighting are older than sixteen years of age.

e) Authorization by the parents, tutors, or legal representatives of minors under twenty-one years of age.

f) Certification by the Bullfighting Sector of the National Entertainment Syndicate, in which it is stated that the fighters who are to perform are registered members; as well as a certificate from the Bullfighters' Fund, showing membership in it.

g) A certificate issued by the owner of the bullranch, his administrator or legal representative, and extracted from the bullranch's official book, in which is stated the date of birth, name and description of each and every one of the bulls to be fought, including the substitutes.

h) A sworn statement by the ranch-owner to the effect that the bulls have not been fought, nor have their horns been diminished, filed or submitted to fraudulent manipulations.

If the bullfighter performing in any bullfight or *novillada* should accuse the bull of having already been fought, the President, after consulting the other bullfighters and advisors, shall arrange for the retirement of the bull to the corral and his substitution by the extra bull.

The bull withdrawn for said reason will of necessity be killed with the short dagger in the corrals and his owner fined 10,000 pesetas.

i) Certificate of health of the bulls issued by the Official Veterinary of the Township of origin of the bullranch.

j) Certification of the bill of sale for the bulls, duly stamped by the appropriate Breeders' Syndicate.

k) Certification of the contracts of the announced bullfighters, stamped by the Bullfighting Section of the National Entertainment Syndicate.

l) Certification attesting to the satisfaction of Syndicate or Ministry of Labor requirements in force at the time of the petition.

ll) When the Town Councils are the Management of bullfighting events, they must attest that the agreement for the event has been adopted by a majority vote of the Municipal Corporation, and that the latter is up to date in the payment of its obligations, for which purpose they must enclose a certificate issued by the Secretary, which justifies such ends. The said petition will not be considered without the presentation of this certificate.

m) If the event to be held should be at night, there must be a certificate issued by the appropriate Industrial Delegation, showing that the bullring has an adequate general and supplementary lighting system, in proper running condition.

n) When the event in question is of a charitable nature, there must be an authorization from the General Department of Charities.

The presentation of the petition, with the documents indicated in the preceding paragraphs, must be made at least five days before the date of the event, together with six copies of the official program of the same.

Article 48. When it is a matter of holding bullfighting events in makeshift bullrings, the Director General of Security or the civil Governors will give orders to the Mayors and the Civil Guard to prevent all persons who are not bullfighters' assistants from standing about outside the areas set aside for the public, or from intervening in the fighting, and also to proceed to their arrest, which will be accompanied by a fine of 500 pesetas or, in lieu of the fine, consequent imprisonment.

If the area intended for the fighting should be entered *en masse*, the Mayor must cancel the spectacle and the police must clear the bullring.

Notwithstanding the guarantees established in the present Article, if the governing Authorities should have reasons or sufficient precedents to suspect that, under the pretext of a bullfighting event, a *capea* (unauthorized bullfighting spectacle) is to take place, it must prohibit the spectacle.

If someone should end up injured or dead in any spectacle held in contravention of the rules of this Code, the civil Governor must inform the Fiscal Ministry immediately so that the latter, if it considers it appropriate, may proceed to demand before the Courts any liabilities occasioned by the fault or negligence of the Mayor.

OFFICIAL PROGRAM

Article 49. In the official program announcing the event, whatever class it may be, the following information must be included:

a) The place, day, and time it is to be held. The Authorities in charge of approving the program must keep in mind that the duration of the bullfight must be calculated with sunset as the latest point for its termination, allowing a minimum of thirty minutes per bull.

In those bullrings which have an efficient electrical lighting system installed, it will not be necessary to make this computation, provided that the public be informed.

If the spectacle should last until nightfall, the Management is obliged to light adequately all the passageways and galleries of the bullring.

b) The name and category of the bulls, with the name of the bullranch as it is listed in the corresponding Breeders' Syndicate. The owner may, should he wish, and if not more than four years have passed since his acquisition of the bullranch, state the name of the immediately-preceding owner, provided it is printed in smaller type and after the registered name.

If it concerns a bullranch which is in the probationary period, the explicit phrase *"novillada de ascenso"* (promotional *novillada*) followed by the corresponding regulation number, must be stated.

Likewise, there shall be included, clearly visible, the design of the bullranch's brand, the color of the owner's ribboned device (*divisa*), and the registered earmark. If the bullfight concerned is one in which bulls from different bullranches are fought, the latter will be listed in strict order of their seniority, and as for the order in which they are to be fought, the following plan will be observed:

1. If they are bulls from different ranches, they will be fought in strict order of seniority of the ranch:

2. When several ranches are participating, each with a pair of bulls, the two

bulls of the oldest ranch will open and close the event; in the second and next-to-last place will be fought those from the next-oldest ranch, and so on.

3. When the ranches are several, and the number of bulls from each uneven, the fight will begin with one from the oldest ranch, those of the other ranches following in this order. Once all the ranches have had a bull fought in this order, the remaining bulls will be fought in the order agreed to by the bullfighters.

Likewise it shall be stated that the horns of the bulls have not been blunted, cut, filed, nor submitted to any fraudulent manipulation.

When *novilladas* with defective bulls are held, the notice, *"Tienta* (Test) rejects, defective,"* must be printed in clearly visible type. If it is not thus stated, the bulls, when they are examined, will be considered as being in perfect fighting-condition, for all practical purposes, pursuant to Article 74.

c) Names of the bullfighters and of each member of their corps of assistants (*cuadrillas*), those who fight on foot as well as those who fight on horseback, showing separately the names of the picadors on reserve. Persons who have not been announced in the program may not enter the ring or take part in the fighting. If there are more than three matadors on the program, they will be listed by pairs in the order in which they are to fight.

Women are absolutely forbidden to take part in any kind of bullfighting entertainment, although they may fight on horseback as *rejoneadoras,* but without setting foot on ground to complete the killing of the bull.

d) Classification of the tickets and their prices, according to sunny side, sun and shade, and shady side.

Also there shall be inserted literally or in abridged form those warnings referred to in Paragraph 3, Section *c*), of this article (49) ; the last paragraph of Article 52, the second-to-last of Article 58, Articles 60, 62, and 63, and Paragraph 2 of Article 81.

All programs must always show the name of the Management and the name and surnames of its representative, if there is one.

No program shall be approved for any bullfight or fight with *novillos* in which one or two matadors are taking part, if there is not also announced a substitute matador (*un sobresaliente de espada*) , who must of necessity be a *novillero* who has performed in at least 25 fights with picadors during his professional life, in first- and second-class bullrings, which experience must be verified by a certificate issued by the bullfighting section of the National Entertainment Syndicate.

e) In case the Management announces a subscription ticket for a series of bullfights, it must present the program to the Authorities for approval at least eight days in advance, stating the number of fights included, the combination of matadors contracted for fighting in each of them, and the ranches providing the bulls to be fought, which information must be verified in the manner set forth in Sections

j) and k) of Article 47, and the dates and times when the subscription holders may pick up their tickets. In no case may there be included more than two bull-ranches per fight announced in the series, except when the bullfights are for competition between bullranches.

Once the program is approved and the bullfight announced, the bulls to be fought in that fight may not be substituted, in their entirety or in part, except in unforeseen and unavoidable cases, or if they are rejected in the examination prior to the fight.

The Management will not be obliged to provide more bulls than those announced, whether or not the event is part of a subscription series, even if they haven't put up much of a fight, or even if one or several have been sent back to the corral or have been disabled in the course of the fight, in which case the matador whose turn it is to fight will be passed by as if he had killed the bull. If the disability or disqualification should occur before his entrance into the arena, the bull must be returned and substituted by the extra bull, without the matador losing his turn.

Those bulls not killed in the ring will be slaughtered immediately after the bullfight is over, in front of the delegate of the Authorities, the breeder, and Management, or their legal representatives.

Article 50. Disregarding the fact that the holding of a bullfighting spectacle may have been approved by the appropriate authorities, they may suspend it for reasons of public order, national mourning, or if an epidemic should be declared to exist in the town.

Article 51. Managements may offer subscriptions for complete seasons or for a series of bullfights, on the occasion of fairs or traditional festivals, in which case the posters and programs on which the information is indicated will be adjusted according to the formula established in Section e) of Article 49.

The value of the series will be deposited by the Management in the Bank of Spain or in some other bank having accredited solvency, in the name of the Director General of Security, in Madrid, and the civil Governors, in the provinces, who once the bullfight is over, and charging it to the deposited sum, will authorize the Management in writing to withdraw the amount allocated to the fight held.

The subscribers will have only those rights granted them by the Managements at the time the subscription is issued, on the posters and programs of each season or series of fights, once the former are approved by the appropriate authorities.

In case a subscription is issued, the Management is obliged to respect the right to renewal of reserved seats of those persons who held them in the previous subscription, as well as to reserve, for the period of one day, their seats for special, non-scheduled bullfights, and a half day for *novilladas*.

If, due to modification or reorganization in the distribution of seats, one of the subscribers should lose his, the Management will be obliged to reserve him another in the same class, if there is one, or if there is none left, the one closest to it, after having first satisfied those subscribers who have not been affected by such loss.

Article 52. The Management will be obliged to reserve for each bullfighting spectacle a box for the Director General of Security in Madrid, for the civil Governor in the other provinces, and in places where the latter do not reside, for the Mayor, and another for the Captain General, where there is one.

Also excluded from sale will be: the box set aside for the President, and another for a small party of the Civil Guard, two seats for those who are to provide spiritual aid, in case it should be necessary; and the number of seats necessary for the surgical staff and the veterinary personnel, whose seats must always be the same and located in the spot nearest to where they perform their services. In those rings where there are installed coverts in the arena alley for the members of these services, the said reservation will be cancelled.

Also holding free entrance to the bullring are: the Chiefs of the General Police Corps, the Armed Police, Civil Guard, or Municipal Guard, as the case may be, and officers and Service Forces under their command.

The only persons permitted to be in the alley between the ringside section and the arena fence are the bullfighters, the agents of the Authorities, and the Ring employees, the latter only in the places mentioned specifically in this Code.

Article 53. When His Excellency the Chief of State attends the spectacle, the Management must take care to decorate the box which he is to occupy in the most suitable manner, to which end the governing Authorities, or that body entrusted with matters of protocol, will make available the necessary items.

Article 54. Managements may establish as many ticket-offices as seem necessary in relation to the dimensions of the ring, in closed premises in different places in the towns, which must be open on the dates and times specified by the Managements, and in all of them, in full view, there must be displayed signs on which is stated the price of the seats. The price must also be printed on each of the tickets.

Tickets may be authorized to be sold by private persons, groups or associations which solicit permission from the authorities, agreeing to make the sales on closed premises, which will in no way inconvenience the public, and not to charge a commission more than 20% above the ticket price.

Article 55. Managements may not dispose of the amounts taken in by the ticket-offices without permission from the authorities until the spectacle is over.

When the authorities consider it suitable, they may require of Managements sufficient guarantee to cover the general expenses, which guarantee may consist of a bank or personal deposit down.

Article 56. Once the ticket-sales have begun for an announced bullfight, if for unforeseen reasons it should have to be postponed, or one or several of the matadors advertised have to be substituted, the bullranch changed, or half the bulls have to be substituted by bulls from another ranch, the Management, having obtained the approval of the authorities, must inform the public, by means of notices posted in the ticket-offices and in the main places where posters are usually put up. The holders of tickets who are not satisfied with the change, will be entitled to have their money returned in a period of time to be no less than one day; when the changes take place on the day of the fight, the ticket-holder will be able to get his money back up until an hour before the time announced for the beginning of the fight.

Also, it shall be announced to the public at the bullring, opposite the main gate, at the two first side-gates, and in the Patio of the Horses, which—if any—bullfighters' assistants cannot take part in the bullfight, and those who are to substitute for them, a copy of the announcement being remitted to the President's box.

The Management will be fined 250 pesetas for each individual who performs without being previously announced.

Article 57. In no case may the Management sell all the tickets in advance, since necessarily there must be available to the public at the ticket-window, ten per cent of the total number of tickets in the bullring, until the day before the spectacle.

Article 58. Once the ticket sales have begun, the Management may not cancel a bullfight without the consent of the Authorities, which it may obtain if it considers it advisable, by making a request of the acting President. The Management's petition must be presented before the separation of the bulls immediately before the fight.

When rain has fallen after the separation of the bulls, leaving the surface of the arena in bad condition for fighting, the matadors will be consulted and, in his capacity as arbiter, the President will decide—giving weight to the majority opinion expressed by the matadors if it is in order or not to cancel the fight spectacle, in either case drawing up the appropriate affidavit.

The same procedure will be followed in case the wind, because of its force, constitutes a serious risk for the fighters.

The decision to cancel will be announced by the Management in a clearly visible fashion in those places indicated in Article 56; if it should take place at the time the spectacle begins, the announcement will be made over the loudspeaker, if there is such a system, or by a trumpet-blast if there is not, the attendants proceeding to take down the flag flying on the outside of the bullring, as well as removing from the President's box the hangings which decorate it.

If the bullfight should be cancelled after it has begun for reasons which, in the judgment of the Appellate Court, are beyond control—the spectators will not have their tickets refunded.

When the announced bullfight is cancelled before it begins or during its celebration for reasons imputable to the Management, the Authorities will punish the Management with a fine of 5000 pesetas for *novilladas,* and 10,000 for full-fledged bullfights.

4.

THE SPECTATORS

Article 59. Bullrings will open their gates two hours before the time announced for the beginning of the spectacle, and when it is over they will remain open until the ring is completely emptied.

Article 60. The grandstand, gallery, and upper gallery spectators may not go to their seats nor leave them during the fighting of each bull, in order not to bother the other spectators. This prohibition will be communicated to the general public, the pertinent warning being printed on the back of the tickets.

Article 61. For any communication or urgent and truly necessary announcement which the Management wishes to make aloud in relation to the public, utilizing the loudspeaker system if there is one, it must have the previous authorization of the President.

Article 62. All spectators must remain seated in their own seats during the fighting; only agents of the Authorities or Management employees will be allowed to stay in the passageways. It is absolutely prohibited for spectators to utter insults or words which offend public decency and morality, to toss away lighted matches and burn papers or other combustible items, to strike, poke, or yank the banderillas out of the bull if he should leap the fence into the alley, or pass next to the first row of seats in those rings without an alley; to throw into the ring pillows or any object which could hurt the fighters or interrupt the fighting.

The violators will be punished with a fine of 500 pesetas, and in lieu of payment, they will be subjected to the appropriate subsidiary arrest.

Violators of the prohibitions in this article will be placed at the disposition of the President, and if he should not be able to take cognizance at once of all the infractions committed during the spectacle, they will be punished afterwards by the Authorities, who will impose the fines corresponding to the violations committed.

Article 63. The spectator who, in any kind of bullfight, leaps into the area during the fighting, will be taken out by the service aides and by the personnel of the *cuadrilla,* who will conduct him to the alleyway where he will be handed over to the agents of the Authorities, who will impose upon him a fine of 500 pesetas which, if it is not paid, will be substituted by the appropriate arrest. In case he should make any resistance on being removed from the arena, he will receive, in addition, another fine for the same amount. Ring employees as well as members of *cuadrillas* who show obvious negligence in preventing the performing and in effecting the withdrawal of the *espontaneo* (anyone who leaps into the ring to try his luck or skill), will be fined in the manner set forth in Article 34 of this Code for ring employees; with 1000 pesetas a piece for members of the performing *cuadrilla,* and with 5000 pesetas for the matador.

Espontaneos may not take part in any taurine festival for a period of two years starting from the date on which they leap into the ring, and they will have their Professional Syndicate card (if they have one) taken away for the same period. To make this punishment effective, a file will be kept by the Director General of Security in Madrid and the civil Governments in each province, in which is contained the name and complete personal description of each *espontaneo,* with the date and *plaza* where he committed the infraction, and before authorizing the programs of any taurine festival, the said files must be consulted in order to eliminate from the program those who are in the period of punishment.

In order to keep the said file up to date in the General Department of Security, the respective civil Governors must send by special delivery to the said department, and the latter to the other civil governors, as well as to the National Entertainment Syndicate, the necessary information to complete the file of every *espontaneo* to whom this measure must be applied.

Managements will be responsible for any infraction committed in regard to the individual party, for which they may request background information from the files, by writing to the General Department of Security, or to the respective civil Government, or to the National Entertainment Syndicate, before making up the programs; for, if it is determined that an individual subject to prohibition has performed, on account of being advertised with a false name or through any other circumstance, a fine of 10,000 pesetas will be imposed upon the Management.

Article 64. Managements will post copies of this Code, scrupulously abridged and in perfectly legible and durable form, in the quadrants of all floors of the bullring and in the Patio of the Horses; all ushers must have on their persons a pocket-size copy, complete, to show it if necessary to the spectator who makes a complaint.

5.

THE PRESIDENCY

Article 65. The Presidency of bullfights of all classes corresponds, in Madrid, to the Director General of Security; in the other provincial capitals, to the Civil Governor; and in the remaining towns, to the Mayor; they may delegate this position to an officer of the General Police Corps, where there is one, or if there is none, to a Deputy of the Mayor, every effort being made to select a person suitable for the duties involved.

The President, that he may be aided in the performance of his duties, will have under his immediate command an officer of the General Police Corps, where there is one, and there not being one, a non-commissioned officer of the Civil Guard, who will act as Delegate of the Authorities; will represent the latter in the signing of all documents related to the spectacle, and very particularly, during its progress, see to it that the orders given to him are carried out, in addition to implementing those originating from this Code; will consider all incidents which come to his attention or which are reported to him; and will take charge in each instance of those persons arrested in order to put them at the disposition of the Authorities.

The Delegate, in company with the Chief of the Public Forces on duty inside the bullring, will occupy during the bullfight a covert situated in the arena alley, below the President's box, with which he will be in communication by means of a telephone line in perfect working order. He will have under his immediate command, besides the Constables, an agent of the authorities, who will act as Secretary of Records, and Liaison Officer; another agent for keeping check on the service of horses and pics, and a third to check on the infirmary.

Article 66. Since the President represents the delegation of the Authorities, it is his duty to attend all those preliminary operations outlined in this Code; to resolve clearly and with strict adherence to the Code all incidents which may arise with the Management, Veterinaries, breeders or their representatives, bull-fighters and managers, and between these different groups, his decisions being considered final; he must report them and the errors or infractions he observes to the Director General of Security in Madrid, the civil Governor in the other provincial capitals, and the Mayors in the remaining towns.

The President will occupy the center seat of the box; to his right will be seated one of the Veterinaries who have taken part in the examination of the bulls, and to his left, a technical expert in artistic-taurine affairs, both of them being limited to expressing their opinions on the particular point about which the President may consult them, the latter being at liberty to accept or reject the opinion given.

The appointment of the artistic-taurine expert, in case of vacancy, will be made by the governing Authorities and must, necessarily, go to a bullfighter of reknown, retired from the profession, or, such a person not being available, to an enthusiast of well-known and recognized competence. For this appointment, the Bullfighting Spectacle Syndicate and the Bullfighters' Fund will submit in writing, when they are so requested, lists of three candidates, from which will be chosen the one who seems the most reliable, judging from the personal, artistic history of each one of the proposed residents of the town where the vacancy is to be filled or of the corresponding province. In case the appointment should go to an enthusiast it must be by free choice of the Authorities. This expert will be paid 300 pesetas in full-fledged bullfights, 200 in *novilladas* with picadors, and 150 in other festivals, which fees will be paid by the Managements.

Article 67. At the exact time announced for the beginning of the spectacle, the President will wave a white handkerchief, which will be the order for the Constables to begin the parade. When the parade of the cuadrillas has ended, the President will hand over the key to the bullpens through the Delegate, to one of the constables who, crossing the arena, will give it to the man in charge of opening the gate of the bullpen.

The duties of the President during the fighting will be: to order the change of all phases of the fight; to order black *banderillas* placed in those bulls which do not receive three good pic-thrusts, except in unusual cases in which, because of an injury suffered or because of excessive punishment received it would be better to reduce said number, in the judgment of the President or by the respectful request of the matador through the Delegate of the Authorities. If this request should not be granted and the matador, on his own initiative, should order the withdrawal of the picadors, he will be punished with a fine of 2000 pesetas.

Further duties will be: to grant to breeders as well as to matadors the trophies which they earn through the bravery of the bulls or the performance of the matador with cape, muleta and sword, respectively; to give the matadors warnings as prescribed in this Code; to arrange for the trained steers to come out in the prescribed circumstances; and lastly, to take all necessary measures to restore public order when for any reason it should be disturbed.

In order to signal the entrance of the bulls, the changes of the phases of the fight, and the concession of trophies to the matadors and breeders, the President will show a white handkerchief; for black banderillas to be placed on the bulls being fought, a red one; to indicate the return of the bull to the corrals and, therefore, the entrance of the trained steers, a green one; and to indicate the granting of a turn around the ring to the bull, a blue one.

The spectacle will be considered over when the President leaves his box.

Article 68. The trophies for the matadors will consist of: the turn around the ring, the grant of one or two ears of the bull which he has fought, and the exit on the shoulders of his fans through the main gate of the bullring. It is absolutely forbidden to cut off the bull's hooves for a trophy.

Only as a great exception may the President grant the cutting of the bull's tail.

These trophies will be awarded in the following manner: the matador will take the turn around the ring himself attending to the wishes of the public which will express its approval by applause. The awarding of one ear will follow upon the President's affirmative response to the majority request of the public; that of a second car of the same bull will depend exclusively on the President's judgment, for which he must keep in mind the quality of the bull fought, the manner in which the fight is directed and controlled, and the *faena* accomplished with the cape, the muleta and the sword-thrust.

The cutting of appendages will be done in the presence of the Constables who will, in turn, be those responsible for handing them to the matador. If, once the matador is in possession of the trophy and, responding to a minority which expresses its disapproval of the award, he should throw it on the ground, said act will be punished with a fine of 3000 pesetas for matadors of bulls and 1500 for matadors of *novillos*.

Exits on shoulders through the main gate of the bullring will only be permitted when the matador has been given the trophy of two ears, as a mininum, during the fighting of his bulls. When this occurs, the distance to be covered by the enthusiasts carrying him must not exceed 300 meters, measuring from the exit gate of the bullring. The Chief of Public Forces on duty inside the ring will take the necessary measures to prevent the exit of matadors who have not been granted the award specified.

Article 69. When, because of the extraordinary bravery and excellent responses of the bull fought, the majority of the public demands a turn around the ring, the President will so order the muleteers by showing the blue handkerchief.

A turn around the ring for the breeder or the Chief Herder may be taken when the public demands it with insistent applause.

6.

PRELIMINARY OPERATIONS

Article 70. The veterinary station described in Article 11 will be sealed off twenty-four hours before the arrival at the bullring of the bulls to be fought in the first bullfight and unsealed when the bullfighting season is over, operations which shall always be effected in the presence of an Agent of the Authorities appointed for said purpose.

If, during the course of the season, the Management should need to utilize the station for taking care of any bulls it may have in the bullring corrals, on any date other than that on which some fight is held, it must request from the appropriate Authorities the presence of one of their Delegates in order to effect the unsealing and resealing up of the station, once the operation in question has been accomplished. In both cases, the appropriate affidavit must be drawn up.

Article 71. The transportation of the bulls from the ranches of origin to the bullrings where they are to be fought, will de done by train or in trucks, under the proper safety conditions, it being absolutely forbidden to move them on foot.

The Chief Herder who brings the bulls will be entrusted with the position of a Sworn Guard, and he will be responsible for their safekeeping from the time of their departure from the ranch until their examination after they have been killed.

If, for some justifiable cause, the bullfight should be cancelled, the Management may demand from the breeder that he maintain the watch over the bulls, and assume the responsibility for any clandestine operation affecting the bulls' horns during a two-week period. After this period, whatever fraudulent operations may be observed on the horns at the time of the official examination, will be the sole responsibility of the Management of the bullring, in which case the said Management will be punished with a fine of 50,000 pesetas for each bull thus interfered with; if the infraction is repeated, with a fine of 100,000, and should it occur a third time, with a fine of 250,000.

Article 72. The Veterinaries who are to conduct the examination at the bull-ring of the health and fighting condition of the bulls, will be appointed by the Director General of Security in Madrid and by the civil Governors in the provinces, from the nominations of the Provincial Departments of Veterinary Health.

In full-fledged bullfights and *novilladas* with picadors, four Veterinaries will be appointed: two for the examination of bulls and two for the examination of horses; in *novilladas* without picadors, and amateur calf-fights, only two will be appointed, and one in bullfights of lower category.

These functionaries will each receive from the Managements the remuneration set by the General Department of Health, in addition to travel expenses if it is necessary for them to travel to a town other than that of their residence.

When, in the act of examination, the appointed Veterinaries observe that the animals examined are afflicted with contagious or parasitical diseases capable of transmission to the human species, they must take the appropriate provisional health measures and inform the proper Authorities so that the definitive measures required by the situation may be adopted.

Article 73. Before the bulls are examined, the breeder or his Foreman must give the Veterinaries on duty the health records of the animals.

The professional examination of the fighting condition of the bulls will be conducted by the appointed Veterinaries in the presence of the Delegate of the Authorities, the Empresario and the breeder or their representatives, one day before that of the bullfight, or three at the most, if the Management should so request.

There must be examined, as a minimum, one bull more than the number announced in the program if the bullfight is of six bulls or less, and two if it is of eight, which will be the extra, or substitute, bulls. The latter will be from a different bullranch than the one announced, but always from a ranch affiliated with the appropriate syndicated group. The same criterion will be observed in *novilladas* and other bullfighting entertainments.

In case of disagreement between two veterinaries, the Provincial Inspector of Veterinary Health (where there is one) will arbitrate, and where there isn't, a Veterinary delegated for that purpose.

When both Veterinaries reject, at this first examination, the entire lot of bulls or part of it, the Management or the breeder may take the matter before the governing Authorities which shall dispose that one or the other, or both at the same time, appoint a Veterinary to represent them and the Authorities will name another, all of whom, being previously advised by the first Veterinaries, will conduct another examination on the following day, and they will declare whether or not the lot should be rejected, the Authorities having the final word.

The first examination will be subject to a check, which will take place before the appointed persons two hours before the time indicated for the separating of the bulls.

A certificate in duplicate will be made of the final results of these examinations, which will remain in the hands of the Delegate of the Governing Authorities and the Management.

Should the substitute bull or *novillo* enter the ring, the ranch from which he comes must be announced on a sign placed above the gate of the release-pens. These substitute bulls may not be offered by either the bullfighters or the Management to be fought after the announced bulls have been fought. This may be done only in bullfights involving a single matador.

Article 74. The examinations referred to in the previous article will be based on health, age, estimated weight (in third-class bullrings), horns, fitness for the fight, and, in general, upon everything required by the zoological type of the fighting bull.

Bulls intended for fighting in bullfights must be from four to six years old, to which end, once the bullfight is over, in the *post-mortem* examination made by the Veterinaries on duty, they must check to see that the bulls at least have their six permanent teeth completely developed.

Article 75. The weight of fighting bulls must be: 460 kilograms in first-class bullring, 435 in second-class rings, before cleaning and gutting and 410 in third-class rings, when they are dragged out, or their equivalent of 258 when they are cleaned and gutted.

In first- and second-class rings, the weighing will be done on a platform scale of appropriate dimensions, in the presence of the Delegate of the Authorities, the breeder or foreman who has come with the bulls, and the Management, or their representatives. In third-class rings, the weighing will be done on a platform scale or an adequate steelyard scale, either at the dragging-out, or after they have been gutted, one or the other method being chosen by the breeder or his representative when the first examination is made.

The weight of the bulls in first- and second-class rings will be given to the public in the order in which they are to be fought, and likewise in the bullring at the entrance of each bull into the arena.

Insufficient weight in third-class rings will be punished with the sum of the terms of an arithmetical progression, whose ratio and first term will be of 100 pesetas, and the number of terms being that of the kilos lacking, with a limit of 5 considered as lost during the fighting, up to the limit of 30.

Article 76. The Veterinaries will reject all bulls who do not meet the conditions enumerated in Article 74.

If the Veterinaries declare in their certificates as fit for fighting bulls which do not meet the required conditions and which, for said reasons, are sent back from the arena, the governing Authorities, having been duly informed and at the recommendation of the Provincial Department of Veterinary Health, will impose the appropriate punishment on the Veterinary who is responsible.

Article 77. Of the bulls intended for the fight, one *banderillero* from each *cuadrilla* will make up as fairly as possible as many lots as there are matadors taking part in the fighting, it being decided by means of a drawing by the *banderilleros* in the presence of the Delegate of the Authorities, the managers of the bullfighters, the Ring Management, the breeder, or their representatives, which lot of bulls is to be fought by each of the matadors.

When the drawing has taken place, the previously mentioned representatives will come to an agreement on the order of placement in the release-pens of the bulls which have fallen to the lot of each matador, the President having the final word in case of doubt. If the bullfight should be announced as a competition between bullranches, the order for the placement of the bulls set forth in Section *b*) of Article 49 must be kept in mind.

The substitute bulls will go into the drawing as if they belonged to the announced bullranch.

Article 78. At twelve o'clock of the day on which the fight is to be held, the separation of the bulls will take place, which act, if so authorized by the Management, may be witnessed by the public in those bullrings with the necessary facilities for it, by paying for an admission to the corral and release-pen balconies, unless it should be permitted free of charge, it being obligatory to place in full view adequate signs warning that it is forbidden to attract the attention of the bulls under penalty of a 250 pesetas fine and immediate expulsion from the area, without hindering the right of the Management to exact responsibility from that person who might by his imprudence cause them some harm.

Article 79. After the verification of the bulls has taken place, during the separation, and while the bulls remain in their pens, until their entrance into the arena, a guard will be set up with the chief herder of the breeder, a representative of the bullfighters, and two cowboys from the Management, for the purpose of preventing all persons who could cause them injury or weaken them, from entering the areas where the bulls are kept. Those employees who, on opening or closing the gates to let the bulls through, do not do so smoothly and carefully to avoid hurting them will be punished in the manner described in Article 34.

Article 80. In the corrals there must be ready at least one group of three bell-oxen so that, in the event it is necessary and so ordered by the President, they may enter the arena led by the cowboys, with the purpose of leading out the bull which, on account of entering the ring with some physical defect, or on account of the official time limit having transpired without the matador having accomplished his objective, or for any other unforeseen circumstance, may not be killed in the bullring.

Article 81. On the morning of the day on which the bullfight is to be held, there shall be outlined on the surface of the arena, in paint of a sufficiently strong color, two concentric circles, with a distance of seven and nine meters, respectively, from the buttress of the ringside fence. The picadors may not advance across the first line on placing themselves for the action of picing, and the bull may not go beyond the second line upon being placed in position for the pic.

Before the event begins, the arena of the bullring must be sprayed, removing the uneven surfaces which might harm the fighters; it may be sprayed again when the fight is half over, if the matador directing the fighting considers it necessary. Whether or not the arena is sprayed a second time, the Ring employees shall proceed to repainting the circles described in the previous paragraph at those points where they have become erased due to the fighting.

Article 82. Once the bull has been dragged out, the horns must be cut off at their base, pulling out, if possible, part of the bony base, and, duly sealed and numbered according to the order in which fought, they will be deposited in a zinc-lined box, the key of which will be kept during the entire bullfight and used only by the agent of the Authorities appointed by the President, until they are examined.

If for any reason, the breeder, because of the bravery of the bull, or the matador, should request the Authorities to grant him the bull's head, they may accede to his wishes, although first its horns must be examined by the Veterinaries on duty to make sure that they have been in no way altered.

HORSES

Article 83. The day before the bullfight, the Management shall have delivered to the bullring stables at least eight horses, fit for the purpose for which they are intended. If the Management should agree to have the service contracted out, it will do so always under its own direct and sole responsibility.

The horses must stand at least 1.47 meters high, and weigh 450 kilograms as a minimum in bullfights, and 400 in fights with *novillos,* and they must be examined in the presence of the Delegate of the governing Authorities by both Veterinaries on duty, who must reject all horses not fit for the action of picing or which show symptoms of infectious diseases, in which case the steps described in Paragraph 4 of Article 72 must be taken.

In a suitable spot in the Patio of the Horses there must be an iron measure, at the height established in the previous paragraph, in case it should be necessary at any moment to check the height of a horse.

Article 84. All the horses, once weighed and provided with their protective padding, must be tested by the picadors on the morning of the day of the bullfight, before the shutting-up of the bulls to be fought, in the presence of the Delegate of the Authorities, the Veterinaries on duty, and the Management, in order to make sure that they offer the necessary resistance, that they are accustomed to the bit, that they can present their side and step backwards, and are responsive to directions, each picador in order of seniority choosing the one he is to use in the fighting, but under no circumstances being allowed to reject those which in the judgment of the Veterinaries meet the required conditions.

When the test is over, each picador will choose the saddle he is to use, which he will adjust to his liking and height, so he may not be delayed, under the pretext of adjusting his stirrups, or any other excuse, when it is time to make use of the horse. The required stirrups will be the common ones, called *de quilla* (like the American Western riding stirrup, covered, of wood and leather), but without any sharp edges which might harm the bull.

Those horses rejected in the examination mentioned in the previous article and in the first paragraph of this one, as well as those made vicious as a consequence of the fighting, in the judgment of the picadors and in agreement with the Veterinaries, may no longer be utilized in these spectacles, to which end a perforation of a centimeter and a half in diameter will be made in the middle part of the left ear.

In order to prevent the already-approved horses being changed, the Authorities shall arrange, besides the suitable guard, that there be placed around the neck of each of the approved animals a metal tag on a red cord.

The customs snippers will always be in the possession of the Authorities, who will order the tags to be removed when the bullfight is over.

The Veterinaries on duty must submit, with the approval of the Delegate of the Authorities, a certificate in quadruplicate of the examination, test, and review of the horses considered fit, giving one copy to the Management, and two to the Delegate who, in turn, will give one to the agent of the Authorities on duty at the Gate of the Horses.

PROTECTIVE PADDING

Article 85. The Management must see to it that the necessary harnesses, saddles and trappings are kept, in good condition, in the tackroom. Likewise, it must be equipped with no less than six sets of protective padding for the horses, the essential characteristics of which must be the following: two pieces of waterproofed canvas, stuffed with cotton which is also waterproofed, stitched together as in quilting, a caparison-flap of sufficient length to protect the inner thighs of the horse; its edges must be bound with leather; it must have thongs or straps for fastening and unfastening; and straps in the center part to prevent the stirrups from rising. Its finished weight may not exceed 25 kilos, allowing for a leeway of 5 kilos possible increase after repeated use.

Twenty-four hours before the fight is held, the sets of padding to be used will be inspected by the Delegate of the Authorities, Management representatives, and bullfighters, and those which meet the established standards will be tagged. An affidavit testifying to the results of this operation must be drawn up, signed by those present, and handed over to the Authorities along with the report of the results of the fight.

The approved padding will be stored in the assigned place in the tackroom until an hour before the bullfight begins; at that time, it will be untagged by the Delegate of the Authorities in the presence of the Management and bullfighters, in order to be placed on the horses.

Those which, because of their design, the materials used in their fabrication, and weight, do not meet the prescribed conditions, shall be rejected, the Management being obliged to replace them at once; or a fine of 2000 pesetas will be imposed for each one. If, four hours before the appointed time for the beginning of the bullfight, the violation has still not been made good, the fine will be increased to 10,000 pesetas, and the fight will be held with the padding available, which will afterwards be declared unfit for use.

If during the fighting it should be ascertained that one or several of the approved sets of padding has been substituted, the Management will be punished with a fine of 5000 pesetas for each one. Likewise, the picador who knowingly enters the ring with his horse equipped with rejected padding will be fined 1000 pesetas.

PICS

Article 86. The *puyas,* or pics, to be used in the fighting of bulls must be to the number of three per announced bull; they shall only be used for one bullfight, and they shall be previously stamped on the cord-wrapped part by the Livestock and Bullfighting Spectacles Syndicates and shown by the Management, before the enclosure of the bulls, to the Delegate of the Authorities, in sealed boxes, to be opened by the Delegate; thre shall also be shown an equal number of shafts for the pics, of beechwood, slightly warped, from which each picador will choose and mark two.

The pics shall have the form of a triangular pyramid, with straight edges, and be made of cutting and piercing steel, sharpened on a grindstone, attached to the shaft not with a socket-screw but with a riveted spike-screw; and their dimensions, measured with a templet gauge, must be 29 millimeters long on each edge by 20 wide at the base of each face or triangle: they must be equipped at their base with a stop-plate of wood, covered with glued cord, 5 millimeters wide at the part corresponding to each edge, 7 counting from the center of the base of each triangle, 36 in diameter at its lower base and 75 millimeters long, ending in a fixed cross-piece of steel, its arms in cylindrical form, 52 millimeters from their tips to the base of the stop-plate, with a thickness of 8 millimeters.

The Delegate of the Authorities must always have in his possession a gauge for checking these measurements.

When the pics are mounted in the shafts, care must be taken that one of the three faces which form them is turned upwards, that is, coincides with the convex part of the shaft, in order to avoid ripping the bull's flesh, and the cross-piece in a horizontal position parallel to the base of the face referred to.

The total length of the spear, that is, the shaft with the pic already screwed in it, must be from 2 meters, 55 centimeters, to 2 meters, 70 cm. The Delegate of the Authorities present at the act of inspection of the pics must require the presence of the representatives of the Management, the bullfighters, and the breeders, and an affidavit shall be drawn up and signed by the above-mentioned representatives and the Agent of the Authorities, who will act as Secretary.

The spears (*garrochas*) will be put away in a chest set aside for the purpose, the key of which will be taken by the Delegate of the Authorities after this inspection has taken place, and when the bullfight begins, they will be placed in full view of the public at a distance of 6 meters, as a minimum, from the Gate of the Horses, in charge of an Agent of the Authorities, and handed over to the picadors by an employee of the Management, who will collect them when the picing is over or the horse is changed, not allowing them to be left in any other place, and no representatives of the picadors or breeders will be allowed to intervene in said operation.

Article 87. The use of pics with specifications different from those described in the preceding article may not be authorized; the manufacturer who produces them without meeting the required specifications will be punished with a fine of 2000 pesetas for each one and seizure of all those already manufactured.

The picador who knowingly uses a pic which does not meet the established standards, will be fined 2000 pesetas, and in case of repetition of the offense, he will be dismissed from work for the period of time deemed suitable by the Authorities.

In order to make these rules effective, the pics, whatever the specific place of their manufacture, must be stamped in Madrid by the official agencies indicated in the previous article.

BANDERILLAS

Article 88. Also there shall be presented to the Delegate of the Authorities for inspection five pairs of ordinary *banderillas* and four pairs of punishing ones for each bull to be fought. The *banderillas,* which must be straight and of strong wood, shall have a length of 70 centimeters of stick and 6 of iron, and the harpoon should be 4 centimeters long and 16 millimeters wide.

The punishing *banderillas* must be of cutting and piercing steel, with a stick-length of 70 centimeters, wrapped with curled black paper, with a 7-centimeter white fringe or band in the center.

The steel must be 6 millimeters wide and 120 long, of which 40 must be for inserting into the stick. The harpoon-point must be 61 millimeters long, by 20 wide, and the space between the end of the point and the body of the harpoon, 12 millimeters.

Article 89. Managements must have complete freedom, within the required standards, for the acquisition of bulls, horses, trappings, pics, banderillas, and other items used in bullfights, without being subject to any demands by the bull-fighters, nor the breeders, on their own account or in the name of the Organizations they may represent, to acquire the bulls from any specific bullranch or organization, nor to purchase the other materials from contractors or manufacturers designed by them.

The Management which does not take advantage of this freedom and later finds faults or attributes them to outside pressures, will be punished with a fine of 5000 pesetas.

7.

THE PICADORS

Article 90. The number of picadors participating in bullfights shall be equal, as a minimum, to the number of announced bulls, in addition to the reserve picadors provided by the Management, who must remain mounted, in back of the Gate of the Horses, from the beginning until the end of the picing phase (*suerte de varas*), ready to enter—being reserves—the moment that those on regular duty are injured or dismounted; but they may not be in the arena when the phase is begun.

Nevertheless, the said reserves may give the first pic-thrust in *novilladas*, provided they are so authorized by the acting bullfighter.

Article 91. At the time of the entrance of the bull, the acting picadors will be at the Gate of the Horses, ready to enter the ring as soon as the President may so order.

Once the picing phase has begun, the picador may not dismount nor yield his horse to another fighter, nor abandon it before it is injured; he may do so only in the event that during the course of the picing it has picked up some vicious habit which prevents it from continuing the fight and it must be taken out.

Infractions of this nature committed by picadors will be punished with a fine of 500 pesetas.

Article 92. When the picador is preparing for the phase, his horse must have its right eye blindfolded with a handkerchief, no fighter being permitted to pass ahead, or go beyond, the left stirrup, and no *peon* or groom being allowed to place himself on the right side or in that direction even though he may be quite far from the entrance-place of the bull.

Both fighters and grooms who disobey the substance of the preceding paragraph, will be punished with a fine of 1000 pesetas, for fighters, and in the manner described in Article 34, for grooms.

Article 93. Picadors must fight by challenging the bull straight on, respecting the terrain indicated for them in Article 81, and when they must go after the bull, it shall be done by the one so ordered by the matador.

Notwithstanding the above provisions, if the bull being fought should not charge the horse after having been placed for the third time in the circle laid out for it, it shall be placed into action without taking into account said circle.

Article 94. The picador who, in order to carry out the picing, should cross over the line closest to the ringside fence described in Article 81, or deliberately seeks out the site of another, previous pic-thrust which he has placed in the lower parts or shoulders, or, also deliberately, blocks the exit of the bull, by moving around him, will be punished with thirty percent of his earnings the first time, 40% the second, and 50% the third, as well as those succeeding times should they occur, keeping in mind the classification and category of the bullfighter with whom he is fighting in order to determine the fees which correspond to him under the Labor Laws.

When the number of sanctions imposed on a picador show a persisted repetition, the General Department of Security may, in concrete and specific cases, order him disqualified for the period or number of bullfights it considers suitable.

Article 95. When they are not fighting, the picadors shall by no means stay in the alleyway outside the covert reserved for them next to the Gate of the Horses; he who breaks this rule will be fined 250 pesetas and, in case of repetition of the offense, he will be forced to withdraw to the Patio of the Horses. In those bullrings which do not have an alleyway, they shall stay in the covert assigned to their *cuadrilla*.

Article 96. When, for whatever accident, one or more picadors should not be able to go on fighting, the youngest picadors of the other *cuadrillas* shall take their place. And in case all of the scheduled picadors and the reserves should be incapacitated, the Management will not be under any obligation to provide others and the fight will continue, omitting the picing phase.

Article 97. During the fighting, there shall always be in the Patio four horses, saddled and bridled, duly prepared to come out into the ring, so that the picador will encounter no obstacle whatsoever to returning immediately to the arena, when his own horse has to be replacd for the reasons set forth in Article 91.

Once in the arena, the reserve picador, who was to have entered at the time the accident occurred, will return to the place assigned to him in Article 90.

Article 98. Horses which suffer injuries causing repugnance shall be killed with the *puntilla* on the spot, and covered rapidly with burlap cloths, rectangular in form, of the necessary size, sandcolored, and with eight lead weights in the corners and the centers of the sides; there shall be three such cloths in readiness.

The dragging-out ropes shall not be put on them until the bull has been killed.

8.

THE BANDERILLEROS

Article 99. For running the bulls and stopping them, there shall be in the arena no more than three subalternates, unless the acting matador does it by himself, the remaining members of the *cuadrilla* being obliged to stay in the alleyway; the subalternates will stop the bulls as soon as the latter enter the arena, preventing pointless running and their leaping into the alleyway; they must fight to one side only, always taking care to run the bull straight on; they may as an exception fight to both the right and left sides, if the matador so orders.

It is absolutely forbidden to turn the bulls too sharply, to tangle them up in the cape, blinding them to get them to collide against the ringside fence or deliberately to make them charge the fence or the coverts, with the intention of making them lose their driving strength, hurt themselves, or be rendered useless.

Failure to comply with this rule will be punished with a fine of 500 pesetas. If, because of the rule being broken, the bull should suffer some harm to his physical integrity, those guilty will be fined 2000 pesetas.

Article 100. *Banderilleros* shall enter the ring by pairs, alternating according to seniority, but he who makes three false starts will lose his turn and be replaced.

Article 101. The number of pairs of ordinary or punishing *banderillas* to be placed in each bull will be decided by the President, with regard to the circumstances present in each case.

The *Banderillero* or bullfighter who places unauthorized *banderillas* after the change of phase has been announced, will be punished with a fine of 500 pesetas.

When the *banderillas* are placed by the matador, this phase of the bullfight will be considered finished the moment he decides not to go on with it, even though he has not succeeded in placing a single pair.

Article 102. Once the second phase of the fighting is over, the fighters will turn in the unused *banderillas* to the groom who keeps them, and those which have fallen to the ground will be removed to the service rooms as soon as the position of the bull permits, without anyone else being allowed to take possession of them.

Article 103. When, due to some accident, the *banderilleros* of one *cuadrilla* are not able to go on fighting, the youngest of the other *cuadrillas* will take their places.

9.

THE MATADORS

Article 104. No matador announced in the program may fail to take part in the bullfight, unless he justifies his absence by virtue of a legitimate cause which, if it be due to illness, must be supported by a medical certificate, stamped by the appropriate Provincial Health Inspector. When this justification is lacking, the governing Authorities shall, without prejudice to the civil rights protecting Management, impose—in addition to the fine of 10,000 pesetas—the prohibition from fighting in the bullrings of the province where the rule is broken, or in all bullrings.

Both fines and the prohibition from fighting in provincial bullrings shall be determined by the respective Civil Governor. When the said fines and prohibitions go beyond the powers of the said Authority, or the disqualification is extended to bullrings outside the province, they shall be determined, at the latter's request, by the Director General of Security who, in turn, will propose to the Home Office if it seems appropriate, other sanctions of a greater quantity or of a different kind.

When a matador is absent at the time of the bullfight, he will be replaced by the other matadors, who will be obliged to fight the bulls assigned to the missing fighter.

An appeal may be filed against the decisions handed down respecting the rules established in this article, before the Home Office and within a period of two weeks counting from the date of notification.

Article 105. Matadors will compose their *cuadrillas* of two picadors and three subalternates; in the case that one matador should fight the entire bullfight himself, he must employ two complete *cuadrillas* in addition to his own. If the circumstance should occur of there being only two matadors scheduled to fight, each one must augment his *cuadrilla* with one more picador and one more *banderillero*.

One of the *banderilleros* of each *cuadrilla* may act as *puntillero* (the bullfighter who kills the bull with the *puntilla,* or dagger) . When this does not happen, the function will be exercised, in rigorous order of seniority, by one of those inscribed in the Bullfighting Syndicate and at the nomination of the latter, for which purpose the Syndicate representative will give the name of the appointed person to the Delegate of the Authorities on the morning of the day of the fight. This assistant may dress in the suit of lights during his participation.

The matador who authorizes the replacement of one of his subalternates without informing the Management, according to the provisions of Article 56, will be punished with a fine of 250 pesetas.

Article 106. All bullfighters must be in the ring at least 15 minutes before the time set for the beginning of the bullfight, and they may not leave it until the very end of the spectacle. When a matador requests permission from the President to leave the bullring with his *cuadrilla* on account of having to leave that very day for another town where he is to fight, he may be authorized to do so once his part of the fighting has been completed, although he must have the consent of his colleagues and he must give the public the appropriate advance notice.

Article 107. If the announced matadors should be incapacitated during the course of the fighting, the substitute matador (*el sobresaliente*) , when according to the rules there is one, must substitute for them and shall kill all the bulls left. If the substitute matador is also incapacitated, the spectacle will be considered over.

Article 108. Matadors may not bring with them more than one sword-boy and one assistant, who shall wear as a mark of their job an identification tag or armband with the name of their position on it; no other bullfighters' aides will be permitted to stand behind the ringside fence. Those who cannot show this status will be expelled by the Delegate of the Authorities or the agents under his orders.

The sword-boys and their aides shall occupy a covert at the ringside, being forbidden—no matter what the pretext—to leap out into the arena or lean against the fence except at the indispensable moments for handling the bullfighters the articles they need.

If they should have to follow the matador in the alleyway, they must always do so as close to the wall as possible, trying to place next to it, in a manner that will cause the least bother, the sword-sheaths, panniers, and all those things they carry about for the bullfighters' use.

The managers of the performing bullfighters may stay in the alleyway during the fight, in the place assigned to them by the Management.

Article 109. The artistic direction of the fight corresponds to the matador with the most seniority and, as a consequence, it is his duty to order the bullfighters to put the bull in the picing phase, if he does not do so himself, without crossing over the circle of least diameter marked out on the arena; to order the picadors to perform this phase of the action in the form established in Articles 92 and 93; to oblige the picadors to dismount when the horses do not meet the conditions required for the fight or if they have lost them during the action; to see that the subalternates take their places and follow the precepts of this Code in their performances, and that in the placing of the *banderillas* they lose their turn should the case described in Article 100 arise; to arrange in general that the other matadors observe in the execution of the different phases of the action the rules of the art, and to take care that there are never any more than the necessary number of fighters in the arena.

Notwithstanding the provisions of the foregoing paragraph, each matador may direct the fighting of the bulls of his lot, being responsible for this direction, but he may not object to the bullfighter who has seniority making up for and even correcting his mistakes, in the manner provided for.

The bullfighter-director of the fighting who, because of lack of character, negligence, or inexcusable ignorance, in the judgment of the President, does not fulfill all the provisions of this article, causing the fighting to degenerate into a disorder inappropriate to this kind of spectacle, will be punished with a fine of 5000 pesetas.

Article 110. In order to make the *quites* during the first stage of the fighting, the matador whose turn it is to make them will be the only one permitted to stand near the picadors, and he must try to make them from the outside and always paying more attention to preventing any danger occurring to the picador than to his own personal brilliance of performance; the picador's being in danger is the only case in which the other matadors and bullfighters will be allowed to intervene in the *quites;* the acting matador shall likewise prevent the picador from continuing the picing with a faulty pic-thrust, in which case he will make the *quite.*

Article 111. It is forbidden to pull the bulls' tails, and only in cases where it is absolutely necessary in order to save some bullfighter from a goring will it be allowed as a last resort.

Matadors should not pass with the cape, nor place *banderillas* in, another matador's bull, and they may do so only if they have obtained the consent of or invitation from their colleague.

Article 112. Matadors must dedicate their first bull to the President.

Article 113. In bullfights in which more than three matadors take part, they shall participate in the fighting by pairs, in the manner previously announced in the posters, as established in section *c*), Article 19.

The announced matadors will kill, in order of seniority, all the bulls to be fought in the bullfight, whether they are the announced ones or substitutes.

If, during the course of the fighting, one of the matadors should fall injured, bruised, or ill before beginning the kill, he will be replaced in the remainder of the task still to be executed by his colleagues, in strict order of seniority. In case the accident should occur after he has begun the killing, the most experienced matador will replace him without having his turn passed by.

Article 114. When a bull in the arena is incapacitated for the fight and has to be removed or killed with the *puntilla,* the matador whose turn it is will be passed by as if he had made a kill.

Article 115. During the phase of the *muleta,* matadors are to use the real steel sword, and in case one of them should allege a physical deficiency which prevents him from doing so, he must submit to a medical examination by the Chief of the Infirmary before the fight begins. If the fighter's complaint is verified, he will be granted the necessary certification, which will be sent to the President, who will order that, before the execution of the last phase of the bullfight begins, this irregularity must be communicated to the public, there being posted from the alleyway a sign worded in the following way:

"On the basis of a medical examination, the acting matador is authorized to use the imitation sword."

This notice must be ready before the bullfight begins, to avoid having to make one up each time, subjecting the spectators to an unnecessary wait.

The sword used in the *descabello* (killing of the bull by stabbing him in the cervix) must have, as a special characteristic, a fixed stop-plate in the form of a cross, 78 millimeters long, composed of three sections: one, the center, or controlling part, 22 millimeters long by 15 high by 10 wide, its edges bevelled so as not to reduce visibility for the matador when he is lining up for the *descabello*; and two side sections in the form of an oval, 28 millimeters long by 8 high by 5 wide. The said stop-plate must be fixed at exactly 100 millimeters from the point of the sword.

The matador who uses the *descabello* without having first tried to kill properly will be punished with a fine of 1000 pesetas.

Article 116. Members of the *cuadrilla* are forbidden to: push in deeper the sword already placed in the bull, whether the animal is standing or prostrate; kill with the *puntilla* before the bull falls; make it dizzy by turning it rapidly or twisting it about with the cape to make it fall sooner; wound it in the flanks or anywhere else in order to hasten its death; and attract its attention from the ringside when not attempting to prevent a goring.

Violators of these rules will be punished with fines of 500 pesetas.

Article 117. Warning-signals will be given to the matador by the sounding of the bugle or trumpet: the first, ten minutes after beginning the action of the *muleta;* the second, three minutes later, and the third, when fifteen minutes have passed.

At the second warning, the steward of the bullring will have the bell-oxen ready to enter the arena when the third warning sounds, at which moment the matador and the other fighters must retire to the ringside, leaving the bull to be led to the corral or killed with the *puntilla*.

Violation of this rule will be punished with a fine of 1000 pesetas for the matador and 500 for each one of the members of his *cuadrilla* who assists him.

If a matador who is fighting cannot continue because of illness or an accident, the time will be counted for the colleague who replaces him as if the action had just begun.

Article 118. Bullfighters who are disrespectful to the public, either in speech or indecent gestures, will be punished with a fine of 5000 pesetas.

Article 119. When a matador of *novillos* reaches the category of matador of bulls, the most experienced of those who alternate with him in the bullfight in which his new status is conferred upon him will yield to him his place with the first bull, handing over to him the *muleta* and the sword as the alternate, the most experienced matador passing to second place, and the one who follows him in seniority passing to the third, the correct order being reverted to with the remaining bulls.

10.

NOVILLADAS

Article 120. *Novilladas* in which picadors participate will be governed in all respects by the regulations prescribed for bullfights, with the exception of those cases specified in the following article.

Article 121. Bulls fought in *novilladas* may be in perfect condition or defective; in either case, their condition must be stated in clearly visible fashion in the posters announcing the spectacle.

The pics used for *novillos* will be identical to those used for bulls except that the height of the pyramidal part will be 3 millimeters less.

Veterinaries shall examine the *novillos* which, if they are in perfect condition, will conform to the standards established for bulls in Article 74.

As for those announced as *tienta* rejects or defectives, the inspection will be limited to determining whether or not they meet the health conditions necessary for the fight and their horns have not been tampered with; those with one horn broken or missing will be accepted and those which have defective vision, provided that these defects are found on one side only; and those *novillos* which have both horns broken or diseased (these bulls are called *hormigones*), blind ones, completely castrated ones, or those crippled in any of their members, will be rejected on the spot.

The age of fighting bulls in this type of bullfight, in perfect condition or defective, must be from three to four years, to which end, once the fight is over, in the *post mortem* examination made by the Veterinaries, it must be verified that the bulls fought have a minimum of four permanent teeth, completely developed; their maximum weight may in no case exceed that set for bulls, according to the categories of the bullrings.

In first- and second-class bullrings, the young bulls will be weighed on the hoof, and in third-class rings, when they are dragged out, either before they are bled or after they are cleaned and gutted, according to the option of the breeder, pursuant to the contents of Article 136, allowing for a loss of five kilos during the fighting, which amount must be figured into the total weight. This weight may not exceed 410 kilograms at the time of being dragged out or the equivalent of 258, once cleaned and gutted.

For excess weight, the same standard and proportion is to be followed which is set forth in the last paragraph of Article 75, for violations with bulls fought in third-class rings.

The lack or excess of weight will be punished in the manner prescribed in Article 135.

Fines for infractions of every kind committed in these fights will be reduced by 50% from those prescribed for bullfights.

Article 122. In *Novilladas* in which picadors do not participate, the age of the bulls will be from two to three years, whether they are in perfect condition or rejects and defectives, and their weight may not in any case exceed 210 kilos cleaned and gutted. The previous examination of these bulls will be limited to determining whether or not they meet the necessary health conditions, and in the *post mortem,* whether or not they have two completely developed teeth.

For both excess weight and for excess or insufficient age, the same standards set forth in the previous article will be followed.

11.

CALF-FIGHTS, CHARITY FIGHTS, AND COMIC BULLFIGHTING

CALF-FIGHTS

Article 123. By "calf-fights" (*becerradas*) are understood those bullfighting celebrations in which are fought, either by professionals or amateurs, bulls which in no case may exceed two years of age.

The official programs will not be approved by the Authorities if they do not include, as the director of the fighting, a professional bullfighter of the category of matador of bulls or *novillos* (no distinction being made for these purposes between the two), to help the amateurs who take part in the *fiesta*. This provision will not be necessary when those who are fighting are professionals in bullfighting, in which case the one with most seniority will have the role of director of the fighting.

The cattle used for calf-fights must be examined by the veterinaries appointed by the Authorities. This examination must be attended by the director of the fighting, who will determine whether or not the animals offer any danger, which fact he will at once communicate to the Authorities, who will order the special tool chest unsealed in order to diminish or modify the horns of the calves which require it.

Besides the above provisions, the Authorities, in order to prevent accidents, will take all measures they consider appropriate, given the type of spectacle that it is, especially as regards the number of bullfighters.

CHARITY FIGHTS

Article 124. By "bullfighting festivals" (*festivales taurinos*) are understood those spectacles celebrated for the purposes of charity. In this type of celebration,

333

its organizers, upon requesting the appropriate authorization from the Authorities, must include in their documentation the permit from the General Department of Charities, according to the provisions of Section *n)*, Article 47.

In these spectacles, any kind of cattle may be fought, provided they are male and meet the necessary health requirements. The pics will be those for *novillos* or bulls, according to the circumstance, and the number of horses to be used will be three.

The bullfighters participating may be of any of the classes established by the Bullfighting Group of the Entertainment Syndicate, who may fight with no distinctions made in the same celebration (*festejo*). Their *cuadrillas* shall consist of one *banderillero* more than there are bulls to be fought, and one picador for each bull, when the spectacle is with picing.

When the official program is submitted to the Authorities for approval, the provisions of Article 63 pertaining to *espontaneos* must be taken into consideration.

COMIC BULLFIGHTING

Article 125. Comic bullfighting celebrations may be held equally by day or at night.

When they are held at night, the provisions on the lighting installation set forth in Section *m)* of Article 47, and *a)* of Article 49, must be kept in mind; and their duration may not exceed the limits set forth in the laws in force concerning the ending of public spectacles. Delay with regard to the hour set will be punished by the Authorities with a fine of 2000 pesetas, which will not pertain when the spectacle, having begun at the hour announced, ends with a delay less than thirty minutes due to causes beyond the control of the Management.

Article 126. Should the electrical system break down during the fighting, there should exist an adequate amount of supplementary wiring of sufficient intensity so that the public can leave the bullring. Furthermore, the Management must have on hand a sufficient number of torches so that the employees may light them if necessary.

If the short-circuit is due to defects in the interior lighting system of the bullring, the account of the corresponding accusation against the technician who has granted the certification required in Section *m)* of Article 47 must be delivered to the Authorities.

Article 127. Cattle fought in these spectacles must meet the same requirements provided for calf-fights in Article 123.

Article 128. In every comic bullfighting celebration, whether held in the evening or during the day, there must be a serious part in which are fought as many bulls as are to be sacrificed in the comic part.

The serious part of the spectacle will be held at the beginning of the fight, and in the parade, those who take part in the serious fighting shall march in front of those who perform in the comic part.

Article 129. Fighters who take part in functions of comic bullfighting may not use in the fighting any fireworks on the animals, nor drag them, knock them down, pull their tails, or use any instruments which might harm the calves.

In order to prevent accidents, the Authorities must take the necessary measures with regard to the pantomimes that may be presented.

Article 130. It is absolutely forbidden to portray in caricature or by any other indiscreet form any definite Institution or person, to defend or eulogize any vice or crime, which may tend to excite hatred or aversion between the social classes, which may offend the integrity or prestige of the Authorities, their Agents, or the Armed Police.

12.

FIGHTING WITH THE REJON

Article 131. On the program announcing any celebration in which *rejoneadores* take part, the name of the second-in-command (*el sobresaliente*) of the *cuadrilla* must figure, if the bulls to be fought have their horns intact; this not being the case, they will be considered de-tipped.

If they have their points, that is to say, if their horns are intact, once they have been dragged out, they will be subjected to an examination by the Veterinaries under analogous conditions and sanctions, if they are in order, as those provided for ordinary bullfights.

In case the arena is in poor condition, the *rejoneador* shall fight at the moment considered suitable by the Authorities, having heard the opinion of the director of the fighting. This performance may be at the beginning, the middle, or the end of the bullfight.

Rejoneadores shall be obliged to present as many horses, plus one, as there are bulls to be fought with the *rejon*, whether or not the bulls' horns are detipped; if the horns are capped, there shall be one horse for each bull.

The *rejoneador* shall be accompanied into the ring by two assistants, who will help him in his task as he determines, refraining from turning the bull sharply upon itself, weakening it, or making it dizzy.

Rejoneadores may not pierce any one bull with more than three punishing *rejones*, and three or four *farpas*, or pairs of *banderillas*, to be decided by the President, who will signal the change of phase for the horseman to use the *rejones de muerte* (the lances of death), of which he must place two before dismounting. If he has not killed the bull within five minutes after this signal, the first warning will be given, and two minutes later, the second, at which moment he must withdraw or dismount, if he is to kill it, at which task he may not employ more than

336

five minutes; at the end of this time he will be given the third warning and the bull will be returned to the corrals. When the announced *sobresaliente* of the *cuadrilla* is charged with killing the bull, he will be governed by the standards set forth in Article 117.

Article 132. The punishing *rejones* must be of a length of 1.60 meters, and the pike (*la lanza*) must consist of a socket or case 6 centimeters long with a 15 centimeter double-edged blade for *novillos* and an 18 centimeter blade for bulls, the blades being 25 millimeters wide.

The upper part of the socket will have a cross-bar 6 centimeters long and 7 millimeters in diameter, going in an opposite direction to the blade of the *rejon.*

The *farpas* must have the same length as the *rejones,* with a harpoon or blade 7 centimeters long by 16 millimeters wide, and the *banderillas* must measure 80 centimeters long with the same 7 centimeter harpoon.

The *rejones* of death must have the following maximum measurements: 1.60 meters in length, with a 10 centimeter socket and double-edged blades; 60 centimeters long for *novillos,* and 65 for bulls, and 25 millimeters wide.

Rejoneadores who use the so-called *rejon* of death before the time set for it will be punished with a fine of 3000 pesetas.

Article 133. All the items specified in the previous article must be inspected by the Delegate of the Authorities on the morning of the day of the celebration, before the shutting-up of the bulls, and once the described dimensions and characteristics are ascertained, they will be put away in the box used by the *rejoneadores,* which—duly sealed—will be placed in the chest in which the pics are kept until the very hour the fight begins, when it will be moved to the alleyway and there unsealed and kept ready for use the moment it is needed, being duly guarded by an Agent of the Authorities appointed by the President.

If, once the above-mentioned items are inspected, either part or all of them do not have the described dimensions, they must be rejected and the *rejoneador* required to present others up to an hour before the fight; if he does not do so, he may perform, but he will be punished with a fine of 10,000 pesetas and the loss of all his equipment, both that left over as well as that used, which equipment will be taken charge of and put out of use by the Agent of the Authorities appointed for the guarding of the same.

13.

FINAL OPERATIONS

HORNS

Article 134. When the bullfight is over, the inspection of the horns will be made by the Veterinaries in the presence of the Delegate of the Authorities, a representative of the Management and another of the breeder, the appropriate affidavit being drawn up, a copy of which will be sent to each of them, and another to the General Department of Security. The unjustified absence of any one of the above-mentioned representatives shall not be an obstacle to the decisions taken by the Authorities as a result of these inspections.

If, the inspection having been completed, one or more of the horns show signs of having been fraudulently manipulated, they will be put aside and stored in sealed boxes to be sent, with another copy of the affidavit, to the National School of Veterinary Health, where they will be examined again.

The same procedure will be observed with the horns from any bullfight which the governing Authorities judge to require further examination.

Each horn must bear on its surface a paper seal, which goes around it, stamped with the seal of the Delegation of the Authorities, in such a way that part of it is printed on the paper seal and the remaining part on the horn; the horns of each bull should be paired and tied together so that they may not be confused with those of the other bulls. Also, they may bear, for purposes of easier identification, the seal with the brand of the bullranch, if the owner provides one.

At the base of the horns there must be placed a wad of cotton soaked in a solution of 10% formaldehyde, with the object of preventing, during their transportation, the decomposition of the soft substances in the base of the horns.

Once sealed and in a maximum group of four, the horns must be properly packed in wooden crates. If the number of horns to be sent is greater, as many boxes as are necessary should be prepared.

The packing crates must be of strong wood, one centimeter thick, and with the dimensions of 40 by 40 by 25 centimeters high, lined on the inside with zinc. There must be placed on their locks a stamped seal and they must have two steel straps, one encircling the box horizontally and the other longitudinally, which will guarantee the inviolability of the contents.

These boxes with the horns, once sealed, must be sent by the door-to-door services of the RENFE (National Railway System) or a moving-van company to the Police Headquarters in Madrid, where the integrity of the seals will be ascertained, and in this office they shall be handed over to the National School of Veterinary Health, by means of an affidavit affirming that the container has not been opened, or stating any irregularities observed.

In the examination and analysis carried out by the Veterinary Services, there shall intervene one veterinary appointed by the General Health Department, and another by the Breeders' Syndicate, from the appropriate chapter, the first representing the Authorities, and the second, the breeder or ranchowner. Notwithstanding this arrangement, a veterinary appointed directly by the breeder may also intervene, provided he requests it, to prepare, together with the others, the experts' report. In case the latter does not come to the examination, after having been summoned, the General Department of Veterinary Health will pronounce its verdict assuming that the breeder has renounced this right.

For each bull whose horns should appear to have been artificially blunted, cut or filed, the General Director of Security will impose the fine of 50,000 pesetas on the owner of the bullranch; in case the violation is repeated, the fine will be 100,000 pesetas, and if there is a third violation, he shall be restricted from having his bulls fought for the period of one year, even if during the course of the said year he has the bullranch transferred to a different name. All without affecting the responsibilities incurred for falsifying certification to which reference is made in Section *h*) of Article 47.

If the bulls subjected to this examination are the ones corresponding to another bullfight not yet held, and the two weeks prescribed in Article 71 have since passed, the Managements will be responsible for the fraudulent manipulations observed, thereby incurring the punishments indicated in the same article.

If the fraud is flagrantly committed by order of the Management or a bullfighter, evading the vigilance of the breeder, his representative, foreman, or employees, a fine will be imposed by the General Department of Security upon those responsible, of 50,000 pesetas per altered bull, the repetition of the violation carrying with it the fine of 100,000 pesetas, and if a third violation should occur, the matadors will be prohibited from fighting for six months, counting from the date on which the fraud was perpetrated, and the Management will be punished by being forbidden to organize bullfighting spectacles for the period of one month, or in lieu of this, by paying a fine of more than 100,000 pesetas, to be imposed by the Home Office, on the recommendation of the Director General of Security.

The interference of procedures against such sanctions will not paralyze the action of the same.

AGE

Article 135. In like manner, the Veterinary on duty, in the presence of the Delegate of the Authorities, Management, and the breeder, or their representatives, must examine the bulls fought with the purpose of determining their age, in conjunction with the provisions of Articles: 74, for bulls; 121, *novilladas* with picadors; 122, *novilladas* without picadors; 123, amateur fights; 124, charity fights; and 127, comic bullfighting.

If it turns out that one or more of the bulls is not of the required age, the corresponding affidavit will be drawn up, and will be signed by the witnesses, to each one of which will be sent a copy. Another copy will be sent to the General Department of Security.

If failure to meet the age required of bulls fought in bullfights is ascertained, the ranchowner will be punished by the Director General of Security with a fine of 15,000 pesetas for each bull, the first time; 25,000 pesetas the second time, and in case a third violation should occur, with 50,000 pesetas and the restrictions on the bullranch under the same conditions indicated in Article 134.

In case it is proven that in a *novillada* without picadors the bulls were over three years old, which is the limit established in Article 122, the breeder will be fined 15,000 pesetas for each one of them, and in case of repetition of the violation, 25,000 pesetas.

Without any effect on or hindrance to the sanctions previously established, the breeder shall also be held responsible for falsifying the certification referred to in Section g) of Article 47.

WEIGHT

Article 136. In third-class bullrings, and in the presence of the representatives mentioned in the previous article, the weighing of the bulls will be done immediately after they are dragged out of the arena, either with the body intact and unbled, or after they are cleaned and dressed, according to what the breeder or his foreman has decided at the time specified in Article 75, for which in all the bullrings there shall be on hand a scale of adequate size and properly balanced. The appropriate affidavit of the weighing will be drawn up, a copy being given to each one of the witnesses, and another being sent to the General Department of Security.

If *novillos* are concerned, the provisions to this effect in Article 121 must be kept in mind.

The Management is required to post the weight given for the bulls in full view, at the exit of the bullring.

The President of bullfights held in the provinces must wire the weight of the bulls being fought to the Director General of Security, specifying, when it is a matter of bullfights held in third-class bullrings, whether the weight has been verified at the dragging-out or after the cleaning and gutting.

MEAT

Article 137. At the end of bullfights, the veterinaries on duty will proceed to the health examination of the animals, granting the appropriate certification with the approval of the Delegate of the Authorities, one copy of which must be given to the contractor who is to remove them for public consumption.

Once the inspection of the flesh, viscera, and offal of the fought bulls has been completed, should they be the object of forfeiture, the Veterinaries will inform the Management in writing, the latter being empowered to make an appeal to the local Authorities within the period of four hours after the notification.

PUNISHMENTS

Article 138. In regard to bullfighting spectacles, fines may be imposed only in those cases strictly set forth in this Code, without impediment to those punishments of every kind which, in accordance with the laws in force, correspond to crimes or violations committed during the celebration of said spectacles.

These fines being intended as the imposition of punishments of a personal character, no one will be forced to be subrogated in the payment of the same, even though it is so prescribed in the clauses of the contracts, which shall be considered null and void.

FINAL DISPOSITION

The following Decrees of this Ministry, and the Bulletins which have been issued for the enforcement of these decrees, are hereby repealed: the decrees of July 25, 1930; January 10, May 8, June 27, August 28, September 2, and December 23 of 1931; June 3, July 22 and 27, and August 14, 1932; March 20, 1933; August 3 and 17, and September 11, 1934; January 6 and April 30, 1936; February 25 and June 3, 1942; April 28, 1943; February 12 and March 12, 1948; February 21 and August 12, 1949; February 10 and July 2, 1953; March 20, April 23, and July 6, 1956; April 9, 1957; July 24, 1958; April 11 and 15 and July 23, 1960.

Madrid, March 15, 1962.

INDEX